'I don't think I particularly balance anything. I just make it work. I'm really religious about this; I don't think women should feel as if they have to do it all and make it look easy, because it's not easy and we shouldn't have to try to do everything, and I don't. We must not pretend we're superhuman, because that sets a false expectation and it also leaves the impression that we shouldn't need support.'

Jacinda Ardern

'One female journalist asked me how I was going to cope without a husband. In response, I asked her, "Excuse me, would you have asked a question like this of a male candidate?" And then she immediately realised what she had done. But it was very strange that, being a woman, she thought, in a very sexist way, I wouldn't cope if I didn't have a shoulder to cry on at home.'

Michelle Bachelet

'In Malawi, there is a saying that a bull goes to the farm to pull a cart, a cow is kept at home for milk. So, people in the opposition said, "How unlucky are we to end up with a cow pulling our cart?" It was vicious and cruel and could only be used because the person at the end of the insult is a woman.'

Joyce Banda

'I'm proud of the campaign I ran but I wish I had known then what I know now. I went where nobody else has ever gone and it was really, really hard. But it opened doors. It has motivated people and encouraged people, and that's all to the good.'

Hillary Clinton

'It's raining men! So how do I feel about being there? I feel like challenging them, especially when I am in the chair. Because very often they don't even realise how gendered it is. It is the frame they are used to.'

Christine Lagarde

'A few years ago, I was in a lift in the House of Commons and there was a young woman, and I commented that she had a nice pair of shoes on, and she said, "Your shoes got me into politics." She saw somebody, me, who she viewed as human, because I am known to like shoes. And that's what got her watching politics. And there she was working in the House of Commons.'

Theresa May

'I did get a particular feeling when I went to meetings of the cabinet and everyone else was a man. I had established myself as someone of strength and that is where the term "iron lady" came from, because on fiscal matters I was quite strong. They respected me but they didn't really see me as part of the team. I was the stranger commanding things.'

Ellen Johnson Sirleaf

'One of the things people often say about me is that I'm always calm. Naturally, I am calm as a person, but I've also had to learn to be so. If a woman becomes too aggressive, too agitated, then I think people react to it.'

Erna Solberg

women
and
leadership

REAL LIVES, REAL LESSONS

Julia Gillard
&
Ngozi Okonjo-Iweala

The MIT Press
Cambridge, Massachusetts
London, England

First published by Penguin Random House Australia Pty Ltd.

This book was set in Minion Pro by Midland Typesetters, Australia.
Printed and bound in the United States of America.

Library of Congress Cataloging-in-Publication Data is available.

ISBN: 978-0-262-04574-2

10   9   8   7   6   5   4   3   2   1

Contents

Prologue

Why are we writing this book?

Two frantically busy women chat on the sidelines of meetings held all around the world. What do they agree to do? Take a holiday? Sneak off for a day of relaxed sightseeing? Have a leisurely dinner? All enticing possibilities. But the answer is that we decided to write a book – this book.

At first blush that might seem like a bit of a weird choice, and there have been moments when we have whispered underneath our breath, 'What on earth were we thinking?' Most of the time, though, we have felt a real clarity of purpose and sense of urgency. The high-octane fuel that propelled us on is a mixture of passionate belief in gender equality and tearing frustration that we have not yet achieved it.

We know we are not the only ones who feel driven and dismayed all at the same time. However, not everyone channels that itchy kind of energy into writing a book, and we owe you an explanation as to why we did.

Our shared story starts in 2011 when, as Nigeria's Finance Minister, Ngozi came to Australia for the Commonwealth Heads of Government Meeting, which Julia chaired. Bringing together the leaders of more than fifty nations in a meeting focused on democratic norms and values is serious business. Talking about it now makes Ngozi laugh, though, as she recalls trying to explain to some of her colleagues what it meant when the biographical notes on Julia said she had a partner, not a husband.

Unfortunately, the two of us met only briefly at that event but, a few years later, we ended up becoming acquaintances and then friends by being at the same international meetings. We found ourselves at many global events in our roles as chairs of major international development funds. Ngozi chairs Gavi, the Vaccine Alliance, which seeks to provide children in the developing world access to affordable vaccines that help prevent diseases like diphtheria, measles, pneumonia, polio and malaria. Julia chairs the Global Partnership for Education, which focuses on school education in the poorest countries in the world.

In the margins of these meetings we started to have hurried conversations about women leaders. There was always something happening to a female prime minister or president that we thought might be the result of gender biases, but we wanted to talk it through.

Out of these discussions, we started putting theories to each other about what was happening. However, we could never quite get to the bottom of it. 'Something is going on,' we would mutter to each other. 'Women leaders all seem to be facing the same kinds of problems,' we would say. 'Why is it as bad as this and not getting better?' we would cry out in frustration between ourselves. Then Hillary Clinton lost the US presidential election, and our talks took on a new earnestness.

At some point, we started to move beyond anecdotes to more structured conversations. Both of us felt the fact that we are very different people brought a richness to our exchanges. It seemed to help us puzzle out more together than we could have done alone.

Slowly but surely, we inched our way forward to the big question: should we try to write something on women and leadership, which would further our own thinking and hopefully inform and inspire women?

Like all big projects, we started seized with inspiration, felt the muddle of the middle and had to persevere to get to the end. As we were finalising the book, the Covid-19 pandemic swept through humanity. Both of us joined the billions working from home while worrying about family, friends and the future. Ngozi's workload was accelerated given her key role in the global organisation responsible for vaccines, and the need to advocate for immediate assistance to African nations as they confronted the virus. Importantly, Ngozi became a special envoy for the global initiative to accelerate the development, production and delivery of Covid-19 vaccines, therapeutics and diagnostics. Julia also experienced new demands helping the Global Partnership for Education as it urgently worked to maintain some form of educational continuity for the poorest children in the world. Tragically, prior experience with epidemics like Ebola has shown that without extraordinary efforts, child marriage soars and the most marginalised girls never return to school. At the same time, demand surged for the services of Beyond Blue, the innovative mental health body Julia chairs.

Yet out of all this pressure, doom and gloom, there are fresh insights about the value of caring work, the need for empathy and the importance of community. At the time of writing, we are both still asking ourselves the question, can we emerge from this stronger? Will we see a new global understanding about the true value of so much of what has been historically defined as 'women's work', a determination to address growing inequalities, an embrace of telework to provide family-friendly flexibility, and a new spirit of kindness based on the dramatic reminder of our shared humanity? Rather than resorting to the trite saying 'Time will tell', in our own ways, we want to be participants in distilling the lessons learnt. For now, we are pleased that we found the time needed to finalise the book between so many urgent video conferences.

In all the travel and writing time it has taken, there have been plenty of differences of opinion, but no cross words. The sense that our diversity is a huge strength has never left us.

We came to our collaboration as experienced women who had already formed our core values and outlook on the world. Let us give you an insight into our individual perspectives.

A message from Julia

I have always been a feminist. For as long as I can remember, I have believed women and men should be equal in every way. While I was a student at the University of Adelaide, I developed a deeper understanding of why and how the world was failing to live up to this simple ideal. The knowledge I absorbed came to me not through a formal course of study, but as a by-product of becoming involved in the student movement, which included many feminist thinkers.

This new life of ideas and activism started because I was incensed by the decision of a conservative federal government to cut back funding for university education. My anger gave me courage and propelled me into becoming one of the leaders of the local component of a national campaign by students and academics to fight back. Amazingly, we won some concessions from the government and the worst of the changes were reversed. I learnt from this experience that, joined in common cause with others, I could make a difference.

From there I was increasingly involved in the student movement, becoming education vice-president and then president of the Australian Union of Students (AUS). At campus, regional and national levels there were positions available as Women's Officers, dedicated to leading the fight for gender equality. In fact, the AUS secretariat had a special department that was overseen by an elected Women's Officer.

In university debates, including those within AUS's decision-making structures, there was a high degree of discord between many of the women who chose to devote their time exclusively to the feminist fight and those who did not. This was not simply a difference in priorities, but mirrored the debates of the time about the efficacy of women's separatism, with its philosophy that, to find true liberation, it was vital for women to be in spaces separate from those defined and designed by the men.

Within AUS, this gave rise to all sorts of tensions: practical, political and personal. Just from the point of view of budgeting and staffing, it was fraught to manage the resourcing of a Women's Department that insisted on autonomy from the rest of the union. Politically, AUS faced two existential threats: right-wing students campaigning to have universities disaffiliate, and conservative governments enacting anti-union legislation. Both aimed to destroy AUS's ability to raise money through receiving a small amount out of the fee each student was required to pay to be a member of their university student union. Time and again, the more radical, hard-to-defend policies that the Women's Department supported were held up to ridicule by these conservatives. On a personal level, all of this pitted the women who supported the purest version of autonomy in the Women's Department against women like me who were involved in the rest of the union. You could have cut the air with a knife when, as AUS president, I attended meetings of the committee that ran the Women's Department. On more than one occasion I was referred to as an 'honorary man'.

I finished my term of office at AUS in 1984, at the age of twenty-two. I came out of this intense experience still an ardent feminist, but definitely a mainstream one. In the years that followed, as I completed my university education and started working at a law firm, I was increasingly attracted to pursuing a career in politics. My motivation in doing so was to make an impact on public policy for all, not to be a specialist focused on what were seen as 'women's issues'. If you had asked me at the time, I would have said my ultimate dream was to serve in a federal Labor government as Minister for Education, given this was my first public policy passion, or Minister for Industrial Relations, an area I viewed as ripe for reform because of my job as a solicitor practising in employment law. In my parliamentary career, I was ultimately fortunate enough to do both.

There is always a gap between forming an ambition and realising it. For me, in the very factionalised environment of Australian Labor Party (ALP) politics, that gap was measured in years and failed attempts to get preselected, followed by narrowly losing out on a Senate position in the 1996 Australian federal election.

I could have become disillusioned and given up. Instead I kept at it, in the highly charged and divisive atmosphere of internal ALP politics. I became a leader of a strongly bonded group of party activists and trade union officials, men and women, who thought that the current structures of the ALP's progressive wing were undemocratic and exclusionary. Ultimately, we broke away and formed our own faction. As a result of winning the votes of local party members and receiving support on the central candidate selection panel, I was preselected for the federal seat of Lalor and finally became a member of parliament in 1998.

While all this was happening, I was strongly involved in securing a rule change to implement a target for the number of women the Labor Party needed to preselect for national and state parliaments. Getting this required campaigning to win hearts and minds, but it also relied on negotiation, bluster and even threats in order to work a way through the ALP's formal and informal power structures. In addition, I helped establish a Labor women's organisation called Emily's List, with a mission of supporting and fundraising for pro-choice, pro-feminism and pro-equity candidates.

Once I became the Member for Lalor, I worked incredibly hard and honed my craft in parliament, policy, media and campaigning. I won enthusiastic support from some, and grudging recognition from others that I had the skills and ability needed to climb up the ladder to the ministerial ranks. At the time I was elected Labor was in opposition, and the years that followed included uncertainty about the way forward and divided opinions about who was the best person to lead the party.

As I grew more senior, I was not a bystander in all these discussions and machinations. I was increasingly able to influence people and rely on their support. When necessary, I was good at counting numbers. These skills would have made little difference if my parliamentary colleagues thought I lacked the ability to connect with the public and develop policy. In high-stakes portfolios and situations, I showed I could do both.

I really do not want readers to conclude that the foregoing summary means politics is unrelentingly grim, with noses to the grindstone. You do work incredibly hard, so much so that it feels as if you live life at two speeds, completely full-on or at dead stop, having fallen over exhausted. Finding the space for dinners with friends, seeing films, even attending family events, is extremely difficult. But the compensation is that you are translating your values into policy action. In addition, with your close colleagues – both elected and political staff – you feel an incredible bond of camaraderie. You ride the ups and the downs together, finding time for plenty of laughter along the way, even if it is only a gallows style of humour.

In my third parliamentary term, in 2006, I was elected deputy opposition leader, alongside Kevin Rudd as leader. In 2007, the ALP won the election, making Kevin prime minister and me the first woman to be deputy prime minister. In 2010, I became the first woman to be prime minister, having advised Kevin that I was challenging him for the leadership. He chose not to run against me in the subsequent party ballot.

Inevitably others have different perspectives on the events of 2010, but I know in my heart of hearts that, having been a loyal deputy, I acted only to try to put an end to the chaos and dysfunction in the government.

I went on to be prime minister for three years and three days, leading a government that, despite its minority status, was the most productive in enacting new legislation in Australia's history. We delivered nation-changing reforms, many of which continue to make the country stronger and fairer.

Politics rolled back around in June 2013, when Kevin Rudd defeated me in a party-room ballot. At the election held shortly afterwards, I exited politics, and in the years since I have scrupulously avoided being a commentator on Australia's domestic political affairs. I leave that to the current generation of parliamentarians.

I am acutely aware that many reading these paragraphs will conclude that my pathway to power, from the moment I first started handing out leaflets as a student activist at Adelaide University to becoming prime minister, is a story about playing the boys' game and being good at it.

Please excuse me if I bristle at that analysis. Politics is inherently full of contests. At its core it is a battle of values, as expressed through political party creeds and policies. Come election time, voters decide who should emerge victorious. Within parliamentary parties, there are always more people wanting to become pre-selected candidates, ministers or leaders than there are positions available. While some get the nod unopposed, overwhelmingly people get these various positions by competing and succeeding. Tarring all of this as the 'boys' game' circles us back to the same divisions and discussions I had in AUS in my early twenties.

Living through this experience, I was very conscious of the status and role-modelling impact of being the first. I did want to show that women could stand tall and win in the very adversarial environment of Australian federal politics, including its robust Question Time, which is characterised by cheering, jeering, occasional witticisms and, frequently, outright abuse. It is so tough that visiting politicians from the United Kingdom, where our Westminster system of government was born, have walked away shaking their heads in amazement.

It is therefore true that I accepted the parliamentary rules and norms rather than trying to change them. In the theatre of the House of Representatives, I gave as good as I got. There is a physicality to projecting yourself in that environment; performing in parliament is about more than what you say. Your adrenaline kicks in and your senses are heightened. I enjoyed it, and at my best I dominated in the chamber.

These skills are displayed in what has come to be known as the 'misogyny speech', my take-down of my political opponent, the leader of the opposition, in October 2012. It became a viral hit, has been sung by a choir and, somewhat bizarrely, enjoyed a recent renaissance on the video sharing app TikTok. Women all over the world have asked me how I was able to give a speech like that. My best answer is that I had, in reality, been developing my ability to speak with force for years. Add a big dose of cool anger, and voila.

Outside of contests in the House of Representatives chamber, I much preferred politeness and discussion to rudeness and conflict. I have always disliked personal confrontations and despised belittling, whether deliberate or inadvertent, by the powerful of those with less status. If you truly want to judge someone's character, watch how they respond to the person who waits on their table or serves them at a counter. I always want to work with people respectfully, with the aim of finding an agreed way forward. Time and again, in very different sorts of situations, I have experienced the delight that comes with forging a disparate group into a loyal, high-performing team.

These consensus-building skills stood me in good stead as I navigated the complexities of delivering big reforms while leading a minority government that needed to rely on the votes of a small political party and key independents in order to get legislation passed.

All that means my leadership style was certainly a mix of characteristics people would think of as stereotypically 'male' and 'female'.

When I became prime minister, I understood that being the first woman would be seen as momentous news. I therefore did not see the need to point to the fact myself or campaign on the basis of gender. I also assumed that the maximum reaction to my gender would be experienced early in my period of office and then it would all normalise to business as usual.

But in fact what I found was the longer I served as prime minister, the more shrill the sexism became. Inevitably governments have to make tough decisions that some people like and others hate. That is certainly true of the government I led. What was different was that the go-to weapon in hard political debates became the kind of insults that only get hurled at a woman. That emerged as a trend alongside what was already a highly gendered lens for viewing my prime ministership. Every negative stereotype you can imagine – bitch, witch, slut, fat, ugly, child-hating, menopausal – all played out.

If I had that time again, I would certainly do two things differently. First, I would point to the bias early in the hope of defusing it a little. If, during my initial period as prime minister, I had raised some examples of sexism, perhaps I could have provoked a debate that would have set some new norms. Second, I would reach out to community leaders beyond the world of politics, men in particular, and try to get them involved in calling out the sexism. These voices would have been seen as more objective than my own.

But by offering these conclusions I do not want to mislead you into believing that I have developed fixed answers on the many issues that surround women and leadership. Despite my long political experience and exposure to feminist thought, I find myself still working things out. Believe it or not, almost forty years of contemplation is insufficient time to solve this puzzle.

When I left the prime ministership and sat down to write the account of my experiences, *My Story*, I set myself the task of including one thoughtful chapter on what I then called 'The curious question of gender'.[1] In preparing to write it, I studied academic papers on gender and leadership. That really helped, both in opening my eyes to new evidence and ideas, but also by enabling me to put my individual experiences into a broader context.

However, I was still left with a frustrating sense I did not know enough, and that collectively as women we did not have available a deep enough research base. In particular, we lacked clear, evidence-supported solutions to overcoming all the barriers to women becoming leaders and having their leadership fairly evaluated. After serving a few weeks as a visiting professor at King's College London in 2016, I pitched the idea of developing a global institute that would concentrate on generating and popularising more of this kind of research and evidence. I first raised the idea over farewell cocktails with the team, but the longer we held the idea up to the light in the sober months that followed, the more we liked it. In April 2018, we launched the Global Institute for Women's Leadership (GIWL) in London at King's, and there is now a sister institute at the Australian National University in Canberra.

The work of GIWL has helped me further develop my own thinking, so now I believe I am a better-equipped advocate for women's leadership than I was when I was prime minister.

Yet, for me, this has been more than an intellectual journey. It has caused me to question whether all those years ago, in adopting my practical, can-do version of feminism, I lost some of the stirring, almost spiritual aspects of sisterhood and solidarity. I wonder whether, on my journey in politics, I was an active and analytical feminist, but not a sensitive one.

By that I mean when, as often happened, I found myself at a decision-making table full of men, I would be motivated to look for ways to get more women in the room, but I didn't really think about what would shift in the interpersonal dynamics of the meeting as a result. When I saw a woman achieve a first, I was happy to tick the box of another battle won, but I did not really feel the joy of celebration. If a woman complained about being over-looked for promotion, or talked over in a meeting, or patronised, I would want to help her push through, but I may not have been the best empathiser.

In some ways, my 'get it done' approach helped as a protective shield when political times were ugly and gendered. I was not given to hours of talking about sexism and misogyny. I would rather be getting on and doing something. But now in my life post-politics, as each year goes by, I increasingly feel the emotional tug of my feminism. The need to unpack with colleagues and friends my sense of anger when the pulse of public discourse about a leader is different solely because she is a woman. The real sense of con-nection and energy I get from gathering with women and talking about our experiences. The urge to console when things go badly for a woman and whoop with delight when they go well.

What does that make me? Older and wiser? Less in need of the protective cloak? I am not sure. On one of the few occasions I have returned to the Australian Parliament since exiting politics, I did so to watch a young and talented woman, Marielle Smith, give her first speech as a senator. Marielle came to work with me after I moved back to Adelaide and was pivotal as I set about creating my life after politics, and we became firm friends. The only good part of watching the election results come up in May 2019, when Labor unexpectedly lost, was seeing her win through. Tears sprang to my eyes as she thanked me for my support. The reaction of one of my former Labor colleagues who is still in the parliament was, 'Jeez, you've gone soft, Gillard.' Maybe that is the explanation. Maybe I have.

For me, all of those things rolled together is the motivation for writing this book.

I wanted to be intellectually engaged, to keep learning more about women and leadership, and bring to readers facts, evidence and insights. However, thinking alone was not going to be enough for me. I also wanted to feel, to revel in women's stories, to absorb the passion and the power of them speaking in their own words. To invoke, through bringing these stories to you, a sense of connection and solidarity, a nourishing of the spirit.

Feminism of the heart and the head. I hope you take the same pleasure in reading it as I have in working on it.

A message from Ngozi

Julia describes herself as a feminist and I describe myself as a womanist – a word invented by the writer Alice Walker and further elaborated and put into good usage by my own aunt, Chikwenye Okonjo Ogunyemi, a writer and critic. I use the word womanist to describe my enduring respect and admiration for women everywhere; for their ability to do so much, love so much and endure so much. Womanist describes my belief in gender equality. The notion that girls and boys, women and men, should have an equal chance in life and equal opportunity to make progress.

Objective statistics on women in leadership positions in politics, finance or business, and statistics on the gender pay gap, coupled with my own life experience, show we have some way to go on gender equality. And it may be harder if you are a woman of colour. You may be at the bottom of the power pecking order that positions white men first, then men of colour, white women, and women of colour. I have not let this reality dampen my optimism for life or diminish my passion for the work I do. Both qualities have helped me power through adversity and manage triumphs.

For some years now, I have wanted to capture my journey to share with other women. But I was busy being a public servant and a technocrat thrown into politics. The latter role led to profound and searing events that meant that before I could get to this book, I had to write another book on issues of transparency, good governance and fighting corruption, which were at the centre of my last four years in government. That book, *Fighting Corruption Is Dangerous: The story behind the headlines*,[2] was completed by mid-2018 and shared my experience of what it means to fight vested interests and build institutions in government.

Having disposed of that important matter I turned to this book – another important matter. Unlike Julia, who joined politics early on as part of her career, I was not your typical politician. I was selected into a position in government and found myself thrust into politics with little or no preparation. Nigeria has an American-style presidential system. This means that the president can look beyond elected politicians to bring others – for example, technocrats, people who occupy senior positions in technical fields – into government. I was selected into government twice, by Presidents Olusegun Obasanjo from 2003 to 2006 and Goodluck Jonathan from 2011 to 2015. I became the first female and, to date, the longest serving Finance Minister of Nigeria, and briefly the first female Foreign Minister. My departure from government in 2015 created the opportunity to reflect on and distil my experiences, and I wanted to share these with younger women managing their careers and aspiring to or already in leadership positions in politics or the private sector. I wanted to talk about what it takes to be in high-stakes positions and work your way to a leadership role. But, frankly, I also wanted to share, in the form of a book, a self-defence.

There are still surprisingly very few working women role models in top leadership positions in the public sector, and women leaders of colour are even more scarce. So, I frequently get asked by younger women what it takes, and how they should manage their careers and balance their lives between work and home. They want to know how I juggled tough jobs with having a family. How did I navigate a husband, four children and a career with frequent overseas travel, they ask? Young women who approach me want mentorship, and I consider this an honour. That people want to learn from me is humbling. But true mentorship is intensive and exhausting, and one can only take on so many women and, yes, men at a time. I would always feel guilty when I had to say to the next young person, 'Sorry, I cannot take on any more.' So it seemed to me that a book was one way to reach more people and answer the myriad questions that women have asked me about managing a pathway to leadership or career success, however that success is defined.

As I mulled over these issues in the years after 2015 and thought about my own bittersweet journey as Nigeria's first female Finance Minister and Foreign Minister, I observed a series of events unfold around the world that unseated women leaders like Presidents Park Geun-hye of South Korea and Dilma Rousseff of Brazil. Hillary Clinton lost the 2016 US presidential election, Joyce Banda took a break from her country, and so on. Women leaders seemed to be having a tough time and I began to wonder, what were their leadership pathways? What had got them to the point they were now at? What successes and failures could they share? What could other women learn from their leadership journeys? I began to discuss these issues with Julia Gillard, the first female prime minister of a fellow Commonwealth country, Australia. We were both members of the International Commission on Financing Global Education Opportunity chaired by Gordon Brown, and I was drawn to her because she was a woman who had also been through tough times, in her role as prime minister. Julia was of course elected, a prime minister and seasoned politician compared to someone like me who had been selected into a political post. Nevertheless, I thought we had quite a lot in common. I found Julia to be a self-proclaimed feminist with a direct and engaging manner, and a sharp and clear mind that had also been reflecting on the fate of women leaders around the world. We exchanged views on several occasions, and we thought there were some narratives emerging from the experiences of women leaders, and some hypotheses we could formulate and test that might capture career and leadership journeys in a manner useful to women. But to get there we would need to talk to other women leaders and test these hypotheses against their experiences and our own. Some of the circumstances surrounding the rise to leadership and fall of certain women leaders were truly unique, and we thought those instances were probably too special to extrapolate from. So, we focused on leaders whose career paths and experience in politics and government could be more readily drawn upon. That gave rise to the women you see in this volume, to their stories, their leadership paths, their and our real-life experiences that prove or disprove various hypotheses about women and leadership.

I hope you will read and relate to these stories, and smile at the familiarity of some of the narratives. Above all, I hope you can garner something to help you with your own pathway.

Thank you to our women leaders

While our own efforts and perspectives are a key ingredient of this book, this project would all have amounted to nothing if eight women leaders had not given freely of their time and spoken with candour. We sincerely thank Jacinda Ardern, Michelle Bachelet, Joyce Banda, Hillary Rodham Clinton, Christine Lagarde, Theresa May, Ellen Johnson Sirleaf and Erna Solberg for the trust they put in us, and we hope they feel that this book is true to what they wanted to convey.

Another important ingredient of this book is the work of academics and others who try to elucidate issues around gender. Thank you for your intelligence and insights.

Our particular thanks go to those who work directly with us and the friends who have offered support and guidance along the way.

Last but not least, a shout-out to our families for putting up with us being in what we called 'book prison', locked away writing.

We each hope that the youngest girls and boys in our families will inherit a world in which leaders are selected or elected based on fair evaluations of their wisdom and capacity. This book is our contribution to getting there. We hope the content informs and inspires, and that you enjoy the occasional laugh out loud.

1

Doing the numbers

How many women have won an Academy Award for Best Director? The answer is one: Kathryn Bigelow for the film *The Hurt Locker*. That makes one woman and ninety-three men across the history of the Oscars.[1]

A dispiriting result. Yet it could be worse. Far too often, the answer to a question that starts with the words 'How many women . . .' is zero. Let's try a few.

How many women have led the United Nations or the World Bank? Zero.

How many women have held the office of President of the United States, France, Nigeria, Mexico or Japan? Zero.

How many women have been Prime Minister of Italy, Spain, Sweden, Malaysia or Singapore? Zero.

Only fifty-seven countries out of the 193 nations that are members of the United Nations have ever had a woman hold the highest political office with executive power in their nation, whether that be president or prime minister. This means 70 per cent of nations have always been led by a man. If we add in the women who served in an acting or temporary capacity, the number rises to seventy-two, meaning over 60 per cent of nations have never seen a woman in the top job even as a stand in.[2]

Only thirteen countries have had more than one woman lead, and of those, only New Zealand and Iceland have had three women leaders.[3] No country has ever had four or more women leaders.

A different way of looking at these numbers is to ascertain how many women are leading nations at any one time. In 2010, fourteen UN member nations had women leaders. By 2019, the number had risen to a historic peak of eighteen women leaders holding office in the same year. In 2020, at the time of writing, the number has fallen to thirteen, or just under 7 per cent of UN member countries. Growth in the number of women leaders was faster in the prior decade, moving up from a base of four in the year 2000. The last year in which there were no women leaders was 1978.[4]

While the numbers have moved around year by year, taken as a whole it means when the councils of the world meet, those bodies are overwhelmingly male.

Take for example the G20, which is a regular forum that brings together the leaders from the twenty places on earth with the largest economies. When it is convened today, Chancellor Angela Merkel of Germany is the only female national leader sitting around the table. Fortunately, she is not completely alone. Ursula von der Leyen, the President of the European Commission, attends because the European Union is accorded country status. Kristalina Georgieva also attends as the head of the International Monetary Fund (IMF).

Both Ngozi and Julia have been to G20 meetings, but not at the same time. During the days of the global financial crisis, Ngozi went in her capacity as managing director of the World Bank, and she was briefly a sherpa, which is the name given to the key officials who hammer out the communiqué. This descriptor is a term borrowed from mountain climbing and fits with the whole event being seen as a 'summit'.

As prime minister, Julia attended G20 meetings to represent Australia. Women leaders were always dramatically in minority. At the 2012 meeting, Julia saw the most women. Angela was also in attendance, as well as President Dilma Rousseff of Brazil and President Cristina Fernández de Kirchner of Argentina. Christine Lagarde was there too, representing the IMF. On the gender balance of G20 meetings, things have gone backwards since then.

Julia also attended meetings of the Asia-Pacific Economic Cooperation forum, which brings together the leaders of economies that make up 60 per cent of the world's output and 47 per cent of global trade. The twenty-one members, which include countries like the United States, China, Chile, Mexico and Japan, are home to almost 40 per cent of the population of our planet. When Julia went to the APEC meeting in Hawaii in 2011, she was the only woman leader in attendance. When APEC last met, in 2018, two women, Jacinda Ardern of New Zealand and Carrie Lam of Hong Kong, attended. A step forward but nowhere near enough.

Given there are almost four billion women and girls alive today, how can it be that the odds are still so severely stacked against them having a woman lead their nation? Indeed, how can it be that so few women represent them in the parliaments of their nations? Only one in four parliamentarians globally today are women. In the past twenty-five years the number has doubled, which is progress.

Yet somehow it is hard to get too enthusiastic about a result that means three out of every four political decision-makers in 2020 are men.[5]

The results are worse the more senior the level in politics. Of the 3343 ministerial positions examined by the World Economic Forum in 153 countries, only 21 per cent were held by women.[6]

The gender limitation in the number of women parliamentarians and ministers has a pipeline impact. While political systems vary enormously, in many countries it is not constitutionally possible to become a nation's leader unless the individual is first a parliamentarian. This is true of Westminster-style systems in which the highest executive office is that of prime minister.

Even in countries without this specific structure, it is common for people to have experience in an elected position before seeking the top job. If women are not equally included in the levels of politics, including local and regional decision-making forums, as well as the layers of national politics, then that bias will likely carry through to who will be in contention to fill the ultimate leadership spot.

This book endeavours to find answers to the profound questions raised by the dearth of women national leaders in today's world. While we focus on political leadership, the same kinds of gender issues touch every part of our lives.

For example, the businesses women deal with as consumers and workers are disproportionately shaped by men. The *Fortune* 500 is a list of the largest companies incorporated in the United States. Many of the businesses are global household names. In June 2019, a gender record was attained: the number of women chief executive officers of these companies was at its highest level ever. This milestone number was 6.6 per cent.[7]

The FTSE 100 Index includes the biggest companies on the London Stock Exchange. While the location may be different, the number is the same. Only six of the one hundred CEOs are women.[8] The Hang Seng Index details the largest companies that trade on the Stock Exchange of Hong Kong. Here the picture worsens. Out of the top fifty companies listed, only one has a female CEO.[9]

As citizens who want to stay in touch with news about what is happening in the world, it is most likely that women will end up reading about or listening to bulletins written by men, presented by men or about men. Only 24 per cent of persons heard, read about or seen in news media are women. Even worse, only 4 per cent of news stories clearly challenge gender stereotypes.[10]

At the end of a long, hard day, women who want to wind down by watching a movie or television show, or settling in with a good book, can still find themselves reading, hearing or seeing men.

Pick one of the top one hundred box office successes and the likelihood is the voices will be disproportionately male. An annual study of these movies conducted for twelve consecutive years concluded female speaking characters filled only 30.9 per cent of all roles.[11]

Turn on the television, whether broadcast, cable or streamed, and women characters make up less than half of those depicted onscreen, and when they do feature they are more likely to be playing a personal-life orientated role – being a mother, for example – than a work–life role.[12]

Want to watch some sport? While a woman spectator might never be able to imagine herself performing the same physical feats as the professional athletes she admires, at least she can identify with the gender pay gap. Looking at the pay of all working women globally, for every dollar a man earns, a woman earns

63 cents.[13] Being an amazing sportsperson does not end gender pay problems, and that number sixty-three comes up again but in a different context. Serena Williams is the only woman on the list of the one hundred highest paid athletes in the world today, and she comes in at sixty-three.[14]

Try reading, perhaps by selecting a novel by a Booker Prize–winning author. If you do, the chances are that author will be a man, given thirty-one men and sixteen women have won that award. What about the works of Nobel laureates in Literature? The odds worsen. That prize has been awarded to 101 men and only fifteen women. The fact that the awarding committee was mired in a sexual misconduct scandal in 2018 might be seen as a capstone to those figures.[15]

Of course, Nobel Prizes are given for other important accomplishments, including contributions to peace and scientific research. Across the whole spectrum of prize categories since the awards started in 1901, over nine hundred individuals have won a Nobel Prize. Only fifty-three of them have been women.

Whether women are relying on seatbelts and airbags for protection in the event of a car accident, or carefully measuring out the dose of a medicine prescribed to them, it is likely the research behind those features of modern life came out of testing that was of greater relevance to men than women. The crash-test dummies that are used to inform the design of vehicle safety features are almost always man-sized and man-shaped. As a result, the equipment meant to protect works less well for women, who are 17 per cent more likely to die in an automobile accident.[16] Women are also far less frequently the subjects of pharmaceutical trials. The reason given for this is money, because it is more expensive to control for hormonal variations associated with menstruation.[17]

Worryingly, we are at a major risk of not leaving this kind of gender skew in innovation behind us, given the historic barriers to women entering the fields of science, technology, engineering and maths. As a result, much of the work of designing and shaping the products and services of the future is being done by men. In big data and artificial intelligence, women are an estimated 26 per cent of the workforce, in engineering just 15 per cent and in cloud computing a mere 12 per cent.[18]

The gender statistics in the venture capital industry, which defines through its investments what new ideas will survive and thrive, are even worse. For example, only 12 per cent of the people in the United States who decide where venture capital funding should go are women.[19] In terms of who receives the funds, currently only 2.7 per cent goes to companies founded solely by women and 11.8 per cent to mixed-gender teams of founders.[20] That means money is predominantly being invested by men in men and their ideas for what should be our shared and gender-equal future.

There are so many more dimensions to gender discrimination: sexual violence, early marriage, human trafficking, honour killings, the denial of reproductive rights, and the list goes on.

But describing all the characteristics, repercussions and ripple effects of the maleness of the world around us is not the purpose of this book. Rather, our mission is to examine the many obstacles holding women back from becoming leaders, with a view to working out how best to clear those hurdles out of the way.

We see the task of having an equal number of women leaders in politics and business around the world as an urgent one.

The World Economic Forum has calculated that, if we continue to improve at the current rate, closing the global gender gap in political representation will take ninety-five years.

So slow is the pace of change that not only will we not achieve gender equality in our lifetimes, it will likely not be realised in the lifetimes of children who are born today.

Our choice is between having the world crawl towards the dawn of political gender equality in the year 2115, or acting more dramatically now. While fast change will undoubtedly be difficult to achieve, to simply wait would be intolerable.

We hope you share our mindset of fixed determination coupled with extreme impatience. Let's get this done.

2

Our framework

Judging by the wild popularity of criminal investigation television shows, it seems human beings are fascinated by what happens in morgues. Autopsy sequences are good for ratings.

In real life, most of us would probably find the blood and guts too much to take. But let us imagine, for a moment, that we managed to put aside any squeamishness and spent a day chopping up brains. What would we find? The answer is lots of pinkish-grey squishy stuff, with folds and creases.

What we would definitely not find is consistent, obvious differences between male and female brains. Many *Men Are from Mars, Women Are from Venus*–style books give the impression that neuroscience can take stereotypical male and female attributes and show what is causing them in the brain. This bit controls communication and is bigger in women. Men have a larger lobe that relates to spatial awareness. And so on and so on.

These kinds of simple stories are more fiction than fact.

Scientists have found some differences on average between men and women. Men tend to have bigger brains than women, but that is consistent with men having bigger organs generally, like larger livers and kidneys. There is no study that correlates sex, brain size and human intelligence. A UK study of around five thousand brains, thankfully done by MRI scans on living patients, found that on average, adjusting for age, women tended to have a significantly thicker cerebral cortex compared to men.[1] Adjusted for brain size, there were fourteen regions where men had higher average brain volume and ten regions where women did.

It certainly is tempting to put labels on what functions those subcortical regions are associated with, create a theory of male brains and female brains, and then use it to explain gender differences in our societies. But such an approach smacks into some pretty big hurdles. First, the complexity of a human being's destiny, let alone the structures and power relations within our societies, cannot be extrapolated quite so easily from the spongy stuff in our heads. It is by no means clear how differences in brains relate to behaviour. Or, put another way, presented with four brains on a slab and told these organs belonged to an astrophysicist, a poet, a tyrannical dictator and a saviour of the poor, other than a fluky guess, a coroner would not be able to match brain to person.

Second, none of this really gets us anywhere given our brains literally change shape depending on how we use them. Albert Einstein's brain was much dissected and studied after he died, with every fold, cortex and connection between hemispheres remarked upon. But even after so much study, it is impossible for scientists to tell how much of the variation between Einstein's brain and an average one explains his genius, as opposed to how much his life of deep thinking sculpted his brain.

This is an individual example of the structural plasticity dilemma: are any structural differences in male and female brains the explanation for differing male and female behaviour, or are variations explained by gendered environments, stereotypes and consequently life experiences, which mean men's brains get more of a workout in one area and women's in another? Perhaps one day we will not be so marooned between cause and effect. But right now, here we are.

Some have suggested it is not so much the structure of the pinkish-grey matter in our heads as it is the hormones humans are dosed with before and around birth that create male and female brains and behaviours. Most of us will recall from high school science classes that chromosomes and hormones differ between men and women. Biology teachers persevere through much adolescent sniggering to explain that a Y-chromosome means a foetus will develop male genitalia. The same foetus will also experience a surge of testosterone from around the eighth to sixteenth weeks in utero. A second, smaller wave of testosterone hits newborn boys and lasts for around three months.

But in terms of character, do those hormonal surges mean anything, especially given female foetuses are also exposed to some testosterone in utero?

In her marvellous book *Delusions of Gender*, psychologist and science writer Cordelia Fine details the many studies that have tried to take testosterone as the predictor of gender differences.[2] A suite of studies involved mothers who needed to have their amniotic fluid tested during the course of their pregnancy. The amount of testosterone in the fluid was recorded, which was an indirect way of measuring how much of that hormone each foetus experienced.

Then, at various times after birth, the empathising abilities of these children were studied in different ways. Did a high dose of testosterone mean the child would be less empathetic, given empathy is considered to be a more female trait? No straightforward correlation was consistently found, nor were young boys reliably inferior in the social domain. Scientists are continuing to study the kinds of complex and experience-based capacities that matter for leadership and as they do so, the more tenuous claims of links with hormone levels early in life become.

Cordelia's conclusion is that we need to be wary of those over-hyped news reports that tell us there is solid scientific evidence sex differences are hardwired into human beings. Beware neuro-sexism posing as neuroscience.

Even in the future, when the study of neuroscience and sex differences will be more advanced, experts will continue to tell us male and female brains are more alike than they are different. Each one is really a mosaic of characteristics, readily combining some attributes that brain scans tell us are more likely to be found in a man's head and some that most commonly exist in a woman's.

Against that background, is there really a women's style of leadership? Are women more sharing and caring, with a multitasking, team-building style? Do men tend to be more commanding, controlling and competitive, while being inclined to focus on a single task at a time?

Many people would readily answer yes to these questions. For your authors, the picture is a little more complex.

This book has not been premised on the idea that there are inherent, biologically determined differences between how men and women lead. Instead, we believe that to the extent there are variations, they arise because, at every stage of life, men and women are socialised and stereotyped differently.

Think about how many times in human history, after the news of the birth of a baby has been imparted, the first question asked was 'Boy or girl?' From that moment on, that child is steeped in an environment of gender differences. In some parts of the world the stereotyping now starts even earlier, when the parents hold an elaborate 'gender reveal' party months before the baby is born.

Think about how many times the child organising the playground games has been described as a 'natural leader' if they are a boy, and a 'little miss bossy boots' if they are a girl. Or how the images of authority that surround us and spring readily to our minds are images of men, in suits, in uniforms, in robes and so very definitely in charge.

Of course, around the world, millions of people push back against this gender stereotyping every day, including many parents who valiantly strive to bring up their children in an environment free from it. But inevitably societal expectations seep in and a frustrated parent can find themselves at risk of losing the argument when their young daughter says, with complete certainty, 'Pink is for girls.'

From childhood and throughout adulthood, socialisation and stereotyping are part of what shapes women and men, including their leadership styles. In our interviews, we have endeavoured to tease out the impact of any assumptions about being female that surrounded our women leaders when they were growing up, starting out, moving up or leading.

Yet this book aims to do more than analyse the biases, conscious and unconscious, that swirl in our thoughts about gender. We also look at the structural barriers that hold women back, including the glass labyrinth, glass ceiling and glass cliff. Yes, that is a hell of a lot of glass, and for the women who break through there is always the nasty consequence of being surrounded by jagged, dangerous shards. However, each separate glass barrier does need to be understood.

The glass labyrinth is a way of capturing the obstacles that hold women back as they seek to make their way up from an entry-level job.[3] The way these barriers halt the progress of many women gives rise to the pipeline problem: the chant that there cannot be equal numbers of women presidents and prime ministers because there are not enough women parliamentarians, or ministers, or members of political parties, and it is impossible to end up being the leader without first being in one or all of these groups. In charting our leaders' pathways to power, we learn about negotiating this labyrinth.

The glass cliff is the documented phenomenon that organisations reach out and embrace women's leadership when they are in trouble. The term was first coined in 2004 in response to claims on the front page of *The Times* of London that, in the top one hundred firms, increasing the number of women on boards was 'wreaking havoc' on share prices.[4] On deeper examination, researchers found a stable share price was the usual precursor to a man being appointed to the board of directors, but often a woman was selected after a period of poor share price performance.[5] When 'steady as we go' was good enough, then a regular male appointment was made, but if there was a crisis, it was time to try a woman.

Further research has demonstrated that, when times are bad, employing a manager good at helping people get through the crisis is seen as desirable.[6] As a result of searching for that nurturing skill, which is stereotyped as a female one, selection panels were more likely to choose a woman to lead in the worst of times. This attitude of those making the appointment may well be compounded by the attitude of the new recruit. Only a female outsider might consider taking such a high-risk position. For her, that may well be a rational choice, because unless she seizes the opportunity and challenge, she is unlikely to be offered another job at that level. Whereas for a man with more options, the smart choice may be to say no. Some of our women leaders in this book have survived the glass cliff and talk about it. Your authors also know the experience.

Then, finally, there is that high, hard glass ceiling that confines a woman to the role of number two and prevents her getting to number one. We also talk about what it is like to smash your head on one of those.

Our women leaders talk about these barriers in both a very human and an analytical way. We hear about the times when the hardest thing to overcome was their own doubts, and when the political system, with its structures and rules historically determined by men, worked to exclude them.

This book is about leadership and gender. When we use that word, we are referring to the socially constructed characteristics that are ascribed to women and men, and the relationship of each group to each other and to power. Our starting assumption has been that while gender constructs vary by nation and culture, there is actually more in common than different around the world in terms of gender and leadership. This is a proposition we analyse and test.

We know there is more to achieving diversity in leadership than simply having more women leaders. Anyone who went off the grid for a few years, missed all the political chatter and then came back would still be right more often than not if they guessed their prime minister or president was a heterosexual man from the most privileged racial group in their country.

All of us would love to see a future in which meetings of the United Nations Security Council or the G20 are as diverse as the people of planet Earth. In particular, it would be wonderful to see leaders of all races and sexualities, who identify as men, women or non-binary. What would be even more thrilling is if each of them were then judged on the calibre of their contribution, not the colour of their skin, who they love, their appearance or whether their gender identity matches their biological sex.

When we reach that place, then a broader and more inclusive language about sex and gender will be needed by writers to discuss and analyse contemporary leadership. But, given who holds political power in today's world, it has been sufficient to use the traditional binary of female and male, women and men, in writing this book.

Getting to that better world will require profound change, and we believe all types of exclusion must be studied, discussed and campaigned on. This book does not aim to cover this vast range of issues. It is devoted to the seismic shift needed to enable women to have equal and fair access to leadership.

This book is also about getting, holding and using power. The feminist movement embraces many who challenge the pyramid-shaped power paradigms of our societies, including the political ones. There is a desire to move beyond adversarial systems filled with winners and losers, leaders and followers.

Your authors respect these arguments but do not believe the cause of women's leadership equality should be parked until more consensual decision-making processes emerge. Both of us share a sense of urgency about democratic renewal and more community engagement, with flatter structures and less distance between voters and national leaders. However, we think strengthening our democracies and promoting women's leadership are causes that can and should be pursued at the same time.

Given we live on a planet that is in peril from pandemics and the ravages of climate change, as well as being home to violent conflict and crushing poverty, many who are sympathetic to gender equality may still query whether it, and a particular focus on women and leadership, are truly priorities. We understand, indeed applaud, the drive to prioritise sustainability and development, but it would be an error to allow gender equality and women's leadership to fall down the to-do list.

When the world, through the United Nations, adopted seventeen goals to guide activities on sustainable development from now until 2030, gender equality was included for hard-headed, not feel-good, reasons. It was a response to the evidence that shows women disproportionately bear the burden of being denied education, health care and economic opportunity, and dramatic change can only be achieved through female empowerment.

For example, research has demonstrated that having women involved in the negotiation of peace agreements in societies emerging from civil wars and other forms of conflict increases the probability that stability will last more than fifteen years by 35 per cent. According to one economic study, attaining gender equality could increase global gross domestic product by up to US$28 trillion, or 26 per cent.[7]

All this means the most peaceful and prosperous version of our planet cannot be reached without better including women. Part of enabling women to see and embrace this better future, to imagine themselves achieving in the world of work and the task of nation-building, is women's leadership.

A seminal study in India has proved this point conclusively.[8] It showed that as a result of seeing female leadership in their village, adolescent girls were more likely to want to wait until after the age of eighteen to marry, and to aim for a job that required an education. They were less likely to want to be a housewife or have their occupation determined by their in-laws after marriage. The impact was not just limited to rising ambition. After seeing two women leaders, the gender gap in educational outcomes between boys and girls was either erased or reversed. Women's leadership changed the lives of the next generation.

It is therefore our belief that peace, shared prosperity, gender equality and women's leadership are not four different destinations. Each is effectively a thread in the interwoven fabric of fair and sustainable societies. Ignoring or deciding to wait until later on to focus on women's leadership does not work. Doing so pulls out a key strand and the whole is ruined.

Political leaders, women included, often publish biographies, and inevitably acres of news commentary is written about them. Consequently, it is fair to ask, what is this book seeking to do that all of those already published words do not? The answer is that this book takes a different approach to the usual rendering of the stories of women leaders in three respects.

First, there is power in this book being more than one woman's story. It is hard for a woman to talk about gender issues and not be criticised for it. Even in memoirs, women leaders can shy away from dealing deeply with gender questions, fearing a backlash if a book is seen to be complaining in tone. By inviting a number of women to speak directly about gender, we have created a more open space to put forward perspectives. Our interviewees were each asked the same set of questions and knew the other women were also answering them. That helped lift the burden of potentially being seen as an individual on a crusade for sympathy.

Second, this book is global. Ordinarily, news and analysis about the treatment of a woman leader does not travel. The number of times gendered moments in one woman's leadership come to global attention are few and far between. One example is Julia's misogyny speech, which was widely reported. At best, there is occasional national analysis of highly gendered moments and the way in which a female leader dealt with the situation. At worst, there is silence.

This leaves no quick and easy way of scanning across countries in order to understand what is happening to a number of women leaders. This book makes a deliberate attempt to correct that lack of worldwide perspective. Using the standard set of questions enabled us, across cultures and continents, to contrast and compare women's experiences.

Third, the predominant frame of our exploration of the experiences of women leaders is the available psychological research. It is wonderful that in so many places in the world, researchers are now corralling people, often students, and analysing in a theoretical fashion their attitudes to gender generally and to women leaders in particular.

However, real life is a world away from such laboratory conditions. We wanted to see what carries from the psychological test to the punishing arena of politics. For us, the whole process has been revealing. We have been left with a new understanding of the tightrope on which women leaders must balance if they are to be viewed as 'man' enough to do the job but feminine enough to not be viewed as unlikeable, or even held in contempt.

Out of all of this examination, we have proposed a series of strategies for change – insights for aspiring women, supportive men, parents, the media, all of us. Ultimately, change happens because in societies around the world, women and men in their millions say to themselves and to each other, 'Let's fix this.' It is our aim that this book helps inform and equip.

What would the world look like if we had approximately equal numbers of male and female leaders, and their leadership was not evaluated through the prism of gender? As authors, we think this question needs careful consideration.

It is tempting to say that the rise of empathetic, nurturing, team-building women leaders would give us a kinder and gentler world. But this reasoning bakes in gender stereotyping of women. Are we really aiming for a world in which a self-centred, egotistical, ruthless man can still claw his way to the top and be viewed as a successful leader, but a woman can only get there if she is caring and sharing?

There are two alternative answers to that question. We can say to ourselves that, in an equal world, no one should make assumptions about leadership style based on gender. Some women leaders would be hard, demanding and competitive. Some men would be self-effacing, team-orientated and nurturing. Or, we could say that we value traits like being communal and compassionate, which are historically associated with women, and as voters we will demand all leaders display such attributes.

In addition to not requiring women leaders to pick up the burden of always being the nicer person, we have to be careful about justifying women's leadership on the basis that they secure better outcomes than men.

This has been much done in the corporate world. Today it is often said that putting more women on corporate boards increases profits. Yet this kind of bald statement runs way ahead of the research findings, which are that the two are only reliably corre-lated in countries with greater gender equality.[9] Then, as every researcher tries to pound into our heads, correlation does not explain causation.

In the political realm, there is a similar reach for empirical justifications of the case for women's leadership. Some of these arguments have force. For example, there is evidence that more inclusive political leadership teams bring different issues to the fore. Of course, it is possible that a man could devote his political life to advocating causes like reproductive health, access to child care and the eradication of domestic violence. But the evidence to date tells us that these issues have tended to be brought to the decision-making table by women, many of whom can speak with the clarity and conviction that only comes from personal experience.

But, ultimately, the case for women's leadership is a moral one. In a democracy, a population should be able to look at its leaders and see a reflection of the full diversity of society. What kind of democracy is it that bestows a vote but not a real prospect of becoming the person voted for?

We passionately believe that every child is unique, but each should be endowed with the same rights and opportunities. Each should be able to dream the same dreams, including wanting to become a president or prime minister. None should encounter extra obstacles if they aim to become a leader.

3

Pathways to power: Introducing our women leaders

Ever played the 'perfect dinner party' game? Who would you invite to share a meal and conversation if you could pick from anyone in the world?

Selecting which women leaders to interview for this book has felt a bit like trying to answer that question. What a group of women to swap stories with over fabulous food! But in reality, we brought a little more science to the task of selection.

While we could have selected women leaders from many walks of life, we decided to focus on political leaders. Partly, that choice naturally grew out of our life experiences. We have both served in office and are enthusiasts about the power of policies and politics to bring change. In a world of increased cynicism about what can be achieved by governments in democracies, we both still truly believe that serving as a political leader is an honourable and impactful life choice, whether you run for office as Julia did or are selected to serve by a president, as was the case with Ngozi.

But the choice also grew from our belief that every dynamic that plays out around women and leadership is at its highest extreme in the pressurised, intensely public environment of politics. While women leaders in other domains are also frequently in the public eye, none are more exposed to judgement than those whose fate is determined by voters.

We knew we wanted to cover different contexts and cultures. In fact, our desire to write the book stemmed from a set of discussions in which we compared what we knew of the experiences of women leaders in developing countries and emerging economies with those in the developed world. Our sense was that those experiences were much more similar than would be expected given the often sharp differences between locations.

Initially, we thought that this set of choices would lead us to women who have served or are serving as presidents and prime ministers around the world. Indeed, we have included women who have held or are currently wielding power in Chile, Liberia, Malawi, New Zealand, Norway and the United Kingdom.

But how could we not include Hillary Clinton, a woman who came so close to becoming leader of the most powerful nation in the world? After all, out of anyone she is the woman with the most visible experience of gender and politics. Surely her lessons from having walked a unique path could teach us a thing or two about leadership. Seeing Hillary in New York went on our to-do list.

So did seeing Christine Lagarde, who, like Ngozi, was politically appointed to serve as her country's first female Finance Minister, a crucial and difficult position. Christine went on to become the first woman elected to lead the International Monetary Fund. We thought it would be a big mistake to miss out on the insights of a person who smashed a number of glass ceilings, assumed a major international role at a time of crisis and attended global leaders' meetings, including the G20.

As described in chapter 1, Chancellor Angela Merkel of Germany has been a continuing presence at G20 meetings since their inception. First elected as chancellor in November 2005, she has announced she will retire from that position in 2021, making her one of the longest serving female political leaders of all time. Of course, we would have liked to interview her for this book but, given the huge pressures on her time, we were not able to do so. Angela has rarely spoken about gender and leadership. We are certainly hoping that in her post-political years she contributes to this vital conversation.

Together, our interviewees form a dynamic and diverse group of eight from across the political spectrum. Some are global, even household names. Some are lesser known outside their own nation. Like all politicians, they have their diehard fans and dedicated detractors. As authors, we have taken the view that each of these women should tell their own story and explain the world through their eyes. We have not weighed their words against the criticisms of others and pronounced who is right and who is wrong. That means the views expressed here are subjective and for you to judge.

Let us introduce you to these leaders and have them explain their pathways to power.

Meeting Ellen Johnson Sirleaf – President of Liberia, 2006 to 2018, the first and only woman to be elected to office as President in Liberia and the first woman to be elected as a national leader in Africa

Every year in late September, the United Nations holds what is known colloquially as 'Leaders Week', a specific time for national leaders to come to New York and participate in UN affairs person-ally, rather than through ambassadors or foreign ministers. While the main set piece for leaders is their address to the United Nations General Assembly, the week has become a whirlwind of meetings, press events and earnest discussions over breakfast, lunch and dinner.

For leaders, every minute of the day and night is full because while everyone is in town it is a terrific time to meet one to one, or at least delegation to delegation, with other leaders. Speed dating for politicians.

If the week only included leaders and their entourages, security teams and motorcades, that would be enough to tip the traffic of Midtown Manhattan from bad to atrocious, and the security arrangements from the usual level for this big global city to a higher degree of alert. But the presence of so many leaders attracts thousands with a cause, and thousands more who want to report the goings-on. That brings the traffic to a standstill and shifts the security to fortress-like.

We had arrived in New York the weekend before the whole jamboree was due to kick off. Both of us had enough past experi-ence with Leaders Weeks to know what to expect. Eighteen-hour days, starting with breakfast meetings at 6 am and ending with dinner discussions that finish late at night. Getting from place to place, for those of us without a motorcade, is best done on foot. As if in protest against the extra demands placed on it, New York City routinely manages to turn on atrocious, humid, wet weather for the occasion.

No one would call all this fun. But for those of us with causes like educating and vaccinating every child, it creates key moments of engagement and visibility at the highest levels. It was also a good time for us to catch a now-retired leader. Former President Ellen Johnson Sirleaf was also in New York, pursuing her own causes.

Despite the nature of the week to come, we had a mounting sense of excitement as we took what seemed like an endless Uber ride out to Long Island for the interview.

Born Ellen Johnson in Monrovia, the capital of Liberia, on 29 October 1938, she became the first woman to lead a nation in Africa. In 2011, her efforts in bringing peace, development and women's rights to her country were recognised when she was awarded the Nobel Peace Prize.

The history of Liberia and its population of 4.8 million people is inextricably linked to American slavery. It was the view of many abolitionists that freed slaves should return to Africa, so in January 1822 the first ship sponsored by the American Colonization Society landed in what was to become Liberia. Understandably, the local indigenous people had other ideas about the best use of their homeland. Between the ravages of fighting, disease and famine, the death rate of those who arrived on a series of ships over the next twenty years is among the highest in accurately recorded human history.

Tragically, war and disease have also racked modern-day Liberia. Two civil wars were fought between 1989 and 2003. The Ebola epidemic struck in 2014. Ellen was the president who led her nation as it rebuilt from war and confronted this deadly disease. Her life's journey includes being jailed for her beliefs, fleeing into exile and leaving an abusive marriage.

Finally, we arrived at a suburban home that gave no sign it was housing such a distinguished leader. It was the home of Ellen's sister, Jennie, and here, around a dining room table with bowls of nuts and soft drinks at hand, we interviewed President Johnson Sirleaf.

Even in this informal setting and dressed in casual clothes, Ellen exuded an air of firm resolve. As she spoke to us, her intelligence and sense of precision were obvious. Ellen, who was shortly going to celebrate her eightieth birthday, was clearly a woman who had spent a lifetime being listened to and having her every word weighed, so she used them neither quickly nor recklessly.

Yet Ellen's life is full of moments where she chose shock and awe over measured and mild. Or, put another way, Ellen knows how to give a hell of a speech.

Not long after finishing high school in 1956, at the age of seventeen, Ellen married James Sirleaf. She had four sons quickly. In fact, her first two boys were both born in 1957, the first in January and the second in December. James was seven years older than Ellen and had studied agriculture in the United States. While his aim was to work for the Liberian Department of Agriculture, it took him a while to achieve it.

For the first few years of her married life, as James worked towards his goal, the couple and their children lived with James's mother. This enabled Ellen to work, first as a secretary and then assisting an accountant. Even though the paid work was a necessity, taken to help the family make ends meet, Ellen looks back on this period as the start of her career in finance.

Ellen and James set up their own home in Monrovia when he succeeded in getting the departmental job. Their fourth and youngest son was born in 1961. She describes this period in her life as one of mothering her children, household drudgery and low-paying jobs.

She still yearned, even in the midst of this exhaustingly full life, to further her education and have her own opportunity to succeed in a career. Her best friend, Clave, went to college in the United States, and Ellen could not help but notice the pitying looks Clave gave her when visiting for the holidays.

In her early twenties, Ellen saw an opportunity for change. James had been awarded a scholarship to study for a Masters of Agriculture in the United States, and she strived to go with him. She sat an exam, lobbied and pleaded in order to get her own scholarship. She was successful, and in 1962 the couple went to Wisconsin so James could attend university and Ellen could study at Madison Business College. This was the real start of her pathway to power, but, as we discuss in chapter 8, to take those first steps Ellen had to make the heart-wrenching decision to leave her children in Liberia.

This was not the only formidable challenge Ellen faced. James was a jealous man, prone to drunken rages, and his abuse increased as he felt he was losing control over his wife, who now had her own life and ambitions. At its worst, he would hold a gun to Ellen's head and threaten to shoot her. Ellen has spoken publicly about living through this kind of terror. To us she simply says, '*That violence strengthened me. It made me more determined to go forward.*'

By the time she returned to Liberia two years later, Ellen had her first higher education qualification, an associate degree in accounting. She started work as a public servant in Liberia's Ministry of Finance. She, James and the children recommenced family life together, but the domestic violence continued. In the late 1960s, Ellen was driven to the conclusion that the marriage must come to an end when her oldest son, then around eight years old, tried to protect her as James waved a gun around.

Under Liberian law, the father took custody of the children in the event of a divorce. For Ellen, this meant separation from three of her four sons. One son, her third child, Rob, demanded to stay with her, and that was ultimately allowed. Her two older sons went to boarding school, and her youngest ended up living with James's brother and following his uncle into the medical profession.

The courage to go on is part of Ellen's character, as is the courage to speak out. Four times in her life, the spectre of going to jail has haunted her words. On one occasion she actually ended up behind bars. As she tells it:

'*In 1969, even though I was just a junior official in the Ministry of Finance, I made a really strong speech about how the government's policies were not working. In response, the government took the decision to send me to jail, but that didn't happen. I guess after that speech my whole life began to take a different turn because that is how eventually I got to Harvard. A Harvard leader at the conference made the arrangements for me to get out of Liberia.*'

This incident in Ellen's life shows the best and worst of human nature. The ugliness of a government prepared to lash out at criticism from any quarter. The generosity of the academic, Professor Gustav Papanek, who realised Ellen would be in trouble. He enabled her to leave Liberia, get a degree in economics and then go on to study for a Master of Public Administration at one of the most prestigious institutions in the world, the John F. Kennedy School of Government at Harvard University.

Ellen returned to Liberia by ship, accompanied by her sister, Jennie. As they journeyed, their homeland entered a new era. On 23 July 1971, President William Tubman, who had led Liberia for twenty-seven years, with a mixture of what Ellen describes as 'old-world charm and iron-fisted control',[1] had died from prostate cancer at the age of seventy-five. For the public, this came as a huge shock because no one knew he had been unwell, and he had always seemed invincible.

The vice-president, William R. Tolbert, became president, and his brother, Stephen Tolbert, a successful businessman, became the Minister for Finance. Ellen was invited by Stephen to become the appointed Deputy Minister for Finance.

President Tolbert saw the need for profound change and was nicknamed 'Speedy' because of his desire to get new reforms moving. However, he had spent many years as President Tubman's right-hand man, and he was deeply connected to the web of old power. Ultimately, he could not break free of it and the country stagnated. At this moment, Ellen chose to give another major speech. She describes it as follows:

'In 1972, I gave the commencement speech at my [former] high school and I think that speech again became a strong propeller on my road to leadership, first to becoming a political activist, and then eventually to leadership because I really stood out and spoke up about what was wrong in Liberia. This was the kind of event where representatives of the old guard, of the old order, were on stage with me. While there were discussions in government after that speech about jailing me, I still think it was important for me to have given it. Liberia had riots over food – over rice – in 1979, and a year after there was a coup d'état, so if one looks back at that speech, I predicted that calamity would come, and it did.'

Fortunately for Ellen, cooler heads prevailed in the internal discussion, and while her speech was banned from publication and distribution, she was neither jailed nor fired. She was sidelined, though, and as a result reached out to officials she had met at the World Bank to see if there was a position for her there. Ellen secured a job as a loan officer at the head office in Washington, DC.

During her years at the World Bank, Ellen gained a number of promotions and served in a variety of postings, including in the Caribbean, Brazil and East Africa.

But the call of home was strong. In 1975, when a new reform-minded person, James T. Phillips, was appointed as Minister for Finance by President Tolbert, he reached out to Ellen and she returned to Liberia and the ministry. This time she arranged an insurance policy by taking leave from, but not relinquishing, her substantive post at the World Bank.

She arrived home in a country with mounting tensions and severe economic problems. Even in these circumstances, President Tolbert was determined to spend almost a third of the government's budget on building the facilities necessary to host a meeting of the Organisation of African Unity, which would be attended by national leaders from across Africa.

Ellen argued against such profligacy. On this occasion, speaking frankly did not hinder her progress. In 1979, she was appointed Finance Minister by President Tolbert.

It was a position she did not hold for long because her life and her country were thrown into chaos on 12 April 1980 when, in a bloody coup, Samuel Kanyon Doe executed President Tolbert and seized control.

Only twenty-eight years old, Doe was a career soldier with no experience in government. He did have a thirst for vengeance, though, executing by firing squad thirteen senior members of the Tolbert regime. Only four ministers from Tolbert's government were spared. Ellen was one of them. Doe later explained that he allowed Ellen to live because when he was a soldier, Ellen's mother had provided him and his men with water to drink. Ellen's mother had no recollection of this incident, but it may have happened. Whether true or not, while others died, Ellen was appointed to lead Liberia's central bank. Her brother was jailed for a period and her sister, Jennie, and Jennie's husband went into exile, concerned because he had served as a minister in the Tolbert government. But compared to others, her family endured less suffering.

Ellen, who had spoken so many painful truths in the past, continued to do so even in these dire circumstances. She tried to help her nation manage its foreign debt issues but saw the Doe regime increasingly engage in wild spending and corruption. She spoke of these matters at the Booker Washington Institute, a Liberian university, in November 1980 and was warned by a friend that Doe was coming for her. By December, she had used her lifeline and returned to the United States and the World Bank.

She remained there for less than a year before being recruited by Citibank to develop new national markets for the company in Africa. Even when safe, in a well-paid corporate post, Ellen could not leave speaking or caring about Liberia alone. She stayed in touch with the local political scene and decided to run in the first elections Doe called after the coup. She says:

'*In 1985 I got into trouble for a speech I gave in Philadelphia where I had again taken the government to task. And I made one big mistake of calling President Doe and his team "idiots". When I returned home to contest the election as the vice-presidential candidate of my party, they jailed me.*'

Prior to landing behind bars, Ellen was hauled to a meeting and directly abused by President Doe, his generals and top ministers, including being labelled '*a stupid woman*'.

While incarcerated, she was tried for sedition and sentenced to ten years of hard labour in Belle Yalla compound, a notoriously harsh rural jail. Ellen did not believe this was a sentence she could survive.

She was rescued from this grim fate by an enormous domestic and international protest campaign. In fact, she never went to Belle Yalla and served only fourteen days of her sentence. But there was a political price to be paid. President Doe threatened to deregister the party that had nominated Ellen unless they dumped her as the candidate for vice-president. This pressure worked, though Ellen was still put forward as a candidate for the Senate. Ellen was elected in October 1985 but never took her seat, in protest against what she believed was the rigged election of President Doe and his supporters.

Ellen was still in Liberia on 12 November 1985 when a coup was unsuccessfully attempted against President Doe. While Ellen was not an instigator of the planned overthrow of the Doe regime, she was one of the targets at whom he lashed out afterwards. Ellen was rounded up by soldiers and threatened with rape and death. She was jailed for nine months before being allowed to go home. Once again, people in Liberia and around the world campaigned for her release.

Still refusing to take her Senate seat, Ellen was kept under strict surveillance wherever she went. Understandably, she feared that she might be re-arrested at any time or even killed. With friends and supporters, she hatched a daring plan to escape in a private plane. One of her sons was getting married and Ellen knew the people watching her would relax a little on that day, certain that she would be at the wedding. Instead, Ellen used this as the moment to make her escape. Once again her family paid a price in that, for his own safety, Ellen did not tell her son about this plan. He was simply bewildered as to why she was not at his wedding.

Ellen could have been embittered by the time she spent behind bars but, philosophically, she says:

'*When I came out, people wanted to apologise. I told them, "No, don't. Just think of how many poor people get into prison without anyone paying any attention to them." So, I think adversity was part of my life. Each time I was able to successfully overcome adversity, I moved one more step towards what I was going to do.*'

Her ultimate destination was to be elected president, but the path from getting out of jail to her eventual election in 2005 was no more straightforward than her complicated life before. Civil war began in Liberia in 1989, leading to President Charles Taylor overthrowing President Doe. In 1997, Ellen stood against Taylor for the presidency and lost in what many viewed as a fixed ballot. Again, Ellen was forced into exile.

Civil war again broke out in 1999, filling the contemporary history of Liberia with much more bloodshed and pain. However, one thing that clearly shines through is the incredible role women played in bringing peace and supporting each other. Ellen recounts as follows:

'*Conflict in Liberia was brought to an end by the 2003 Accra Peace Agreement, which wouldn't have happened without the work of women. I was not there, I was in exile, but the women took a stand. They just got tired of the suffering and the violence. It was so horrific, so brutal. Christian and Muslim women combined and took a stand.*

Leymah Gbowee was one of the leaders, and they challenged President Taylor. They would put tents on the ground and pray all day. Then they went to Accra, the capital of Ghana, which hosted the peace talks and actually negotiated with different war faction leaders. Eventually the women even threatened to disrobe if a decision was not reached.'

Such an act, deliberate public female nudity, was unthinkable in Liberian culture and, as history records, this campaign by the women played a major role in securing peace.

Ellen was finally able to return home and was elected president for the first time in 2005. After her six-year term, she was re-elected in 2011.

The woman who would not be silenced became the leader of her nation.

Meeting Michelle Bachelet – President of Chile, 2006 to 2010 and 2014 to 2018, the first and only woman to be elected. First Head of UN Women, 2010 to 2013

In the same frantic week, in which the New York City skies dumped rain in a way that was almost monsoonal, we met Michelle in a groovy black-and-silver hotel in Midtown. Over coffee, we dried out and talked.

Michelle is no stranger to the United Nations. She is the current UN High Commissioner for Human Rights, and in 2010 she was asked to lead the newly created UN Women, a body formed to fight for gender equality and the empowerment of women. In our world, where women are at the highest risk of being in dire poverty, locked out of school, married young or subjected to sexual violence, fulfilling the mission of such a global body may seem hopeless. But progress is being made, and Michelle's outlook on life seems to be one of not shirking hard challenges, including twice governing a nation of around nineteen million people, once before her time at UN Women and once after.

Modern-day Chile is a vibrant democracy, with a population that encompasses a number of First Peoples, as well as the descendants of those who came from Spain in search of gold and then to conquer, and more recent arrivals. Economically, Chile always tends to be at the top of indexes that compare economic progress in Latin America.

Though she only recently left the presidency, Michelle does not come to our interview with a large entourage. She is alone, barring one assistant. In person, she is diminutive in stature and softly spoken. What makes an impression is her warmth and kind, open face. Intuitively, she seems the sort of person that in a crisis would be a reassuring presence, a beacon of calm and strength.

Julia and Michelle joke about sharing the same birthday. Born on 29 September 1951 in Santiago, Verónica Michelle Bachelet Jeria is precisely ten years older than Julia. Her father's surname was Bachelet, and she has always been known simply as Michelle Bachelet.

Her life has certainly required an inner fortitude but it started in an idyllic-sounding fashion. Michelle's family lived in various locations around Chile as her father, who was in the military, received different postings. Two years of her life were spent in Washington, DC, while her father filled an attaché role at the Chilean Embassy. This time spent at a US high school enabled Michelle to become fluent in English, one of a number of languages she has mastered in addition to her home language, Spanish.

Urged by her father to become a doctor, on 11 September 1973 she was enjoying medical school and looking forward to her twenty-second birthday. But on that date her world collapsed when right-wing military dictator Augusto Pinochet seized power in Chile. This was the start of a sixteen-year period in which it is estimated that thousands of people were executed or imprisoned for political reasons.[2]

This tidal wave of tears engulfed Michelle and her family. Her father was charged with treason and tortured until his heart gave out. He died in March 1974. While Michelle and her mother were not arrested at the start of the coup, they were impoverished, with all the family's bank accounts frozen. They were also shunned. Michelle recalls people who knew them well crossing the street to avoid talking to them.

Things were to get worse. Michelle, who was active in the Chilean Socialist Youth organisation, and her mother were imprisoned and tortured for a month in 1975. They were both held initially at Villa Grimaldi, an infamous house of horrors under the Pinochet regime. Michelle refuses to speak in detail about this time but has said that she was told her mother would be killed, and because they were held separately, she had no way of knowing whether this threat had been carried out. Her mother experienced the same treatment. Bravely, in later testimony, Michelle said what she endured 'was nothing in comparison to what others suffered'.

Fortunately, an old family friend and Argentinian diplomat, Roberto Kozak, who lived in Chile and worked for the local office of a global refugee and asylum seeker support agency, managed to secure their release. Kozak assisted so many people in this period that he has been compared to Oskar Schindler, the hero who helped Jewish people escape the Holocaust.

With her mother, Michelle fled to join her only sibling, an older brother, who lived in Australia. Out of all this sadness, one lovely connection emerges, which is that Michelle was awarded Australia's highest civilian honour, Companion of the Order of Australia, in 2012 while Julia was prime minister.

In 1975, Michelle and her mother moved to East Germany, which gave Michelle an opportunity to continue her medical training. Getting through her studies was slow. Michelle needed to work to support herself, and become familiar with German. In this period, she also met and married another Chilean exile, Jorge Dávalos, who was an architect. Their first child, a son, was born in 1978.

Even though Pinochet was still in power in 1979, in this period some exiles were permitted to come home. By the time their daughter was born in 1984, the family had returned to Chile.

Michelle resumed her medical studies at the University of Chile and in 1983 graduated near the top of her class. But while she and her family were able to live peacefully in the country, politics still intervened and she was unable to get a job in a government-funded hospital. Michelle found other ways to work and use her medical skills, with a special focus on the care of children. One of her roles was heading up the medical department of a non-government organisation that worked to help children whose families had been 'disappeared' by the Pinochet dictatorship.

Her marriage to Jorge faltered and they separated a few years after the birth of their daughter. Michelle did find love again, this time with a fellow physician, and she had her second daughter in 1992.

This third and final child was born into democracy. Pressure both domestic and international had forced constitutional change and free elections in Chile. While continuing as commander in chief of the Chilean Army, Pinochet relinquished the presidency in 1990. This enabled Michelle to access government jobs, and she worked in a Ministry of Health funded and run medical service. By 1994, she was working as a senior assistant to the Deputy Health Minister.

In 1996, Michelle had her first taste of electoral politics when she ran on behalf of her Socialist Party for an unwinnable seat in a local council mayoral election. Michelle says:

'Well, that was a joke, really. The municipality that I used to live in was where the richest people lived. Of course, nobody from my party wanted to go there because they knew they wouldn't win. So, what do they do? They look at women. They asked me to be the candidate there. I knew it was a completely lost campaign, but I did it and I enjoyed it.'

For almost anyone else, a busy life as a health professional, a political campaigner and a mother of three, including a young child under the age of ten, would have been enough. But somehow Michelle found room for more and became intrigued by an entirely new area of learning. Michelle tells it:

'Chile was supposed to be like the Switzerland of Latin America. We were always so moderate, never confrontational – theoretically speaking. But we had endured a military coup. And one of the things that I worked out is that politicians in my country did not have any conversations with the military. And I never thought that I was going to be president, but I thought, how can we bridge this gap? I decided that militarists understood the language of power. So I said to myself, "I will never be powerful, but I can have the power of knowledge." That's why I decided to study military issues in Chile. I achieved a first in my program. That secured me a scholarship to come to Washington, DC, in 1998 in order to study a short, intensive course on regional security and military issues.'

When Michelle returned from her Washington studies she took on a job as a senior adviser to the Minister for Defence. However, in 2000 she got a big break when she was appointed by President

Ricardo Lagos as Minister for Health. It was back to her original field of work and study, an area she felt comfortable in and one she did not perceive as particularly gendered. She recalls:

'As the Minister for Health, I never encountered any particular problems because I was a woman. I knew the issues because I was a doctor, and I knew the people.'

Successfully overseeing a huge reduction in medical waiting lists, Michelle was seen as a high-achieving minister. This led to her promotion into the pivotal position of Minister for National Defense in 2002. About this very male environment, she says:

'In the military, they have discipline, so if you are the boss then you are the boss. In my first meeting with the chief commanders, I said to them, "Look, I represent all the things you don't want – I'm a socialist, I'm a woman, I'm an atheist and I'm divorced. But I understand military issues, I know what needs to be done, and we are going to work well together." And these guys, who are very religious and conservative, were okay [with that].'

It was serving in this very male environment that turbocharged Michelle's public popularity. In 2002, floods engulfed parts of the Chilean capital, Santiago. Michelle personally and actively oversaw the military's role in rescue efforts, including riding on top of a tank as it surged through the water to get to stranded citizens.

The public were appreciative of these efforts, and in 2004 it became increasingly apparent that she was the only candidate for her political party who could command sufficient voter support at the looming election for president.

About that pivotal time, Michelle says:

'I was at home one night when the big leaders of my party came to visit. They were known as the Barons. And they asked me, "What do you want to do, Michelle?" And I said, "I want to walk by the sea,

hand in hand with a man that I love." And they were all like, "What is she talking about?!" And I said, "That's what I would like. If you're asking me to be a candidate, that is something different. I am available, but it's not what I want."

And I was fine with being the candidate because I knew they needed me, and I also thought they were not going to follow it through to the end. I felt they were going to negotiate something and find another candidate.'

But, as history records, that did not happen, and Michelle became president twice. In the Chilean system, it is not possible to serve two consecutive terms as president. Consequently, Michelle served in UN Women in the period in between her two terms of office.

Of her stellar political career, Michelle shows modesty in these words:

'I was the first female Minister for Health in Chile, and I was the first female Minister for Defence in Chile, and I was the first female president of Chile. This doesn't mean I am fantastic, but it does show how terrible Chile was that they had never had women in those posts.'

When asked if, at the major moments in her life, as she crashed through so many glass ceilings, she felt the weight of history on her shoulders, Michelle says:

'The day I became the Minister for Defence, everybody thought I was thinking about my father and the historical chain of events. But you know what I was actually thinking of? I was thinking I couldn't speak like a girl – I couldn't have this young, feminine voice. I was concerned about having a strong voice from the beginning.

And when these Barons came to see me, I wasn't thinking, oh, this is a historical moment. I was thinking, okay, if I'm needed then so be it.'

Meeting Christine Lagarde – first woman to lead global law firm Baker & McKenzie, 1999 to 2004. Minister in the French government, 2005 to 2011, including the first woman to be Finance Minister, 2007 to 2011. The first woman elected to lead the International Monetary Fund, 2011 to 2019. The first and only woman to lead the European Central Bank, 2019 to date. Known as the 'rock star' of finance

The April before September's UN Leaders Week, we were at another global gathering that attracts people with a cause. This time it was the International Monetary Fund – World Bank Group Spring Meetings, an annual event where finance ministers gather from around the world. To make a real difference in education, health or other sectors, the support of these ministers is vital.

The Spring Meetings are familiar territory for Ngozi, who, prior to becoming Nigeria's Finance Minister, worked at the World Bank for twenty-five years and rose to the second-highest position in the institution as Managing Director, Operations. It is public knowledge that Ngozi was both the first woman and first African to participate in the only truly contestable election for World Bank president in 2012. Backed by Africa's presidents, she put her candidacy forward, and the talk in the international community was that, based on her performance, had she been an American citizen at that time, she would have made it.

Unfortunately, around the key institutions of the World Bank and IMF, there is an informal understanding and decades-old practice concerning the nationality of the leadership. To date, an American has always been chosen as president of the World Bank, while a European always heads the IMF. For the World Bank, this nationality barrier and the gender glass ceiling have yet to be broken.

Ngozi mingled easily at the Spring Meetings, advocating her causes in health and climate change. Julia felt on familiar ground too, given that the Global Partnership for Education, which she chairs, is hosted at the World Bank.

But as the meetings ended, word came through that we could interview Christine Lagarde, the Managing Director of the International Monetary Fund, which is the global body tasked with maintaining the stability required for nations to trade and thrive. The IMF and Christine were central to managing the world's response to the global financial crisis of 2008 to 2009 and the subsequent fallout in Europe.

Christine greets us with hugs and kisses in her office, exuding intelligence and poise at the same time. She was born Christine Lallouette in Paris on 1 January 1956. Lagarde is the name of her first husband, Wilfred Lagarde, who is the father of her two sons.

Here is a woman to be reckoned with. In her early sixties, she has succeeded in the corporate world, national politics and on the global stage, and she still has more to do.

Christine describes her first career, her legal career, as follows:

'I was lucky to be in an environment that was extremely avant-garde. In my firm, each and every partner from anywhere in the world had the same vote, the same weight, the same voice as any other. I was lucky to have been hired by the Paris office, because that office was the only one led and managed by a woman. She was fierce, caring, demanding, and a good role model for me.

I was also lucky that Wallace Baker, the eldest son of the firm's founder, was one of the partners, and he was a very modern man in many ways. He was interested in everybody's contribution, he had no gender bias, he was one of the first lawyers in the world I think to talk about corporate social responsibility. I was lucky to have these two as mentors and role models.'

That seems like a lot of emphasis on being 'lucky', but Christine goes on:

'I worked my butt off and proved myself. In those days it was a very tough life being an associate in a big law firm.'

In her view, the existence of clear metrics to establish who was doing well in the firm – measurements like attracting new clients, generating profits and managing associates – helped take gender out of the equation when picking who should be the next partner. In her words:

'I think women tend to feel less comfortable in an environment which is more discretionary and subjective, where you have to do more "clubby" stuff and be part of a boys club.'

But she notes gender did have an impact:

'It was sixteen hours of work, day after day, and young female lawyers who also wanted to have a family found it tough.'

A mother of two herself, Christine acknowledges that she too found the lack of work–life balance a problem, and describes in chapter 8 how she got through it.

Christine was subject to the glass cliff phenomenon when she was approached to become the first female global chair of Baker & McKenzie at a time when 90 per cent of the partners were men. She says:

'The firm went through a really tough time financially and tech-nologically because we had embarked on building this incredible platform that was supposed to do the work without any involve-ment by anybody. When this turned into a complete mess as a result of being engineered by the big egos of men, the nominating

committee came after me and said, "Please come and help sort this out."'

Not only was she elected by her peers, she did fix the problems the firm was facing.

Given the weight of responsibility that has been on Christine's shoulders at so many times in her life, it is jarring to hear her describe herself as irresponsible. But that's exactly how she sees her decision to move into chairing the law firm and then into French politics. She says:

'I think throughout my life I have sometimes taken "irresponsible" risks. When I was asked to become chair of the law firm, I shouldn't have done that. The firm was going down the tube, partners were leaving, I was comfortable in our Paris office, and I could have just run away with my clients and set up shop anywhere. So why did I agree to dump all that to try to turn around the firm? That was dumb and irresponsible, but it was a big challenge and I thought, okay, nobody wants to do the job; fine, I will do it.

When you look at my decision to join the French government it was stupid as well. I was happily cherished in Baker & McKenzie, I had turned the firm around, partners loved me, and they had reconfirmed me once again with a 97 per cent majority. I could have sat back and waited another year and a half to collect my pension, since I had enough years to do that. Instead, when the French president Jacques Chirac and the prime minister Dominique de Villepin pick up the phone and ask me to join the government, I don't ask how much my pay will be, I don't ask what social security protection I have, I don't ask anything except, "Do people work as a team?" "Of course," they say. "Yes, absolutely!" And like a twit, I believe them, so I pack up my bag and I go.'

Christine's only explanation for this apparent act of madness is patriotism. She says:

'I was getting utterly fed up. When you live abroad you cherish and love your country much more so than if you were back home. I heard my compatriots constantly complaining about the government, the policies and the taxation. So, I said, "Okay, it's time to engage."'

Ngozi can relate to this. She accepted her first Finance Minister job in 2003 precisely for these reasons. There is also another interesting connection between Ngozi and Christine. On Christine's very first day on the job as a minister in 2005, she was assigned to oversee the negotiations for relief of Nigeria's debt. Ngozi led the Nigerian delegation in these discussions. The two women struck a friendly chord that helped move the debt deal in a constructive direction.

Christine served initially as Minister for Trade, and then Minister for Agriculture. She recalls being very much an outsider in the following terms:

'Politics is a very "clubby business" and I wasn't in the club. People grow up together, they know things about each other, they hold things against each other and that gives them the room to manoeuvre, to say, "I'll scratch your back, you scratch mine," "You accept this amendment here, and I will vote for this thing here." Politics is full of that crap and people can get totally compromised.'

As she makes these remarks both Julia and Ngozi nod. They can relate to this. Ngozi pipes up that this is exactly what she felt in Nigeria. Christine notes that a male colleague who was also an outsider received similar treatment, and so she does not put it down to gender. None of this stopped Christine's promotion to Finance Minister in 2007, with responsibility for the economy and industry. Here, she does see gender playing a role. She recalls:

'*Major trade deficits continued to be recorded by France and there was a lot of speculation about whether or not I would keep my job as Finance Minister. It was the first time the French Finance Minister had been a woman. There was a lot of envy, with people rumouring that I would be gone before the autumn. I remember being at an international meeting in Tokyo and a lift door opening, revealing a group of French journalists who were all asking me whether it was true that I had submitted my resignation letter just before I left France. This was the spirit.*'

In the months that followed, the global financial crisis hit economies. She dryly says:

'*After the crisis started to really roll out, the speculation I would resign or be sacked was gone because nobody wanted my job.*'

Her career story then intertwines with that of another crisis. On 14 May 2011, Nafissatou Diallo, a maid at a New York hotel, accused Dominique Strauss-Kahn, the former French politician and serving head of the IMF, of sexual assault. On 18 May, Strauss-Kahn was indicted and he resigned his position.

In an atmosphere of global shock, the IMF needed a new leader. Christine, who was still serving as Finance Minister in France, stepped forward to contest the position and was quickly endorsed by key countries. Agustín Carstens, former Secretary of Finance in Mexico and former Governor of the Bank of Mexico, also sought the position.

Whoever won, history would be made. Electing Agustín would have meant that, for the first time, a non-European held the job. Electing Christine would give the IMF its first elected female leader.

In this contest, Christine believes gender worked in her favour, in the sense that the IMF really needed to be seen to be doing something different than business as usual after such dramatic events. This was a glass cliff moment. Somewhat sardonically, Christine captures this need for change with the words:

'I don't think another French man would have been appointed for the job.'

Christine received overwhelming support, and the importance of her attaining such prominence in the field of finance and economics, which has traditionally been so dominated by men, cannot be underestimated. Christine jokes that, when you look at the photos of international finance meetings:

'It's raining men! So how do I feel about being there? I feel like challenging them, especially when I am in the chair. Because very often they don't even realise how gendered it is. It is the frame they are used to.'

But once again she is quick to point out that success does not come easily. Christine says:

'The IMF has respect for academic credentials, citations, papers published and rating in the academic world. I could not check any of those boxes. I was not an economist. On top of it all, I was a woman. There was a lot of scepticism in the first meetings I chaired. But my saving grace was, having been a finance minister, I had been a client of the IMF for four years. I had been on the other side and that was helpful. But I had no natural credentials from their perspective, so how did I deal with that?

I worked like a dog! I literally ate and digested files. That's what I did, and what women always do. We over-prepare, overwork, we are over-briefed. Where a man would flip pages and look at the headlines, we look at every single paragraph and read thoroughly.'

In November 2019, Christine took office as president of the European Central Bank. Another first for a woman.

Meeting Joyce Banda – Vice-President of Malawi, 2009 to 2012, the first and only woman to be elected. President of Malawi, 2012 to 2014, the first and only woman to serve. The second woman to serve as a national leader in Africa

Malawi is a landlocked nation of just over eighteen million people in the south-east of Africa. A mainly agricultural and still largely rural country, it is heavily reliant on crops like maize and tobacco. Malawi has made a great deal of progress since gaining independence from the United Kingdom, but it is still classified as a low-income country, with an average annual income per capita of US$389 dollars.[3] The nation has huge aspirations to move up the income ladder and assure a more prosperous life for its citizens.

Julia has wonderful memories of being in Malawi with renowned recording artist and fashion icon Rihanna, who serves as Ambassador of the Global Partnership for Education. Hundreds of schoolgirls squealed upon catching sight of Rihanna and then followed her around singing her songs, illustrating that in our interconnected world, teenagers in Malawi are not much different from those elsewhere.

Despite its continuing challenges with poverty, child marriage and other social issues, Malawi is known as 'The Warm Heart of Africa', a nickname given because of the friendliness of its people, not the nature of its climate. Joyce Banda is a fine example of Malawian personal style. With a flashing smile, she wants to fold people in her arms as a greeting and hold hands as she talks.

Unlike Ellen's native Liberia, the history of Malawi is one of peace rather than civil war. It emerged in the 1990s as a multi-party democracy, having been a British colony until independence in 1964 and a one-party state for thirty years after that.

Joyce and Ellen's journeys to power are very different but they start in a similar place, with an early marriage and the need to leave an abusive spouse. Joyce was born in Domasi, Malemia village, in Zomba District in the Southern Region of Malawi, on 12 April 1950, and was christened Joyce Mtila. She takes us back in time when she says:

'I got married at age twenty-one and by twenty-five I had three children. My husband was appointed as a diplomat to Kenya and I was there in 1975 when the United Nations Decade for Women was declared. If I had been in Malawi I wouldn't have woken up, but in Nairobi I started hearing more about violence against women and the women's movements. I started looking at my own life, and I realised I was being abused and I didn't even know it. It began to dawn on me that I could walk out. However, I come from a society where you have to stay in the marriage no matter what. But in 1980, I finally decided I wasn't going to stay anymore. I left for me and my children, because I couldn't see how this alcoholic was going to be a role model to them.'

Back home in Malawi, after the end of her marriage in 1981, Joyce had to find a way to live as a single mother. She went back to work and also started a small business to supplement her income.

Two years later she found the love of her life, Richard Banda, a lawyer and judge. Joyce and Richard married and had two children. Her husband helped her grow her business so that, by 1990, she was one of the richest women in Malawi. But her searing life experiences had galvanised her to help others. In her words:

'I made it a mission to help my fellow sisters escape from abuse at the hands of their partners. The key to this is economic empowerment.'

One way Joyce did this was by establishing the National Association of Business Women in Malawi in 1989. It was a huge success, and by 1997 this organisation had mobilised fifty thousand women, with twenty thousand receiving microfinance support. Joyce was rewarded for her efforts by global non-profit organisation The Hunger Project, who named her co-laureate, along with President Joaquim Chissano of Mozambique, of the 1997 Africa Prize for Leadership for the Sustainable End of Hunger. Joyce says:

'The Association began to give women a sense of power. They felt that they had someone who was fighting alongside them. I became someone they could go to whenever they had a problem. If they had problems paying their children's school fees, the solution was to see Joyce Banda; if a woman was being abused, the situation would be reported to Joyce Banda. So, finally the women came out and said, "Don't you think you should be sitting where the laws are made so you can help change those laws that negatively impact on women and girls?"'

However, Joyce resisted such entreaties until Richard retired from his position as Chief Justice of Malawi. That means Joyce's elected political career did not start until she was fifty-four years old, but once it started, she rose rapidly.

In 2004, Joyce won a parliamentary seat in Malawi's third democratic multi-party election. This election marked the transition from President Elson Bakili Muluzi, who had served for two terms, to President Bingu wa Mutharika. Both were members of the United Democratic Front (UDF), as was Joyce. President Muluzi had wanted to change the constitution to enable him to run for a third term, but public pressure prevented him from doing so. President Mutharika then became his chosen successor.

Joyce never served solely as a member of parliament. In Malawi, the president chooses his cabinet from members of parliament, and she was immediately appointed Cabinet Minister for Women and Children Welfare by President Mutharika. In this role, Joyce took many gender violence issues to parliament. During her tenure she also launched the zero tolerance campaign against child abuse and the national call to action for orphans and vulnerable children. She used her power to act against the kind of abuse she herself had suffered. Joyce says:

'The first thing I did was to take the Prevention of Domestic Violence Bill to parliament. It took us two years to pass it. Right after that, in April 2006, President Bingu wa Mutharika told me I had done enough for women and that he was elevating me to be Foreign Minister.'

Joyce served in that position for three years. Further promotion lay ahead. She recalls:

'When President Bingu wa Mutharika won the elections in 2004, he had told me that he was going to groom me to take over from him in 2014. This was a ten-year plan. So, for the longest time, he really empowered me. He would send me to represent him at presidential summits, and that's where I gained experience and confidence. In 2009, while I was Foreign Minister, he asked me to be his running mate for the upcoming elections. In retrospect, I think he wanted the female vote. I did not know that then. But I said no because of how he had mistreated his vice-president at that time. He assured me and my husband that he would never betray me, because by betraying me he would betray all the women of Malawi and they would never forgive him.'

Every aspect of the backdrop to Joyce's decision was vexed. President Bingu wa Mutharika and his predecessor had fallen out.

As a result, in 2005 President Mutharika had formed a new political party, the Democratic Progressive Party (DPP), and he was joined by many members of parliament who had run for the UDF.

Former President Muluzi believed parliamentarians should resist and not change parties. In the midst of this, he was charged with corruption offences and was arrested in 2006. The case is still in court fourteen years later.

Vice-President Cassim Chilumpha, who had been elected in 2004 as member of parliament on a United Democratic Front ticket, refused to change his party. Allegations were made that Chilumpha had been conspiring with others to have the president assassinated. As a result, he was also arrested and charged with treason.

All of this gave rise to constant court proceedings and political disputation. With the situation so turbulent, Joyce thought carefully about what to do. Clearly, this was a major opportunity to bring about greater reform, but accepting the vice-presidential nomination would also be a highly risky move. Joyce's husband, who knew the president well, urged her to do so. Joyce was a founding member of the DPP and its vice-president, so running together made sense because both she and President Mutharika belonged to the same political party. Ultimately, she agreed. As a result, Joyce was elected vice-president. The 2009 elections in Malawi were the only elections in history where a president and his running mate won by over 67 per cent.

As she had feared, that path was a difficult one. She says:

'*The president's brother, Peter Mutharika, was never pleased with me being the running mate, the first time for a woman in Malawi. Then, after the election, I realised that my phone, which had previously rung six to seven times a day with calls from the president, had stopped ringing. My husband, who had a strong personal connection with the president, spoke to him, and he invited us for a cup of tea in his office. He said he was about to announce his cabinet, including portfolios for me. But when the cabinet was announced a week later, I was not allocated ministerial portfolios as he had promised.'*

This discord escalated. The relationship between Joyce, President Mutharika and his brother, Peter, got worse. President Mutharika invited her to State House to tell her he had changed his mind about grooming her to take over from him, and that he was going to groom his brother instead. He asked her to publicly endorse Peter Mutharika, telling her it was the only way she would remain vice-president. However, Joyce refused. To her, this was the betrayal they had talked about only a year earlier.

On 19 November 2010, a car rammed into Joyce's official vehicle. This accident was highly publicised and was viewed as an assassination attempt not only in Malawi but globally. The driver of the other car was never caught, and the incident was not investigated.

In December 2010, the DPP expelled her. In response, Joyce started her own political party. The DPP was not legally able to have her fired from her constitutional position of vice-president because she was elected.

Increasingly, Joyce came to fear for her life and approached international figures for help, including Mary Robinson, the former President of Ireland. In her post-political life, Mary served from 1997 to 2002 as the United Nations High Commissioner for Human Rights, and then from 2008 to 2011 as head of the International Commission of Jurists. In 2007, Mary was selected by Nelson Mandela to be part of an initiative he formed called The Elders, a group of distinguished world leaders who lend their wisdom and expertise to others. Given all these major roles, Joyce believed Mary might be able to help. Joyce and Mary knew each other from working together on the Global Leaders Council for Reproductive Health. Joyce recalls that, during this difficult period, Mary had a confrontation with President Mutharika about Joyce.

Joyce also reached out to Ngozi, who was then Managing Director at the World Bank. Ngozi remembers vividly her state of distress and concern about what might happen next.

Fortunately, ordinary Malawians, men and women, stood with her throughout this ordeal. Joyce recalls:

'On 11 December 2010, I was expelled from the Democratic Progressive Party as vice-president and member, meaning I only remained vice-president constitutionally because I was elected by the people. When I was expelled, straightaway men and women started mobilising themselves and a week later they had formed what they called "Friends of Joyce Banda". In the market they wore T-shirts declaring that they were "Friends of Joyce Banda", and in a few weeks this group grew to five hundred thousand men and women.'

There was an attempt by the DPP to start an impeachment in parliament, but it failed. This deadlock, with the president wanting Joyce out of the role of vice-president and Joyce refusing to leave, persisted throughout 2011 and into 2012. It came to a dramatic end on 5 April 2012, when President Bingu wa Mutharika died of a heart attack. Joyce describes the fateful hours that ensued in the following way:

'The three days following the president's death were full of drama. The Democratic Progressive Party did not want to announce that he was dead. CNN was announcing his death while the DPP government was still saying he was in hospital in South Africa.

In truth, at this point he had already been dead for more than seven hours. I phoned the hospital in South Africa to check on my president's progress and they told me, "There is no president here." That is how serious the situation was and how much we were kept in the dark. The following day, 6 April, there was a cabinet meeting and I was not invited. The law in Malawi says that if the president dies in office then the vice-president must call a meeting of the cabinet. The vice-president must also take the presidential oath of office immediately. But the first meeting of the cabinet was organised without me as vice-president. I quickly wrote a letter to the Chief Secretary, alerting him that they were breaking the law. They appointed Peter Mutharika against the law.

Then on 7 April, in the morning, confused and unaware of what was going on, I contacted the Chief Secretary to find out what was happening, and it was in that conversation he told me he had received information that the president had "just" died, and he was about to make the announcement. I said, "Don't you think you should be announcing his death with me, as the vice-president?", and he refused.

I understood the importance of the army in who was going to be recognised as the new president in this situation. I contacted the head of the army and asked him to come to my residence, and he said he was on his way. When word spread around that he was with me, the Minister of Justice and the Attorney General, who were going to court to take an injunction against my inauguration, abandoned the move and came to my residence to join us. One by one, the ministers began to rush to my house, some almost climbing the fence to be on time for the press conference that I was about to hold. As one of the ministers said later, "We were running around like headless chickens."

By the time I gave the press conference that day, I had fifteen ministers and forty-two members of parliament with me. I began the press conference and told the people, "Our president has passed away, let us all unite and mourn him like a king."

The drama continued as Joyce had to convene her first cabinet meeting, which was filled with people who had been seeking to oust her as vice-president, to deny her the presidency and install Peter Mutharika instead. Walking into the cabinet meeting, Joyce recalls saying:

'Wow, I've missed you. Nice to see you again. I'm sorry we have lost our father.'

She describes the reaction in the following way:

'Everyone was shocked. But during the meeting one minister stood up and put forward a motion "to retract everything that happened yesterday", meaning the attempts to not have me sworn in as president. Everyone seconded it. It is at that meeting everyone agreed I could take oath.'

Despite this reaction, Joyce did not feel secure. She says:

'I was back at home when suddenly I saw two policemen. I rushed to my husband and told him that I thought I was about to be arrested. He went down to find out what was happening and ran back up minutes later to tell me that I needed to get ready. That they had come to take me to be sworn in. The Chief Justice was waiting.

So, if you watch that parade, you realise that I am so lost. I was facing the wrong direction – I was in shock. I only realised when I got to the parliament buildings for the guard of honour and swearing-in that there were thousands and thousands of people who had been walking since that morning and threating to burn down parliament if I didn't take oath that day.'

The situation in Malawi as Joyce assumed the presidency was dire. There was an economic crisis, donors had frozen aid, and the IMF was demanding a devaluation of the local currency. In Malawi's highly polarised political environment, Joyce did stabilise the situation, and the country's economic growth rate rose from 1.8 per cent in 2012 to 6.2 per cent in 2014. During her tenure, progress was also made for women, including the rates of maternal mortality being slashed from 675 per 100,000 live births to 460. When accusations of corruption were made against her administration, Joyce took prompt action by sacking most of her cabinet.

In 2014, Joyce's government organised what were to have been the most transparent elections in Malawi's political history. The Malawi Electoral Commission (MEC) procured a new results management system designed to ensure transparency. The MEC also conducted the first tripartite elections for local councillors, members of parliament and president. Joyce stood for re-election on the ticket of the People's Party (PP), the new party she had founded after her expulsion from the Democratic Progressive Party. Unbeknown to her, Joyce says:

'Things began to unfold in a different direction during the elections, as allegations emerged that the MEC results management system had been hijacked by the DPP, headed by Peter Mutharika.'

Joyce found herself in third position when the results were announced, with Peter Mutharika in first place and another opposition candidate, Lazarus Chakwera, in second place. Joyce says:

'The polls were showing that we were going to win, so I was shocked when the results started coming in. One international observer for the elections said, "We must never call what happened in Malawi an election." The results were disputed, and the Malawi Electoral

Commission announced that there had been fraud and there would be need for a recount but, feeling Malawi deserved better, I called for fresh elections, in which I would stand down as a candidate. When President Sam Nujoma of Namibia, who was the lead observer of the African Union observer team, heard this, he asked if I could stay on for another year to preside over the new elections if my proposal was accepted. But the MEC had started preparing the recount of the ballot papers and we had run out of time, because the laws in Malawi state that whoever is leading on the eighth day after the recount should be declared president regardless, and other contenders should dispute it in court. Justice Kenyatta Nyirenda of the High Court confirmed this law, saying that it was necessary to declare the results. Hearing those results, people started fighting on the streets and one person died that night. It was at that point I decided to concede and leave State House, to avoid further loss of life. Days later, the warehouse housing the ballot papers was burnt down, allegedly by DPP functionaries. So even if any of us wanted to challenge the case in court, it wouldn't happen, because there were no ballot papers to count. The arson was never taken to court, so nobody has been arrested for it six years later. Some indications of fraud that emerged were result sheets altered with tippex, or correction fluid, and my ballot papers having been thrown out on the streets.'

As she looks back, Joyce now says:

'I should have gone to court but I decided not to. I did not want to fight and risk community unrest and violence. It was a decision I made. I knew people would eventually work out who was the better leader, and I am glad I have lived long enough to see this. I think now the woman in me threw in the towel too early. I did not want people to die. Perhaps if I was a man I would have fought till the very end.'

Meeting Erna Solberg – Prime Minister of Norway, 2013 to date, the second woman to be elected as Prime Minister

The prosperity of Norway contrasts sharply with the poverty of Malawi. Norway takes seriously its responsibilities on the world stage and consequently hosts many major international meetings. As a result, both Julia and Ngozi are familiar with Oslo.

But it was to Brussels, the home of the European Union, that we travelled to meet Erna. Norway is not a member of the EU, but its relationship is as close as it is possible to be without actually joining. In between her commitments that day, we met Erna in the Norwegian Embassy, a building of wood and glass.

Erna is a blonde-haired, blue-eyed woman in her late fifties. While not all Norwegians are the descendants of Vikings, it is easy to imagine Erna being cast to play one in a television series – no doubt one who is the leader of her people.

Born in Bergen in western Norway on 24 February 1961, Erna's personal style is best characterised by the word 'openness'. Here is a woman who says what she thinks in a no-nonsense style, which, thanks to the friendly twinkle in her eye, comes across as pleasingly upfront, not abrupt.

Erna's pathway to power started with her choosing the road less travelled by young people in a progressive society like Norway. She says:

'When I was sixteen, I was in a girls' group at my school that discussed politics. All the other ones became far leftists, I became conservative. We were all interested in women's issues, but my view was we don't have to fight down the patriarchy to achieve women's rights and feminism. We can just start by having equal rights.'

Her differences with her school friends led her to saying yes to participating in study circles run by the Conservative Party youth organisation. She recalls her choice to join in the following way:

'At that time, the Labour Party youth group was very left wing, and then there was the Young Conservatives. There was very little in between, so you were either defining yourself as a clear socialist or you defined yourself as a market economist.'

Having made the decision to join, Erna says she *'got very many responsibilities very fast'* but did not plan a career in politics.

'I've always been outspoken but I never thought of myself as becoming a professional politician. There were a lot of young people, especially boys, who were ambitious, and they were not doing their studies. Instead, they would do part-time work, or they would work partly for political organisations because they were aiming for elected office. Most of them were never really successful, because you can't plan for a political career, you have to plan for other things. And I think that was important for me because if you start to think that you are going to become a politician, you might end up not taking a stand on controversial issues and, in a way, you lose a bit of what builds character.'

Erna remembers the environment as inclusive of women and young people. She says:

'When I became active in the late 1970s, the Young Conservatives had a female party leader, Kaci Kullmann Five. She went on to be the first female party leader of the Conservative Party, and I am the second. She was quite a popular figure, even though she was just a youth movement leader, because the party leader at that time took her under his wing. Before every election there was a national question session for each party on television. Kaci appeared on it when she was in her early twenties. It was a first and showed a lot of young girls in my party that we were valued, we were seen.'

She also remembers the spirit of the times making a difference:
'*In the 1970s in Norway, as in many other countries, there were women's marches and discussions about women's issues. Political parties were prioritising more women, so from then on I have never really felt in my political life that being a woman was an impediment. I did sometimes feel that being young could be an impediment and maybe being a young girl could be an impediment. I was hardworking and an extremely serious young person, focused on economics and technical issues. I did that to compensate for the fact that I was younger than the others.*'

But entering parliament did not just happen because of youthful earnestness. Erna had to gain experience and win some fights.

By the time Erna was eighteen years old she was a substitute member of her city council, which was not an easy environment. She says:

'*Bergen, where I come from, was well known for hard fighting in the Conservative Party. On council, I was the only one in my political party who did not support a particular candidate for mayor. I nominated an alternative candidate, even though I was on my own as the single representative from the youth movement. So, I learnt to stand in the storm quite early on and I think that made me a little bit tougher.*'

Clearly, being prepared to do hard things caught people's attention. Erna became a member of parliament in 1989, when she was only twenty-eight.

The Norwegian parliament is called the Storting, and it consists of one chamber of 169 seats. Norway is divided into nineteen counties and each county elects a number of members to the Storting. More populous counties elect more representatives.

Political parties endorse a list of candidates for each county.

Erna recalls her selection by her party to be on that all-important candidate list in the following way:

'There was a vacancy on the Bergen list. There was some fighting, and everyone thought it would be filled by an experienced woman who was already a local party leader and involved in the regional government. But the outgoing member of parliament suggested me. She had the view that it was better to get somebody who you can build up. I was surprised, but I said, "Okay, if you really don't want to vote for the other candidate, you could put me forward in the beginning of the process." I thought when all of the local parties had decided who they wanted, it wouldn't be me. But they did choose me; I think there were some senior members of the party, both male and some female, who saw me as a talent and wanted to give me some possibilities to mature.'

Elected in 1989, Erna was in parliament for Gro Harlem Brundtland's third and last period of service as prime minister. Gro, from the Labour Party, was the first woman to lead Norway. She went on to serve as the head of the World Health Organization and a UN Special Envoy on Climate Change.

In establishing herself as a new parliamentarian, Erna again took the road less travelled. She says:

'When I was young, I had worked in the secondary schools' union. At university, I was the student representative on the governing board. I had been a spokesperson in my city for education. When young people get elected to parliament, everybody wants to put them onto the Education Committee. But despite my background, I didn't want that. Instead, having studied economics, I got onto the Finance Committee in my first year in parliament. Maybe because I was a woman and maybe because I wanted to do other things, I didn't want to do what was stereotyped.'

The Berlin Wall fell during Erna's first year in parliament. Erna explains this resulted in her being offered a new and incredible opportunity.

'*I was asked to be a member of a large government-appointed commission on what the defence policy should be in this new era. It was headed by the former prime minister from my party. I understood that I was in a sort of "grooming" process to learn other things. That was being done to make sure that there were new voices coming through.*'

These early experiences helped put Erna on a path that led to her becoming Minister of Local Government and Regional Development in 2001, deputy leader of the Conservative Party in 2002 and leader in 2004. In 2013, she was elected prime minister, and she was re-elected in 2017.

Unlike Ellen, Michelle, Christine or Joyce, who were married and had their children before entering politics, Erna has been in the public eye for all these stages of her life. In 1996, when she had already been a parliamentarian for seven years, she married Sindre Finnes, an economist who now works for Norway's national employers' organisation. Within the first three years of their marriage, they had two children, a daughter and son.

Meeting Jacinda Ardern – Prime Minister of New Zealand, 2017 to date, the third woman to serve as Prime Minister

On a winter's day in New Zealand's capital, Wellington, we interview a woman who also knows about combining politics with being a mother. Jacinda is sitting in the dining room of the prime minister's residence, and on this Saturday morning, after a budget week filled with politicking, she is casually dressed and seemingly relaxed.

While we are more than five hundred kilometres from Hamilton, where she was born on 26 July 1980, today is still a family affair. Her mother comes and goes with Jacinda's baby daughter, Neve. Her father comes in to say hello. There is a huge pot of tea to be drunk and pastries to eat. Her partner, Clarke Gayford, to whom she is engaged but not yet married, is away filming his fishing television show, so her parents are helping out with the care of Neve.

Jacinda's face is now familiar to the world, as a result of joy and hate: the joy that surrounded her becoming a mother while prime minister, and the hate crime that resulted in the horrific killing of more than fifty people who had gathered for Friday prayers at two mosques in the city of Christchurch. Jacinda led the world in mourning the lives lost.

In person, her face is as open and her smile is as wide as so many photos have led you to expect. But the more she talks, the more you feel yourself drawn to her eyes. It is as if through them you can see her thinking and wrestling with ideas, never glib. As she recounts a vivid memory from her childhood of seeing a boy walking home from school on a winter's day with bare feet, it is still easy to read on her face the sense of injustice she felt that she had shoes and he did not.

These stirrings of social conscience became more and more a feature of her life as she grew. Jacinda was teased about becoming prime minister because, in her small country town of five thousand people, she was the only child interested in politics. But even though she was, in her words, *an angsty teen who wanted to change the world*, she never seriously saw herself in politics or in a leadership role. She dreamt instead of being a psychologist or police officer and assumed she would have a family young. In her words:

'I grew up in the Mormon church, and women in the Mormon church, they all have careers, but they also have families and are often married quite young. So, I just assumed that would be me too. I thought I'd be married in my early twenties, and then I'd have a family really quickly.'

She first took real political action when she was in her late teens. She speaks of her aunt, who helped her get involved, in the following terms:

'She was just a Labour stalwart. She was a door-knocker, she was a pamphlet-deliverer. She was someone who always rallied the troops. She knew I was becoming really interested in politics, so she called the Labour member of parliament she used to campaign for and said, "You've got to get my niece involved." He lived three hours from where I was, but he called me one night and said, "Marie's told me about you. Will you come and volunteer on my campaign?"'

Jacinda immediately took leave from her supermarket job and drove her beat-up old 1979 Toyota down to New Plymouth. She boarded with another volunteer and spent her holidays politically campaigning. She says simply, *'That's how I got my start.'*

Around twenty years later, at the age of thirty-seven, she was sworn in as New Zealand's third woman prime minister.

In the two decades in between, she studied, worked, travelled and developed her adult outlook on the world. During that same period, two women served as New Zealand's prime minister. Jenny Shipley, a conservative, was the first woman to do so, holding office from December 1997 until December 1999. Labour's Helen Clark succeeded Jenny and was prime minister for nearly nine years.

As a young adult, Jacinda reassessed and moved away from her Mormon faith. She was particularly offended by the doctrinaire teachings around sexuality. Fortunately, leaving the church did not cause a major rift with her family.

Her first qualification was a Bachelor of Communication Studies in public relations and political science, which she studied at the University of Waikato Management School from 1999 to 2001. After graduation, Jacinda started working as a political staffer for the then Associate Minister of Energy, Harry Duynhoven. In that job, she accompanied him to many very male environments like mines, oil wells and offshore rigs.

Jacinda decided to combine work with further study. While completing a postgraduate degree in political science at Victoria University of Wellington, she worked for the Minister of Justice, Phil Goff. From there she landed a job with Prime Minister Helen Clark and designed one of the Labour Party's signature policies for the 2005 election – a plan to reduce the burden of student loans on university students.

Jacinda wanted to experience more of the world and so eventually left her job and went travelling. But rather than just sightseeing, she did things like volunteer for a soup kitchen and a workers' rights campaign in New York. While there, she applied for a job in the cabinet office of Tony Blair, who was then prime minister of the United Kingdom. Jacinda got the job, and in 2006 she moved to London. Over the next couple of years, Jacinda was promoted, ultimately to the position of senior policy adviser, and moved from working for Tony into the office of the next Labour prime minister, Gordon Brown. In her various roles, she engaged in policy issues as varied as helping small businesses and improving policing.

Working as a political staff member is a hectic life, but Jacinda found time to be involved in representing young people. In 2008, she was elected president of an international organisation with reach across thirteen countries called the International Union of Socialist Youth. Jacinda was only the second woman to serve as president in its more than one-hundred-year history.

Many young people with a passion for politics would deliberately construct a curriculum vitae like this as part of reaching their eventual goal of being in parliament. But Jacinda did not have her eye on getting elected. In fact, when the call came, she said no. She explains:

'There was growing awareness in the New Zealand Labour Party that, in building our lists of candidates for parliament, there was a need to bring in more women and young people. I was in London and I remember getting a call from a member of parliament saying, "Look, we need more women, will you come back and run?"

And I said, "No. I'm not sure that it's for me."'

Jacinda's reservations were about how she would cope with the combative nature of politics because of her personality. She says:

'Every time someone would say, "Why don't you go for parliament?", all I could think of was, am I tough enough for that? Am I assertive enough for the political environment? Am I strong enough for that environment?

I had seen it up close and I knew what it would take. And I thought, even if I am all of those things and could do it, would I be happy there or would it just wear me down?'

Fortunately, opportunity came knocking again. She recalls:

'The second time I was contacted, they said, "Well, look, why don't you stay in London but go on the party candidate list and campaign to get New Zealanders over there to vote." And I think because in my *mind that wouldn't necessarily lead me into parliament – I might get put in an unwinnable spot on the list – I almost tricked myself into it. I thought, I could do that. I could campaign in London.*

And then it became a matter of, "Well, you know, you need to come back and go through the candidate selection process," and I did that, and it all just suddenly started becoming more and more serious.'

What happened next shows how pivotal the actions of one self-sacrificing person can be in politics. Jacinda recalls:

'We have a process in New Zealand where all of the regions will rank the candidates, and then those regional lists come together and form the national list. So, if you rank highly on your regional list, you're more likely to get into parliament. The order of things goes, usually sitting members of parliament are at the top, and the next spot, right after them, is the key spot that maximises the likelihood of being elected.

I came back to the Wellington region from London for the meeting that set the list. My friend Grant Robertson was seen as the new candidate that the region wanted to back for that key spot. The meeting started and we placed all of the sitting MPs, and then that key spot came up. Someone stood up and nominated Grant, and Grant stood up and said, "I don't wish to be nominated until Jacinda Ardern has been placed." Then he sat down. And so, I then got placed in that key spot and as a result was elected to parliament.'

Grant and Jacinda are still friends, and he is the Minister of Finance in her government.

Elected as a member of parliament in 2008, Jacinda's doubts about whether politics was the right fit for her never went away. She says:

'Even once I got in, I still constantly questioned whether I had the right character traits and personality for that environment, because

I'm a sensitive person, I'm empathetic, I don't like the aggressive side of politics.

I would get graded from time to time on scorecards put together by the media as having been unsuccessful because I hadn't claimed any government ministers' scalps. But that wasn't how I measured success. So, I just decided that perhaps I wouldn't be regarded as the most successful politician, but at least I would be happy with the way I conducted myself.'

Clearly, pursuing her own style did not hinder her advancement. In 2017, Jacinda became deputy leader of the Labour Party in March, then leader in August and prime minister in October.

Jacinda says of her meteoric rise through the ranks of the Labour Party:

'*Every single time I've taken on a role in politics, I've been asked [to do so]. And I can honestly, hand on heart, tell you that, had it not been for the circumstances in each of those cases and having been asked, I wouldn't be in this role.*'

Her appointment as leader so close to an election can be characterised as a glass cliff. Being thrust into a campaign without preparation, and with the former leader having resigned because of poor opinion polls, is a horrible start.

Jacinda faced not just an electoral test but also potentially one of her negotiating skills. New Zealand's parliament has just one chamber, the House of Representatives, to which one hundred and twenty people are elected. Out of that total, seventy-one members are elected by first-past-the-post as the representatives of single-seat constituencies. The remaining forty-nine are elected through the regional party list system Jacinda describes above.

To people from other democracies, the New Zealand system can seem a little strange because each voter gets two votes – one used to elect their local representative and one used to select their preferred political party list. In her career, Jacinda has been both. She was elected as a representative for the electorate of Mount Albert in Auckland in 2017. Prior to that she was elected to parliament because she was on the party list.

There are a large number of political parties in New Zealand in addition to the conservative National Party and Jacinda's Labour Party. It is nearly impossible for one of these two big political parties to form a government without entering into coalitions or arrangements with smaller parties.

Jacinda's opponent in the 2017 general election was the incumbent National Party prime minister, Bill English, who had taken over from the popular and long-serving prime minister John Key, when Key decided to retire from politics in 2016.

While many political pundits would have thought becoming leader of a political party polling at 24 per cent just eight weeks before an election was the ultimate poisoned chalice, Jacinda won through. Her leadership was immediately embraced by the public with an almost twenty-point bounce in the opinion polls and a surge of donations to support Labour's campaign. Ultimately, Labour gained fourteen seats, while the National Party lost four. Even though that meant the National Party still held more seats than the Labour Party, with fifty-six seats to forty-six, Jacinda was able to negotiate the arrangements necessary to create a working majority and a Labour government. In doing so, she became New Zealand's third female prime minister.

Jacinda is very firm about the benefits of coming from a country where two women have been prime minister before her. In her words:

'None of my doubt arose because of a perception that the New Zealand public wouldn't accept me because I am a woman. That's the

difference having two prime ministers like Helen Clark and Jenny Shipley made. I could see that you could be elected and you could be a successful prime minister and be a woman. That's not something that should be taken for granted, how incredibly important that role-modelling is.'

But she is also clear that role-modelling does not take away all the doubts that women feel.

'It never featured in my mind that I can't be in politics because I'm a woman. It just didn't. But it did feature in my mind that I couldn't do it just because it was me. I did question my ability constantly, question whether or not I could take on the roles that people challenged me to take on.

I see this kind of self-doubt in other women. So that makes me think that it's not just my own personality. There is something about our – and I'm making grand sweeping statements here – our level of confidence. You know, that old cliché around seeing a list of traits that you need to possess to take on a role and you only see the ones that you don't have, rather than the ones you do. For women, I think this is absolutely true.'

Meeting Theresa May – Prime Minister of the United Kingdom, 2016 to 2019, the second woman to be elected as Prime Minister

It is easy to see former UK Prime Minister Theresa May as another woman who became a leader in a glass cliff moment. After all, she got the job in the aftermath of a huge shock and inherited a sharply divided political party and nation, as well as the diabolically complex task of carrying out Brexit, as Britain's exit from the European Union came to be known.

In 2010, her predecessor, David Cameron, had become the United Kingdom's youngest ever prime minister at the age of forty-three. He led a coalition government between his party, the Conservative Party, also called the Tories, and the Liberal Democrats. Under his leadership, the Conservative Party improved its result at the 2015 elections and attained a majority in its own right.

With this track record of success, no one attending the Tory election night celebration would have predicted he would be gone in just over a year's time. But that is exactly what happened. On 24 June 2016, he announced his resignation as prime minister following a shock result in the referendum that asked the people of the UK whether the country should 'remain a member of the European Union or leave the European Union'. Cameron had campaigned to remain, and most polls had shown that would be the outcome. Against these expectations, the leave proposition was carried narrowly, and Cameron believed the result rendered his continued leadership of the nation unsustainable.

Two women – Theresa May and Andrea Leadsom – and three men – Michael Gove, Stephen Crabb and Liam Fox – were nominated to replace Cameron. Boris Johnson, who would eventually succeed Theresa and is the current prime minister, was widely expected to run but did not do so after Gove withdrew his backing and nominated himself.

Theresa received majority support in the first ballot. In the Conservative Party system, ballots are held initially among members of parliament. The two candidates with the highest support then face a ballot of party members. Theresa and Leadsom were the top two, but Andrea withdrew in favour of Theresa prior to the party ballot. By 11 July 2016, it was clear that Theresa would be the second female prime minister of the United Kingdom, following Margaret Thatcher, who served for over a decade from 1979 until 1990.

While familiar with the concept of the glass cliff, Theresa says about her selection as leader:

'I think there was an element of wanting something different from the leader compared to what members of parliament had had previously. That was partly about background as well as other things. I don't think there was a huge gender element to it.'

These words are delivered in a croaky voice. Our interview occurs at a coffee shop in Theresa's electorate during the campaign for the 2019 election that gave her successor, Boris Johnson, a huge majority. Theresa had been door-knocking in her constituency, which is situated on the outskirts of London, but earlier in the week she had also been out in Scotland in minus-five degrees Celsius. One can only wonder what an ordinary citizen thinks when answering a knock on the door to find a former prime minister on the doorstep.

Of course, the media had a field day when, with a similar sore throat, Theresa coughed her way through her address to the Conservative Party Conference in 2017. As she struggled on, to add insult to injury, the stage set behind her began falling apart. Like seemingly everything else in life, she handled that incident with stoicism.

In person, Theresa is not the dour figure press portraits would lead you to expect. She is engaging in a businesslike but affable way. You get the sense that while she may not be as extroverted as many others in the public eye, she is comfortable in her own skin.

Her reference to the Tories looking for a leader with a different background is about class. David Cameron is one of twenty

British prime ministers who attended Eton College, the historic independent boarding school for boys that has been educating the elite since its foundation in 1440. Out of fifty-five prime ministers in total, that is a remarkable number. David is what an Australian like Julia would call 'posh'.

In contrast, Theresa Mary Brasier, born on 1 October 1956 in Eastbourne, Sussex, attended the local government girls' grammar school. Her father was the Church of England parish vicar and her mother was a housewife, who supported her husband in his work. Both of their mothers had worked in domestic service as young women.

Of her pathway to politics, Theresa says:

'From about the age of twelve or thirteen, I was interested in becoming a member of parliament. The political bug just caught me at that point. I suppose it was partly because I was an only child, so I was brought up in an environment where the news was on, my parents read the newspapers, talked about things. I just got interested and wanted to make a difference and thought that was a good way to do it, but I never thought, I'm going to be at the top, or I'm going to be the key person.'

She remembers her father's occupation as being an inspiration and a constraint, saying:

'I'm the daughter of a clergyman, and I think the combination of public service and public speaking that they exhibit then came out in me. But I was restricted in what I could do at home because my father said he was the vicar of the parish for everybody, so he didn't want me actually out knocking on doors as a proclaimed conservative. As a result, I went into the back office and started stuffing envelopes.'

She jokes that her political career had an inauspicious start. The history teacher at her school knew she was interested in politics and that a number of others were also keen. As a result, he set up a debating club for them. Theresa says of the first meeting:

'We all had to pick a subject out of a hat and speak on it. When it was my turn, I couldn't think of a single thing to say even though the topic was whether there should be a school uniform, which you would have thought anybody would've been able to talk about automatically.'

While her schooling was different to David Cameron's, like him Theresa went to Oxford University, which can boast that it has educated twenty-eight of the fifty-five British prime ministers. There her debating improved through her involvement in the Oxford Union debating society.

But her approach and path were different from the Oxford men interested in politics. She says:

'Being a woman, I didn't do it quite the way that the men do, because often they'll use their contacts and then go and work for an MP, and that would be the start of their career. I didn't. I always took the view that you must do something else before you become an MP, so you've got other experience. I went into banking.'

While her overwhelming motive for not using connections to go straight into a political job was her belief that it was important to have another career first, she is also clear that had she tried the direct route it would have been more difficult for her. Theresa explains:

'It's more natural for the boys to make the connections. And I think for some of them, they will have had other connections apart from Oxford; they will have school or family as well. So, they'd probably have more natural links into the political world.'

A cocktail of class and gender.

It was at a disco held by the Oxford University Conservative Association that she met her future husband, Philip May. Legend has it the two were introduced by fellow student Benazir Bhutto, who went on to be the first and, to date, only female president of Pakistan. They married in 1980. Theresa has spoken publicly about how the couple wanted children but unfortunately were unable to have them. Philip is highly successful in the finance and investment world.

While Theresa took an alternative route to parliament, she did get there eventually. Tragically, neither of her parents lived to see her elected. Her father, Hubert Brasier, was fatally injured in a car crash in 1981 and her mother, Zaidee Brasier, died the following year as a result of multiple sclerosis.

Theresa first gained practical experience as a local councillor from 1986 to 1994. She put her name forward on a few occasions to be selected as the Tory candidate for a winnable parliamentary seat, but she was unsuccessful. However, she did get a taste of electioneering by standing as the Tory candidate for two safe Labour seats, one in the 1992 general election and one in a by-election in 1994.

Theresa was eventually selected as the Conservative Party candidate for the newly created seat of Maidenhead in the 1997 general election.

Of this period in her life, when she was actively seeking party preselection, she says:

'It was tempting to say, if I lost, "They didn't want a woman." But I actually said to myself, "I must properly analyse my performance. Was there a particular subject I didn't know enough about? Were there questions I didn't answer very well? Was my presentation as good as it could have been?" Rather than just saying, "Well, obviously I'm a woman and that's why I didn't get it."'

The 1997 election was a bad one for the Conservative Party, with Labour's Tony Blair coming to power, but Theresa was successful in being elected. While she was saddened by the election loss, Theresa looks back on this period as one that gave her increased opportunity, describing it in the following terms:

'There were a lot of MPs who had been in government and they found it very difficult being in opposition. Whereas those of us who were new had the sense, we are here, let's get on with it. And so, the opportunities to progress were perhaps greater than they might have been. You know, if there are three-hundred-odd of you in the party in parliament, it's different to if there are one hundred and ninety of you.'

Theresa did rise quickly, becoming the first of the newly elected 1997 members of parliament to enter the shadow cabinet, serving from 1999 as Shadow Secretary of State for Education and Employment. After the 2001 election, with the Tories still in opposition, she stayed in shadow cabinet but moved to the Transport portfolio. In 2002, she was appointed the first ever female chair of the Conservative Party. She used this platform to give a much-discussed, hard-hitting speech about the need for the Tories to change, famously saying at one point, 'You know what some people call us? The Nasty Party.'

In the same speech she took up the cause of diversity, saying, 'At the last general election, thirty-eight new Tory MPs were elected. Of that total, only one was a woman and none was from an ethnic minority. Is that fair? Is one half of the population entitled to only one place out of thirty-eight?'

Theresa not only spoke about diversity, she acted on it, co-founding in 2005 an organisation called Women2Win with a conservative member of the House of Lords, Baroness Jenkin of Kennington. Theresa describes its establishment in the following way:

'I'd been working as party chairman to change our selection process so it was more gender neutral. Inadvertently, it had a bias towards the tub-thumping male in it. But then we recognised that the men had these networks that meant they all talked among each other, they knew the people and so forth. They would be able to say, "Oh, well, John's got that seat, good, he's off the list, now I can go for this one." The women didn't tend to do that, so giving women a network was one of the motivations behind it. In addition, it was about helping women, perhaps mentoring them, talking to them about what it was like being in parliament, so they came with a better understanding of the issues. And there are plenty of women in parliament who are there because of the support that Women2Win gave them.'

Understandably, Theresa is proud of Women2Win but she would still like to see it go out of business, saying:

'Our end goal is that voters and selection committees don't say, "Oh, it's a woman," but they actually just say, "That individual is the person I want to vote for because they're going to do this, or they've got this. I want to select them as a candidate because they've got these skills." We're not close to it yet. But, the perceptions are changing. It's partly because of numbers: with higher numbers of women in parliament, it becomes more natural to imagine a woman candidate sitting there too.'

Theresa's days in opposition ended at the 2010 election. By then she had held a variety of portfolios and been appointed Leader of the House, a key parliamentary role in the Westminster system.

In government, she was appointed to the senior role of Home Secretary. In taking this position she became the fourth woman to hold one of the great offices of state in the UK government, following Prime Minister Margaret Thatcher, Foreign Secretary Margaret

Beckett and Home Secretary Jacqui Smith. She continued as Home Secretary, with responsibility for immigration and citizenship, and national security, including spy agency MI5 and policing in England and Wales, until she became prime minister. For two years, from 2010 to 2012, she was also Minister for Women and Equalities.

About the way she advanced, Theresa says:

'I didn't really feel that I was treated differently from others in the House of Commons, for example. But, then, I chose to do my politics my way. Some of my colleagues actively felt they had to behave like the men, to be in the smoking room of an evening, drinking with the chaps, that sort of thing. Treating it like a club. I didn't. I've always treated it, I'd like to think, much more professionally, and therefore I feel I can do it my way rather than having to fit a stereotype. It's one of my big concerns with women in business and politics, that women often approach things in a different way, but it's equally as valid as the way the men approach it. They'll do just as good a job, but it's different. I don't think that you can't have that difference, that you've got to do it the way the men do it.'

Theresa is also known as a tremendously hard worker, and knows her diligence was noticed. She sees this kind of quieter approach as a female one, stating:

'In reality there's a streak often in women that we think, if I do a good job, it will be noticed, rather than thinking, I've got to tell everybody I'm doing a good job.'

Her time as prime minister came to an end on 24 July 2019, a little more than two years after she stepped in to the job. In that two-year period, her political authority had been eroded by the results of a snap general election she called in June 2017, at which the Tories lost thirteen seats and Labour gained thirty. Her government survived only by coming to a political arrangement with Northern Ireland's Democratic Unionist Party, which held ten seats in parliament. Then her endeavours to deliver a Brexit deal and secure support for it in the parliament failed. In many respects, Theresa's time in office as PM will be defined by the contentious politics of Brexit and by her failure to achieve it. People have speculated out loud whether her being a woman and outside 'the club' contributed to the defeat of the Brexit bills she brought to parliament.

For all the many layers of complexity in this political story, Theresa finds a way to summarise it as follows:

'I think it's difficult to see a gender thread. Boris Johnson, who replaced me, is a Brexiteer, meaning he supported Britain leaving the European Union during the referendum. I think the other Brexiteers in parliament are more comfortable with a Brexiteer and trust a Brexiteer to deliver. Regardless of the actual specifics of any Brexit deal with Europe, because I voted remain, they always felt there was this conspiracy. That we, that all Remainers, were trying to stop Brexit somehow. And therefore, anything that wasn't exactly what the Brexiteers wanted was seen to be part of this plot. So, I think having a Brexiteer there is what's making the difference for some of my colleagues who wouldn't support my deal, rather than a gender difference.'

But her analysis does come back to the clubby nature of parliament and how she chose to do her politics differently. Theresa says:

'I think one of the issues around parliament is the natural instinct to get into gangs, which is largely a male instinct. I was never part of any gang. You know, not all of my male colleagues are either. But for a lot of men, there's that sense you club together in some sort of group. For some, it's their year of entry into parliament or their belief in Europe or belief in another issue, and that does form a very

strong link between them. Of course, in terms of the Brexit, there were women involved in that as well. So, it wasn't just a male thing. But that sense that you were part of this group and you did what the group wanted.

And there were lots of forces externally. The social media work that was being done to persuade people to be against the deal. There was a huge environment of people actively trying to stop the government from getting what it wanted done. Normally, you would expect in parliament that the biggest group you are part of is your party and you have an affinity with it. But unfortunately, because the referendum split parties, their view on Europe has taken over as the group identity for a lot of people.'

Like Jacinda, Theresa believes role-modelling made a difference for her, specifically the fact that the UK had already had a female prime minister. She says:

'There wasn't that sense of the shocking, because it had been done and therefore it was less of an issue.'

She then muses about the impact of female monarchs in the following terms:

'When you think about it, the UK is used to having female leaders. We have had some quite strong queens in the past. So, there's less of a sense of a woman at the top being problematic or unusual. I think back in history, Queen Elizabeth I was a very strong female leader that people will often quote, then there is Queen Victoria. I mean, it is a completely different role, but just the concept of a woman being in that top position is maybe different in the UK.'

Theresa then offers the observation, *'I think it's an interesting question about whether the United States is yet ready to accept a woman as president.'*

On that question, we interviewed the expert.

Meeting Hillary Rodham Clinton – First Lady of the United States, 1993 to 2001. US Senator, 2001 to 2009. Secretary of State, 2009 to 2013, the third woman to serve. Presidential candidate, 2016

Many months after UN Leaders Week, we are back in New York, having travelled from Washington, DC, by train. We have come to interview the most recognisable woman politician in the world, Hillary Rodham Clinton.

Billions of people in the world would figure they know exactly what Hillary looks and sounds like. Yet in person, no matter how many times you have met her, there is always a sense of dislocation between the image and the actuality. Physically, she is smaller than you expect, but the sparkling blue eyes are so much bigger and more captivating.

We meet in her New York office, looking up from time to time at her collection of political badges that, intriguingly, say things like 'Cheese eaters for Hillary'.

Hillary's path to power is so well known it does not require detailed explanation. First Lady, Senator, Secretary of State, first woman to run as a candidate for one of the two major parties for the US presidency, Hillary is a trailblazer. Now in her early seventies, she is still full of energy, ideas and passion for progressive change.

But zooming through the milestones in her life like that loses the sense of just how incredible the roller-coaster ride has been. It is important to remind ourselves, as we live through the long shadow of her defeat in 2016, that Hillary has been chalking up successes for decades. Even before either she or her husband, Bill Clinton, were elected to office, she was making an outsize leadership contribution. She recalls with some sense of pride that:

'I chaired the Legal Services Corporation, which was a national body to provide legal services to millions of Americans who would otherwise be left out.'

She was never a First Lady who stayed out of the policy domain. As First Lady of Arkansas, when Bill was governor, Hillary chaired the committee that completely revamped that state's education system. As First Lady of the United States, she led an effort to reform healthcare policy that she describes as:

'A buzz-saw – it was so difficult, all of the special interests and all of the partisan interests. The comprehensive reform program was not adopted, but we turned around and provided health care for ten million children a year.'

Hillary is the only US First Lady ever to have moved into electoral politics, and as a Senator from New York she provided leadership when rebuilding, both physical and emotional, was necessary after the terrorist attacks of 9/11.

Then, after working in partnership with President Barack Obama, serving with distinction as Secretary of State, she became the first woman nominee of a major party for the presidency. The contest for the nomination was gruelling. Hillary was doggedly opposed by fellow Democratic Senator Bernie Sanders. About that time, she says:

'I was just in the bullseye for the entire campaign. But I won overwhelmingly. I won by twelve points, four million votes. I did become the first woman ever to be nominated and that was an amazing experience, which I'm very, very grateful for. Very proud of.'

But this remarkable life history of achievement and success has left one high, hard glass ceiling un-shattered. Many women around the world, including both those on her side of politics and others who may not have been supporters but respected her and what she stood for in terms of women's achievement, were shocked when Donald Trump was elected US president. Hillary describes it in vivid terms:

'We were over here running a campaign which was like an Obama 2.0 effort. Trump was doing something entirely different, which we had never seen before. We couldn't figure out all that was going on. But in the end, I got three million more votes. I'm proud of the campaign I ran but I wish I had known then what I know now.

I went where nobody else has ever gone and it was really, really hard. But now you've got other women running for the Democratic nomination for the presidency. So, it opened doors. It has motivated people and encouraged people, and that's all to the good.'

We have a fascinating discussion about women and ambition. Looking at our women leaders, none have clearly stated, 'I sought power, I wanted it, I fought for it, I got it.' Instead, our interviewees speak of being asked, of opportunities that came because of crisis, of thinking they would put their name forward only because they were certain someone else would swoop in and get the job. Christine put herself forward to lead the IMF. Erna and Theresa seem to have methodically pursued advancement during their time in politics. None of them describe having taken these steps because they were personally ambitious. Hillary herself has always carefully explained her motivations for running by pointing to the policies she cares about and the people who would be helped.

The conversation with Hillary was sparked because our visit coincided with the release of an interview with Beto O'Rourke, a member of congress from Texas who was at that stage campaigning to be the 2020 Democratic nominee for president. In the

Vanity Fair article, Beto is quoted as saying about the presidential contest, 'Man, I'm just born to be in it.'

Together with Hillary, we muse what would be the reaction to a woman who owned her ambition as squarely as this.

O'Rourke's words go through the Twitter mincing machine and ultimately come to be viewed by the media as a gaffe, an arrogant over-reach. But there is no real reaction to other words in the piece, like, 'You can probably tell that I want to run. I do. I think I'd be good at it.'

Could a woman even say just these words without criticism? Research we discuss later in this book suggests the answer is unambiguously no.

How much of the apparent lack of ownership of ambition is inherent in the internal outlook of our women leaders, and how much is a conditioned response because they have absorbed the fact that ambitious women are viewed negatively? It is impossible to know. We suspect even the women themselves could not quite disaggregate that.

Jacinda is also right that women are less likely to apply for a position if they do not meet all the stated criteria. In a study of over one thousand American professionals, women were more likely than men to give a version of an answer saying they did not put themselves forward because they lacked all the required qualifications. This would seem to indicate less confidence, not necessarily in their ability to do the job so much as the likelihood they would be chosen. Women were almost twice as likely as men to say they did not put themselves forward because they were following the guidelines about who should apply, meaning women tend to view the hiring process as rules based, rather than a more fluid human interaction where is it possible to talk your way into a job.[4] Further work is needed to break down the impact of the confidence effect from assumptions about how people get chosen, but there is hard evidence that demonstrates how men and women behave differently as jobseekers. Data from 610 million LinkedIn users shows that while men and women browse for new employment opportunities in the same way, women are 16 per cent less likely to apply for a job after viewing it than men, and women apply for 20 per cent fewer jobs.[5]

Should we worry about this lack of ownership of ambition? Confidence and competence are not necessarily correlated.[6] Indeed, there is some evidence that the leaders plagued with the greatest self-doubt avoid unnecessary risks and work the most diligently. Yet, somehow, it still rankles that women cannot stand up and simply say, 'I am the right person to lead.'

From all our conversations we find there is no one pathway to power. But there are lessons to take with us.

First, as global citizens, we must never forget that in many parts of the world women risk arrest and torture to become leaders. Ellen, Joyce and Michelle have all had to show physical courage. Ngozi has had direct and harsh experience of violence too. Her mother was kidnapped when she was Finance Minister by those who wanted to fight back against her anti-corruption campaigning. Thankfully, her mother was returned and not physically harmed, though the emotional scars endure.

For those of us who live in easier, wealthier places, our obligations to support women whose pathways to power are more fraught should be always in our minds.

Second, while a glass cliff is a daunting prospect, not all such moments result in a sharp fall. Being prepared to back yourself in a crisis can work. This comes out powerfully through Christine's story.

Third, men are not bystanders when it comes to women's leadership. Michelle's 'Barons' and Jacinda's self-sacrificing male colleague show that being sponsored and encouraged by men and male networks at the right time can be crucial. Ngozi agrees, and notes that almost all her leadership roles came through opportunities offered by men – Presidents Obasanjo and Jonathan selected her as Finance Minister. At the World Bank, Moeen Qureshi, Jim Wolfensohn and Bob Zoellick mentored and promoted her. Men can play a positive role in moving women into leadership positions.

Fourth, and most importantly of all for young women, women leaders are not waking up every morning with an internal monologue of, 'Wow, I'm terrific.' Instead, they share the same anxieties about being unprepared and fears of failure we all do. Any woman or girl who is thinking of becoming a leader but is plagued by worries that she is not good enough should take heart. That experience is not unique, it is held in common with some of the most powerful women in the world. Self-doubt is not a barrier to leadership, but part of it.

Fifth, if the worst happens, there is still tomorrow. Hillary is a model of stamina and grace in the face of defeat. Her example also shows that every courageous effort helps to make more space for the women who come next. Although a woman was not nominated as the Democrats' presidential candidate in 2020, the fact that so many women sought selection and that the ticket ultimately included Senator Kamala Harris for vice president shows that Hillary's run heightened the demand for women to be represented.

Out of all the pathways, there is much to recommend in the approach shown in Erna's Norway, of a network that deliberately opened a door for and then nurtured a talented young woman. We conclude with a note to self: Are we doing as much as we can to make that happen for the next generation? Are you?

4

Hypothesis one:
You go girl

Washington, New York, Brussels, Auckland, London: writing this book has meant planes, trains, cars, a feeling of constant movement. In every place, after every interview, our conversations would be intense and often personal. We came to know more about each other as well as learning about the women leaders who so generously gave their time.

In a beer garden in Brussels on a warm day, while we drank soft drinks and ignored all the alcoholic brews, Ngozi explained that she is the first of seven children, the oldest of five boys and two girls. Born in 1954 in Nigeria, Ngozi is an Igbo, one of the 350 ethnic groups that became the nation of Nigeria as a result of white colonialists drawing lines on a map. Ngozi's first hometown was Ogwashi-Ukwu in Delta State. She lived with her grandmother, a loving disciplinarian who did not spare her from the arduous tasks of walking miles to fetch water from the stream or gathering firewood from the forest. By the time she was nine years old she could cook, clean and keep house.

In Igbo culture, the firstborn child is automatically expected to set an example for the rest. While the weight of this obligation tends to fall a little more solidly if the firstborn is a son, in Ngozi's family it fell heavily on her because there was a large gap between her birth and that of her siblings. She is six years older than the next child and more than fifteen years older than her youngest sibling.

From her earliest days, she was expected by her parents to be a leader in the family and a role model. She was also taught to aim high in education. Her mother had a PhD in sociology from Boston University in the United States and her father a doctorate in mathematical statistics from the University of Cologne in Germany. Having achieved so much themselves, they assumed their children – the girls and the boys – would end up being the holders of doctorates.

For Ngozi and her sister, there was never the slightest hint that they would need to choose between careers and motherhood. Rather, they could be like their mother and their aunts, who were all both mothers and highly educated.

Ngozi said she felt loved rather than pushed to excel, but in her family home she simply absorbed through her skin a culture of high expectations. If anything, she thought more was expected from the girls, that there was more tolerance of a little youthful waywardness in the boys.

With all of that, she did not grow up thinking she would be a leader. Her eyes were on academic achievement and a university career like her parents, aunts and uncles. But looking back on it now, she realises that her family and school environment did build her as a leader. She served as a school prefect – a small-scale, practical experience of leadership – but much more important was the fact her upbringing meant she felt very comfortable in her own skin. When she first went abroad to study at a university in the United States, her father said to her:

'If people discriminate against you because you are black or you are a woman, or both, remember it is their problem, not yours. Use their problem as a source of strength and motivation to do better, not as a source of weakness.'

That became her mantra, and people who know Ngozi marvel at her strength even in the face of adversity.

On the surface, one would not think that the family story of a girl born in Barry, Wales, in the United Kingdom in 1961 would have anything in common with that of a woman born in Nigeria. Yet when Julia told Ngozi her story, there were some clear similarities as well as differences. Julia's early life is the quintessential migrant story, with her mother and father taking her and her sister, Alison, to Adelaide, Australia, in 1966 in search of a better life.

Neither of Julia's parents finished secondary school. Her father was born in Cwmgwrach, a coalmining village in Wales, the sixth of his seven-child family. Simply because of poverty, he was not able to attend school beyond the age of fourteen. Despite being offered a scholarship because of how well he performed in the standard examination administered to eleven-year-olds in that era, his family just could not afford to have him in school. They needed him working, so he took a job in the village shop.

Julia's mother was very unwell as a child, growing up in a home that saw illness and tragedy. Two of her mother's three siblings died as children. One sister survived into adulthood but died from cancer in her forties. Her mother's early life was therefore filled with sadness and many sickness-related absences from school. With no system back then to help a child in this position, Julia's mother drifted away from education before the end of secondary school.

While both of Julia's parents improved their own education through voracious reading and some formal courses of study throughout their lives, there was always a wistful sense of 'What if?'

What if we had completed school? What if we had been able to go on to university? What would the other life not lived have been like?

Consequently, Julia explained that she and her sister grew up in a family environment where they were taught to cherish every day of their education, to think with ambition about their lives, to aim for a university education and a good career.

Having heard each other's stories, we reflected on the fact that we were never hothoused or forced by our parents into thinking we must be leaders. Neither of us was instructed that we must go into politics or aim to be a minister or prime minister. But we were never told we could not be leaders, either. Our early environments were ones that allowed us to grow to be the kind of women who could respond to all sorts of opportunities, rather than being focused on our limits. We were never taught either by word or deed that boys are better and the natural leaders.

In the 1950s or 1960s, or even the 1970s, no one would have said to us, 'You go girl.' Yet that contemporary saying captures what our upbringings were like. It was as if our parents had whispered that into our ears every day.

Family and school are not hermetically sealed cocoons. Whatever we were taught by those closest to us, we still lived in environments awash with gender roles and stereotyping. But as children, especially when very young, the impact of the attitudes of those who loved and directly taught us was pivotal.

Out of our discussions, we developed our 'You go girl' hypothesis: *One key to enabling a woman to become a leader is a childhood in which she is taught she is not lesser than the boys, and to aim high.*

Hypothesis might seem like an unusual word to use, but it has been on our lips since we first began to discuss writing this book. Our shared starting point was a set of best guesses about what might explain the numerical lack of women leaders and the ways we observed that they were treated differently to men. Informing these best guesses were two sources of information: our own life experiences and our understanding of the academic studies about women's leadership.

Neither of us is a credentialed researcher, with a framed doctorate in gender studies sitting above our writing desks, but for many years we have been exposed to and enriched by data and evidence on gender themes. Partly, that has happened because we are inveterate meeting and conference attendees and we have been able to listen to what speakers cite and explain. Partly, it has happened because books and articles on women have caught our eyes. For Julia, the last few years have particularly been steeped in the research on women and leadership because she has the privilege of regularly working in London at a desk in an open-plan office alongside the fabulous staff of the Global Institute for Women's Leadership. As well as being formally briefed about what the team is working on, every day she overhears something new and intriguing.

Our guesses had the benefit of lived experience and all this research by osmosis, but were they completely right, wildly wrong or somewhere in between? We decided that working that out would be at the heart of this book. In each chapter we present one of our best guesses in the form of a hypothesis, meaning it is stated as a proposition that will be tested. In taking this approach we have followed the tried and true processes of inquiring minds across the ages, who have said to themselves things like, *My hypothesis is the earth goes around the sun*, or, *My hypothesis is the earth is flat*, and then marshalled the evidence to work out whether their proposition is true or not.

In total, we present eight hypotheses. Our process of testing involves analysing the lived experience of women leaders and more systematic inquiry into the academic research, with a strong focus on psychological studies. As noted in chapter 2, while we find this body of work intriguing, we can only ascertain how much it carries over into the real world by exploring it alongside the real-life experience of our women leaders.

Each of our interviewees is a fascinating person and we knew that it would be easy to become so wrapped up in conversation with them that we would walk away with wonderful memories but without a body of material directed at answering the hypotheses. Our list of standard questions kept us on track, and for this You go girl hypothesis we asked each woman leader:

1. Did you ever dream about being a leader as a child?
2. Can you talk to us about the key people who influenced your views as a child and helped form who you are today?
3. Can we probe specifically around the influence of your father and mother?
4. Can you please tell us about your education and what role it played, if any, in setting you up for your leadership journey? What were you taught as a young girl about the expectations for your future role in life?

In drafting all our questions, we aimed for open constructions that would prompt discussion, rather than more closed, specific framing that might imply there was a right reply. Depending on what was said, we delved deeper and posed additional questions in a spontaneous way.

In answer, what did our women leaders say?

Of our interviewees, Ellen Johnson Sirleaf was the one who seemed to have been chosen by destiny as a child. Ellen's autobiography is called *This Child Will Be Great*, a reference to a prophesy made by a venerable old man about her when she was a baby. But, as she tells us, over time this grand prediction '*became a family joke*', generating much laughter from her, her mother and her older sister. Given how grim much of the rest of Ellen's childhood story is, it is a relief to know there was also some fun and humour.

The context of Ellen's childhood was strongly shaped by the enduring divisions between former slaves from the United States who settled in Liberia and the indigenous peoples who had always lived there. She describes:

'*My childhood was interesting because I would say I had a foot in both worlds of our country, the indigenous side and the settler side. My father and my mother partly came from the indigenous side but grew up in settler homes and were educated by settler families.*'

The pivotal event of her childhood was the death of her father. Ellen says:

'*I saw my father die. He was the first indigenous person elected to the Liberian legislature. When he was sick for seven years and died, my family crossed over into the other side of want, where my mother had to do things like selling bread to keep us in school.*

My father represented the top person of our tribe and I had seen him rise to such heights, with people like presidents visiting the home when he was well. I had then seen him go down to a place where he sat in a chair and nobody came anymore. After he passed,

I didn't plan it but somehow in my mind I knew we had to regain what my father was forced to lose through sickness. I wouldn't say I had planned my leadership or anything, but I think I felt in my consciousness that he had gone so far and had lost everything because of health, and now someone had to hold that emblem.'

While the death of her father stirred in Ellen the birth of ambition, she clearly identifies a female role model as the one most important to her when she says:

'I must say that my mother was the strongest figure in my childhood. My mother's father was a German trader in the village where she was born. My mother always stood out for her complexion and was seen as different.

After our father's death, she never forgot to carry out his dictate that we should go back to the village where our paternal grandmother lived. Whenever we went back to the village, my mother reached out to everybody. Her life of sharing and teaching is something that I and my siblings have grown up with. She was, for me, a role model, but also the source of my strength. With Christianity she instilled three things into us – hard work, honesty, humility – and my whole life I have attempted to represent those three values. She was a teacher and a preacher, and I just imagined that I would follow in her footsteps.'

As Ellen describes it, her childhood was free from gender stereotyping. She says:

'I thought I could be anything. I could play any game like a boy, I could stand up in class to any teacher, woman or man, and I was taught to do just that.'

It is a long way from Nigeria and Liberia to France, but Christine Lagarde tells a story uncannily similar to Ngozi's about the responsibility of being the oldest child, and one of loss, like Ellen.

Christine is the eldest in her family of four. All the younger children are boys. Christine says:

'From early on, because my parents were engaged in all sorts of activities, I was brought up as someone who was responsible for others, and that is one of the attributes of leadership: you have to take risks and assume responsibility.'

Like Ellen, Christine would play with the boys and think of herself as being as good as them. In fact, she was surrounded by boys at home and at school, because she was in the first co-educational intake of what had been exclusively a boys' school. Looking back, she says:

'I was not exactly shaped to think like a boy . . . but there definitely was no difference made between me and my brothers in our parents' future expectations for us.'

Also like Ellen, she lost her father young and saw how that changed her mother's life. In Christine's words:

'My father passed away from a debilitating disease when I was sixteen. So, very early on, from the age of twelve, because my father went through that disease for about four years, I saw my mother taking over and being the leader of the family because there was no other option. And then, after he passed away, she was a single mother who had to do everything.'

Joyce Banda's early life was not filled with the tragedy of this kind of loss, but it was a life of hardship. Her father was an orphan who strived to make something of himself, he became a police officer and joined the Malawi Police Band. Music was his passion, and he ultimately became the first black person to teach music at Kamuzu Academy, a prestigious school in Malawi.

In Joyce's culture, the first granddaughter in the family would be sent to her maternal grandmother when she was one year old.

Her maternal grandmother would mould her so that ultimately the girl would grow to take over her role as the matriarch of the family. But in Joyce's case, her father refused and said she would stay with her parents five days a week to go to school, but be with her grandmother on the weekends.

This act of rebellion changed the course of Joyce's life, enabling her to get an education and do something other than walk a predetermined path.

Like Ellen, Joyce was also subject to a prophesy. Having interacted with her on several occasions, her Uncle John said to her father, '*I don't know what I see about this child, but she is going to be a leader.*' Joyce remembers her father laughing and replying with the words, '*She is just a girl, what can she be?*' Joyce was sorely disappointed hearing that but believes her father may have come to regret those words, because as she grew up he would frequently say to her, '*Remember what Uncle John said – you are destined to be a leader.*'

It is notable that this spirit of ambition for her was also in her grandmother. Joyce says:

'*I was born in a village called Malemia. A white British woman had come to set up a clinic there. The day after I was born, this British woman was making her rounds and found my grandmother carrying me, and asked what my name was. In our tribe, it would have been traditional for me to take my maternal grandmother's name, given I was born to assume her role. But my grandmother replied by asking this British woman what her name was. She said Joyce, and that it meant 'joy'. My grandmother decided to defy tradition and name me Joyce because she wanted me to grow up and become important like this woman who built clinics and helped people.*'

This was a decision with formidable ramifications. In her ethnic group, bearing the name of her grandmother is more than symbolic. It signifies that the granddaughter will effectively become the grandmother upon her death, including taking her role, inheriting her property and being welcomed by her friends. Joyce's grandmother died when Joyce was twenty-seven years old, but because she did not bear her grandmother's name, many of these things did not happen. Obviously, her grandmother's will for Joyce to become something else, to have a different life, was strong.

A striking feature of Joyce's recitation of her life story is the absence of references to her mother. When probed on this she poignantly replies:

'My mother was only seventeen when I was born, and because she was working and I spent weekends in my grandmother's village, I saw very little of her. She is the opposite of her own mother and of me. She was very quiet. And so sometimes I can have a whole conversation about my past and not mention my mother once, and it is sad but it is true. In so many ways, we were both daughters of my grandmother. However, ten years ago I established a bursary fund in her name that has provided tertiary education for 1500 students in Malawi, including thirty medical doctors. My mum was like a big sister.'

Joyce reminds us, though, that even in families where girls are nurtured and urged to aim high, poverty can flatten everything. She tells us the story of Chrissie, who was her best friend in the village. Joyce says:

'Chrissie was definitely brighter than me. At the end of our primary education we were both selected to go to different but high-quality girls' secondary schools in Malawi. The next holiday, when I came back to the village, Chrissie did not want to see me. My grandmother said she had dropped out of school because her family could not raise the six dollars that Chrissie needed to go back. I remember crying for

hours. That was the first time I woke up to the injustice of this world. It is very painful for me that even today, forty-nine million girls in Africa are not in school through no fault of their own.'

In her own life, Joyce also felt the burn of poverty on education. After she finished secondary school, she says her father told her that he could not afford to send her and her four siblings to college on his salary. As a result, she chose a short course of further education, rather than a longer, fuller qualification.

It is striking that, for our interviewees, being the oldest child came with an expectation of leadership. In Joyce's case, it also meant self-sacrifice.

A world away, Hillary Clinton grew up as the eldest child in her family, with two younger brothers. Pivotal to her sense of self was her father's attitude and guidance. Hillary says:

'I do think that a woman's potential for leadership starts in the family, in the community, and there is evidence, at least in the USA, that the attitude of the father towards the daughter is particularly important. In my case, my father was very encouraging of my education and ideas. He didn't have a set of preconceived stereotypes about what I should be like and how I should act. He also never treated me or my brothers any differently. My mother was also incredibly encouraging and pushed me to be confident, to stand up for myself, to assume little leadership positions within my neighbourhood.'

Being trusted with responsibilities in the girl scouts was one example of Hillary's early leadership experiences. But she also points to the impact of gender expectations outside the home, and especially girls self-limiting their behaviour as they became teenagers. Hillary describes it in these terms:

'What happened in our early teens was that, as girls got interested in boys, the boys' expectations began to limit the public behaviour of

the girls. I remember, in high school, girls worrying that they would get a better grade in a class than their boyfriend. So even when girls heard good messages in school about aiming high, once they got into personal relationships, as a result of the traditional model of how one related to the opposite sex at that time, they began to withdraw a bit from the public arena. It's one of the reasons why I ended up going to Wellesley, an all-girls college.'

She also tasted early electoral success and defeat. She was elected class vice-president during her junior years at high school, but then lost the election for class president in her senior year. Her opponents were two boys, one of whom told her, '*You are really stupid if you think a girl can be elected president.*' Given everything that subsequently happened, these words have an ongoing sting.

Near the top of the world, in Norway, being a girl scout was also a formative experience for another leader, Erna Solberg, who fondly remembers:

'*I was a scout in quite a small group, so when the older ones left for university, I was given more responsibility. When I was fourteen years old, I became one of the leaders of forty scouts. With two fifteen-year-old leaders, I would take this group of girls camping for weekends. When the parents give you that type of responsibility you have to make decisions.*'

Erna jokes that, being the middle of three daughters, she was '*the in-between. I'm the one all of the personality tests say can't succeed.*'

She describes her family as one in which nobody was politically active. But evidently it was one that bred leaders, with both her older and younger sister successful today in their chosen fields.

Her older sister puts this down to the fact that because they never had brothers they never felt that there was a difference or any limits on girls' abilities. From time to time, Julia has also wondered about the impact of being from a family with no sons. The question is unanswerable, but if her older sister had been a boy, would her parents' dreams of the next generation leading a more educated, empowered and prosperous life have been disproportionately invested in him?

Erna simply says, '*There wasn't any activism, but we had supportive parents who said you should try to do what you want.*'

Interestingly, when Erna compares her life to that of her sister who went into business, she believes that politics may have presented fewer gender barriers. Erna says:

'*I think business is different from politics, because in politics you are representing people, but in business it is about money-making. I think there sometimes is a question of whether a female leader will be hungry enough or tough enough to get commercial results.*'

Far closer to the Antarctic than the Arctic, Jacinda Ardern also grew up without brothers. There was only ever her and her sister, who is eighteen months older. She says:

'*From my mum and dad, I just felt as if I could do anything. It was never about gender. When I was about eight, my family moved, and we bought my grandparents' orchard. My father was a policeman and Mum got a job running the high school cafeteria. And we all kept this little orchard going – a very small plot of land, but we still had to work it. So, I grew up with tractors and cherry pickers and motorbikes. I was a bit of a tomboy. I remember helping my dad one day and him saying, "Pass me the spanner, you're the closest thing to a son I've got." I never ever felt as if there were any real stereotypes in my family or any set roles that we fulfilled. But if anything, I felt as though I was probably fulfilling the role that a boy would have if there was one.*'

Theresa is our sole leader who is an only child. Growing up in a village in England in the late 1950s and 1960s, in a household where her mother did not work, it is easy to imagine that she saw her world as full of gender stereotypes. But both her parents' attitude and attending an all-girls' school gave her the sense she could do anything. She recalls:

'My parents always said that it was up to me – that what I did and how far I went was about how hard I wanted to work. There was never any suggestion of you can't do this, or you can't do that.'

Michelle Bachelet effectively summarises the theme we hear from all of the women leaders with the words, *'I had a very enabling environment that let me be myself.'*

She describes the specifics of her own upbringing by saying:

'My father was a very atypical man from the military. First of all, he was very open-minded. He was always very supportive of women, including my mother and me. My mother worked and would always tell me that "Your destiny in life is not to get married and have children – if you want, you can do that, but you can also do whatever you want in life because you work hard." My mother would not have called herself a feminist, but she was. She was very active, had her own thoughts and ideas and so on.

So, I didn't have a typical family. Probably if I had grown up in a very typical Chilean family where male and female roles are so differentiated then it would have been different.'

Michelle is the younger of two children and her older sibling is a brother. Though not the leader of the children in her family, her early years did bring her leadership experiences. She says:

'I never thought of myself being a leader, but looking back I realise that in practical ways I was always leading something. I was always organising at school.'

But as she reflects, she notes that, growing up, she did not think of women as being political leaders or as having power. She had already worked out that female ambition could be perceived as a negative, that it was important for a woman to be seen as pursuing a noble cause, not power for herself.

Her major takeaway from her childhood was that she learnt responsibility. With a hearty laugh, she jokes:

'Responsibility is what has led me my whole life. A lot of the decisions that I've made in my life have been for love, but also because of responsibility.'

The laughter continues as Michelle also remembers being taught to be a good housewife in home economics, including how to cook and clean the silver. Julia says she can top that, because she was forced to study laundry at school.

All jokes aside, what do the recollections of these women leaders about their early days tell us?

First, their words remind us just how much contrast there is in the cultures and contexts from which our women come. Thanks to the World Economic Forum (WEF), we can look at these differences through a statistical paradigm. Each year, the WEF publishes its Global Gender Gap Index, which generates a ranking of countries based on how big or small the gaps are between men and women in four key domains: economic status, education, health and politics. The 2020 index covers 153 countries, with the most gender equal listed first. Julia's home, Australia, comes in at 34, while Ngozi's Nigeria comes in at 128.

Erna's home of Norway blitzes the index, coming in second only to Iceland, which is led by Prime Minister Katrín Jakobsdóttir. Completing the top trifecta is Finland, which is led by Prime Minister Sanna Marin, who assumed office in December 2019. At thirty-four years old, she became the youngest female prime minister ever in the world. Iceland can boast women everywhere because the leader of each of the five parties in the governing coalition is a woman.[1] Erna also knows what it is like to bring together an all-female team. In January 2019, she announced a new coalition in which all four political parties were led by women.[2]

Jacinda has reason to be proud of the fact that New Zealand comes in at 6 in the WEF index. Sitting at 21 is Theresa's United Kingdom, and at 53 we find Hillary's homeland, the United States. Each of these nations is categorised as high-income.

In contrast, Ellen's home of Liberia is ranked 97 and Joyce's Malawi is down at 116. Both are low-income nations.

Michelle is in an interesting position. Chile is characterised as middle-income, but it is not far behind the US in the gender ranking, coming in at 57.

Second, when seeing leaders stride the stage nationally or globally, many would tend to assume they have always led privileged lives and that helped them in their rise. But this easily-leapt-to conclusion does not stand up to analysis in relation to our women leaders.

Undoubtedly, Ellen and Joyce, by the standards of upper- and middle-income countries, come from poor backgrounds. In the environment of their own nations, neither would have numbered among the most disadvantaged children, but their circumstances were hard enough to create real insecurity for Ellen after the death of her father, and to deny Joyce access to full post-school education.

Turning to the rest of our leaders, who come from wealthier nations, their backgrounds are probably best described as middle-class ranging to upper-middle-class. Most were the daughters of employees, with occupations ranging from cafeteria worker and police officer in Jacinda's case, teacher and academic in Christine's, office worker and executive in a public transport company in Erna's and vicar and stay-at-home mum in Theresa's. Hillary's father owned and ran a drapery business, while her mother was a full-time housewife. Once again, the word 'privilege', in the sense of material advantage or social status, does not really seem to be right.

Michelle's father had an upper-echelon position as a general and her mother was an archaeologist. However, any benefit her father's status would have afforded ended dramatically as a result of the coup.

All in all, we believe it is clear that none of our leaders' families are ones from which people would assume national and international leaders are drawn; to which descriptions like wealthy, powerful or aristocratic would apply.

This is a heartening conclusion – a girl can grow into a leader without coming from an elite family.

Third, and most importantly of all, these reflections make it crystal clear that what a girl is told as she grows matters. Our women leaders were never told no, were never told you cannot be a leader – that is for the boys. Each grew up in an environment that empowered them, with an openness about gender roles. Each was the subject of high expectations.

No clear theme emerges about whether the role of the father or the mother is more important. That varies from woman to woman. Interestingly, there is no example of one parent being positive about their girl having a future uncaged from gender stereotypes and the other holding a more traditional view. It would be fascinating to understand how that dynamic would play out for a girl's self-image.

But looking a bit more deeply, perhaps, while not setting boundaries, the parents of these women leaders reinforced a theme about responsibility. That word keeps coming up. Our women leaders were encouraged by their parents to work hard, be responsible, to be 'good girls'. Do we tend to more readily describe a boy as a natural-born leader if he shows an early aptitude for taking command, whereas we praise a girl for showing responsibility? Put another way, do we change the lens from being about who the boy is to what the girl does?

If so, even in the most empowering of families, are there nuances that lead to men having an inbuilt expectation that they will be in charge, while women over-prepare and never assume an entitlement to a place at the top table?

These questions do not have easy answers, but it feels right to offer a hesitant yes to each of them, and to make a mental note about the importance of emphasising responsibility to all children rather than allowing them to develop an entitled sense of self. After all, overconfidence not backed up by actual ability is not a desirable trait in leaders or anyone else.

Another clear theme is that what is taught at home ends up bumping into the gender expectations of the world: teenage girls acting unintelligent, women being punished for ambition. Julia recalls a conversation with her great-niece, Isla, who was just turning four, about attending her older brother Ethan's sixth birthday party. Asked if she had joined in one of the physical play activities, Isla replied that she had not because it was just for boys. Actually, it was just for children who reached a specified height requirement and she did not. No family member would have ever said she could not play because she was a girl, but clearly that is what she had picked up. The world's gender stereotypes get dragged into homes that are trying not to model them.

But given children bring these kinds of impressions about the world back home, in addition to providing a generally empowering environment parents may want to think about having gentle but regular conversations about gender roles and stereotyping – designating a space and time to correct any mistaken impressions that have formed in the minds of both their sons and daughters about what is and is not appropriate.

This seems even more important today given the lack of boundary between home and the outside world. When your authors were growing up, the world beyond their local community only came through the newspapers, radio and television, with access to the latter two time-limited. Now, with mobile phones, iPads and other devices, there are no boundaries and few time limits. The world, for good and bad, is fully accessible, and the primacy of the messages delivered at home is under more challenge.

Beyond talking, there is also the question of what is modelled at home. With the rapid growth of the number of women in the workforce and the lessening of the numbers of women who are continuously at home full-time, many of us would intuitively assume that domestic duties are now more equitably shared. But the statistics show there is still quite some way to go. A time-use study conducted in the United States in 2018 reveals that, on average, women spend two hours a day more than men on unpaid house and care work. The peak difference occurs in the age range of 35 to 44 years old, a time when families may need to look after children and spend time caring for ageing parents. At this stage of life, women are performing 8.8 hours a day of free work, while men are contributing 5.2 hours. Even when men and women both work full time, there is a 22 per cent difference in the time devoted to unpaid domestic and caring work.[3] A look at who manages healthcare needs at home also shows substantial differences. Around 80 per cent of mothers say they are the parent who will take children to medical appointments, and over 75 per cent say they do the follow-up, like ensuring medication is taken. When a child is too unwell to go to school, 40 per cent of mothers indicate they are the adult who takes time off work to look after them, whereas only 3 per cent of fathers say they shoulder that responsibility.[4]

It might be a hard message to absorb for fathers who are not currently regularly wielding a mop, washing the dishes or staying home to look after a sick child, but at-home modelling about sharing domestic duties is another aspect of creating an enabling, non-stereotyped environment. Research has shown that, when asked what they want to be when they grow up, girls were less likely to confine their answers to stereotypically female occupations if they had a dad who not only said he believed in a more equal distribution of domestic labour, but actually did more tasks at home.[5]

With these additions, You go girl is definitely a proven hypothesis and a real lesson for the parents and other relatives of young girls. A family that creates the kind of free-from-gender-limits environment our women leaders grew up in will be empowering her to be a leader.

5

Hypothesis two:
It's all about the hair

Hillary Clinton has been known to joke that she should have called her book about her time as Secretary of State '*The Scrunchie Chronicles: 112 countries and it's still all about the hair*'.

For practical reasons, Hillary, the most travelled US Secretary of State in history, grew her hair long and regularly pulled it back in a ponytail. In words that were surely not meant to be quoted, a State Department official told Rachael Combe of *Elle* magazine, 'As a chick, it's a big pain in the butt. The weather is different, and you're in and out of the plane. [The staff] gets off that plane looking like garbage most days, but she has to look camera ready. She said the reason she grew her hair long was that it's easier. She has options.'[1]

Somewhat ironically, coverage of Hillary's announcement of a gender equality and women's empowerment initiative in Cambodia in 2012 was overshadowed by stories about her staff wanting to ban the scrunchies, the fabric-covered elastics holding back her hair.

In this chapter, we explore a hypothesis about scrunchies and shoes, body shapes and appearance standards, to discover whether for women leaders it does end up being all, or at least disproportionately, about their appearance.

This hypothesis has a few different dimensions. The first and perhaps easiest to come to grips with is, *Women leaders end up losing valuable time on matters related to their appearance.*

Our unnamed State Department official might have thought Hillary had options, but one that was off the table was the efficient approach of appearing every day with a wash-and-wear short haircut, no make-up and dressed in a standard suit, shirt, tie and comfortable lace-up shoes.

That, especially in this era of globalisation, is the defined and accepted male leadership 'uniform'. Equally valid alternatives include military attire, black tie for formal events and an open-necked shirt for casual wear. Another acceptable variation is wearing a country's traditional dress. For example, President Narendra Modi of India wears modernised versions of the traditional bandhgala.

Men who wear the accepted uniform may have other aspects of their appearance critiqued. For example, they may be viewed and described as short or tall, paunchy or lean, balding or thick-haired, but the clothes generally do not take centre stage.

Only very occasionally does clothing become an issue for a man. Prime Minister Justin Trudeau of Canada ended up finding out the hard way that if you have the benefit of a uniform that draws no criticism, it pays to stick with it. On a trip to India in 2018, he adopted traditional dress on many occasions, resulting in the jarring image of him wearing a golden brocade sherwani, which is a long coat, to meet male Bollywood icons who were dressed in plain black blazers. He was roundly pilloried for going over the top and 'playing dress-ups'.[2]

President Barack Obama, who famously told *Vanity Fair* in 2012 that, 'You'll see I wear only gray or blue suits . . . I'm trying to pare down decisions. I don't want to make decisions about what I'm eating or wearing. Because I have too many other decisions to make',[3] almost broke the internet when he turned up at a media conference in 2014 wearing a beige suit. Wits immediately reworked his most famous slogans into 'Tan you can believe in' and 'The audacity of taupe'.[4]

But these incidents are so few and far between, they are truly the exceptions that highlight the rule that the standard uniform works for men.

No equivalent has emerged for female political leaders. Women have an almost infinite number of clothing choices and what they wear for day, cocktail functions and night is going to vary much more than putting on either a suit or a tuxedo. Whether a woman revels in fashion and a wide variety of clothing choices or finds it all a bothersome nuisance varies from person to person, from leader to leader.

But for almost every woman, and especially leaders who are in the public eye, the lack of a uniform means more time and energy goes into working out what to have in their wardrobe and making the choices about what to wear each day. After all, how long can anyone equivocate about which tie to wear?

In many cultures, there are also expectations about coiffed hair, varnished nails and make-up for women that mean, in addition to the time taken on wardrobe, still more is needed for all of that.

In our hypothesis, the time cost is not just paid by the woman leader in getting ready each day. It is also paid because political airtime is used to report on what a leader is wearing or how she looks, rather than what she is doing.

But our hypothesis goes deeper than that, to how *Appearance has historically been and continues to be the basis on which women are judged.* Put baldly, women have tended to be valued more on how they look and men on what they do. Popular culture caught this when stores used to sell outfits for children that were emblazoned with 'Smart like Daddy' for boys and 'Pretty like Mummy' for girls. Not a shred of ambiguity there; judge the girls on their looks!

Thankfully, you cannot buy T-shirts like that anymore, but the fact that this prejudice is less visible does not mean it has entirely ceased to exist.

There is a further difficult-to-describe dimension to this issue of appearance that we want to hold up to the light, namely how people judge and characterise women based on clothing. If each of us was asked to close our eyes and imagine a male and female version of a scientist or surgeon or road worker, the same clothing would appear in our imaginations for both: a lab coat, scrubs, a neon-bright safety vest. But there are all sorts of ways of describing women that come with a defined expectation of what she is like and what she wears that have no male equivalent; try 'yummy mummy' or 'girly swot' or even – and we apologise in advance for using this word to make the point – 'slut'. In our mind's eye we can summon the female images that go with these terms, because these stereotypes do not just come with an expected set of behaviours, they come with a defined wardrobe. The purpose of this exercise is to capture how clothing is seen to speak about women in a way it just does not for men. There is a societal expectation that, even before a woman speaks or does anything, observers can work out likely aspects of her character and conduct from what she wears. How does this play out for women leaders?

Then there is another hard-to-catch leg to our hypothesis, that *We not only judge women on their looks, but we tightly constrain the ideal against which they are to be measured.*

Author and philosopher Susan Sontag put this concept beautifully in her 1972 essay titled 'The Double Standard of Aging':

'The great advantage men have is that our culture allows two standards of male beauty: the boy and the man. The beauty of a boy resembles the beauty of a girl. In both sexes it is a fragile kind of beauty and flourishes naturally only in the early part of the life cycle. Happily, men are able to accept themselves under another standard of good looks – heavier, rougher, more thickly built . . . There is no equivalent of this second standard for women. The single standard of beauty for women dictates that they must go on having clear skin. Every wrinkle, every line, every gray hair, is a defeat.'[5]

So many of the global cultural references for women live up to Sontag's words. Think of the Hollywood actresses who present forty-, fifty- or even sixty-year-old faces to the world apparently unmarked by the passage of time. Compare in your mind the still-smooth features of singer Madonna with the lined face of the James Bond actor Daniel Craig, who is a decade younger.

The lack of a second standard for women is always going to play hard against women leaders, who are unlikely to be girlish in actual age or looks.

To sum up, our hypothesis is that, compared with men, the appearance of women leaders is more scrutinised, that what is acceptable is judged against a different standard and that questions of character are more likely to be inferred from clothing.

In addition, women leaders lose out on opportunities to deliver a substantive message because of the crowding out effect of disproportionate commentary on appearance, and pay a price in extra time spent preparing for public events.

Does science prove or disprove our hypothesis, in whole or part? The truthful answer is it helps a little, but not as much as we would like. Because women leaders are still unusual on the political stage, the research tends to come in fits and starts around particular elections with high-profile female candidates. There is not long-term, methodologically consistent research.

Even if there were, given how women leaders are seen and judged will often be analysed through news reporting, the degree and speed of change in the media landscape makes the research task more difficult. It would be almost impossible to answer the question whether differences over time result from variations in gender norms or variations in reporting approaches.

There are studies on how women are treated on social media and much discussion of how toxic that environment can be. But we lack contemporary studies that get to the bottom of gender-based appearance bias in reporting on women leaders in today's world, in which social media shapes traditional media and vice versa. Studies to date have tended to focus on one or the other, not both and the interplay between them.

Then there is the complication that judgements of a woman leader do not come in a vacuum. There never has been or will be a perfectly constructed election in which equally capable, resourced and supported male and female candidates, of exactly the same age, race and experience, contend and enable us to see what difference gender makes when everything else is the same. Context clearly matters. For example, a Canadian study of contests involving women for leadership of a political party showed that being an unexpected disruption candidate, combined with being younger and blonde, magnified reporting on appearance. In contrast, being the frontrunner meant for a female candidate that even though there were more references to appearance than for her male competitor, the number of references was low and the style perfunctory.[6]

A study of governor races in the United States found that print reporters devoted significantly more attention to women's appearance, personalities and private lives compared to men, who were more likely to be judged by their views on a public policy issue.[7]

One study, which made a good job of wrestling with both the number of mentions of a candidate and the style and tone of those mentions, relates to Elizabeth Dole's bid for the Republican Party nomination for the presidency of the United States in 1999.[8] For a period, Elizabeth was running second in opinion polling to the ultimately successful contender, George W. Bush, and was beating John McCain, another contender. In surveys that compared her to the likely Democrat challenger, Al Gore, she was coming out on top.

The researchers showed that Elizabeth received less coverage than would have been expected given her poll status. There were also more references to her appearance, including very negative ones, and to her character traits, than for Bush and McCain.

Disturbingly, in words that could easily have been written about a woman candidate today, the study found that, 'In reading through the news stories, two predominant images of Elizabeth Dole emerge. One is the more positive image of the intelligent, hard-working, talented, popular trailblazer while the other is the more negative image of the overly cautious, overly rehearsed, robotic perfectionist who oozes charm but lacks substance.'

In the next chapter we focus on these kinds of gendered characterisations of style, but it is worth noting here that, based on Dole's experience, there is a gendered slippery slope on both appearance and personality that seems to easily take women from being described with adjectives like 'polished' and 'poised' at the top to 'Stepford wife–like' and 'inauthentic' at the bottom.

Of course, it is a long time ago that Elizabeth Dole was a contender. However, unfortunately, there is no reason to assume the focus on appearance is diminishing. Research by Dr Blair Williams, an Australian political scientist, shows it is actually getting worse.[9] Blair's work compares the media reaction to the election of the second female prime minister of the United Kingdom, Theresa May, in 2016, against the reaction to the first, Margaret Thatcher, who was elected in 1979. The research shows the coverage is more gendered now than it was then. In particular, Blair found references to Theresa's appearance happened twice as often as references to Margaret Thatcher's, and that the problem was worse in the conservative press.

This finding may well be explained by declining media standards rather than a growth in focus on appearance. After all, forty years ago the media was more measured and respectful in how it covered politicians across the board. But whatever the cause, it does mean voters are living in an environment with more reporting on appearance, not less.

None of this analysis is meant to imply that there is no coverage about how men look, either. President Donald Trump's hair has been frequently discussed and during the election campaign was even pulled by a talk-show host to show it was real and connected to his head. Across the pond, in the United Kingdom, Boris Johnson's blond mop also comes in for commentary.

But while there is interest, there is not the same degree of judgement. When Boris Johnson became the UK prime minister, news and commentary pieces frequently referred to him as dishevelled, but no one suggested his lack of sartorial sense or ability to style his hair was the prism through which he should be assessed.

But a dishevelled, obviously middle-aged woman? One who apparently had so little regard for appearances that she was routinely photographed with messy hair and items of clothing coming untucked? Would she be judged and discarded because her lack of care would be seen to say something profound about her character?

Yet the other extreme of looking glamourous and attractive does not help either. To take one example, Belinda Stronach, a candidate for leadership of the Conservative Party of Canada, who was under forty years old, blonde and attractive. She was consistently reported on with reference to her appearance, with her hair, wardrobe, body and sexual attractiveness analysed.[10] Controversially, at a later point in her political career she was referred to as a 'dipstick', bringing into play the stereotype that women can be beautiful or brainy but not both. Even worse, she was also referred to as a 'whore' by former Conservative Party colleagues.[11]

Given the paucity of research, looking at it can only take us so far in our hypothesis testing. To gain a broader view, we asked each of our women leaders three questions:

1. During your leadership, were your appearance and clothing focused on more than was commonly done for male leaders?
2. What did you do, if anything, to manage the interest in your appearance?
3. Did you view any disproportionate interest in your looks as taking political oxygen from your policy messages?

We found these questions provoked detailed and animated discussions.

Theresa has always been interested in fashion. But even she could not have foreseen exactly how much commentary she would face on her appearance. In the public consciousness, she broke through as a major force in Conservative Party politics when she gave her 'some people call us the nasty party' speech in 2002. While giving this hard-hitting address, she wore a black trouser suit and leopard-print kitten heels.

The headline writers zeroed in on the shoes. For example, the *Daily Telegraph* devoted one third of its front page to a picture of Theresa's shoes, accompanied by the headline 'A stiletto in the Tories' heart'.[12]

Once fixated on the shoes, the media could not let go. Every pair of shoes and other details of the outfits Theresa wore during the days of the conference were reported on. There was much excitement about a red leather jacket.

Commentators came to see her shoes as the symbol of the new Tory party. *The Times* stated, 'When the history of the Conservative Party is written it may record that the Tory revival began not in the Bournemouth International Conference Centre but in a shoe shop across the road'.[13]

Indeed, the coverage had taken a detour into the absurd. But being analytically thin was not the worst of the problems with the media reaction.

The *Daily Mirror* saw Theresa as embodying a 'dominatrix fantasy, with her formidable, finger-wagging, headmistress act . . . The sight of Theresa May in kitten-heeled leopard skin "don't f*** with me" shoes was enough, apparently, to bring tears to the eyes of red-blooded Tories on the first day of the party conference.'[14]

The *Guardian* took this line of reporting even further, with Matthew Norman stating in his Diary column – which, admittedly, takes a wry look at political events – that Theresa, in wearing the red leather jacket, was striking an 'ageing, faintly up-market hooker pose'.[15]

To this nonsense, Theresa gamely replied, 'It beats me why the *Guardian* knows what an upmarket hooker looks like.'[16]

This prompted what was presumably meant as a comedic clarification, that a comparison was being made to 'the sort of game-yet-battle-scarred old bird . . . who hangs around Shepherd Market in the hope of a bottle of chablis and a quick tumble in a three-star hotel'.[17]

More than a decade and a half later, it is hard to imagine these words being published. Does that mean we should conclude the media is better today? In answering that question, consider that as recently as 27 March 2017 the *Daily Mail* put on its front page the headline 'Never mind Brexit, who won Legs-it!' next to a photograph of Theresa with the leader of Scotland, Nicola Sturgeon. Both women are wearing skirts and have their legs crossed.

These two leaders were meeting to discuss the complex question of the future of the United Kingdom. Scotland had voted solidly to stay in the European Union and the looming Brexit was fuelling a new round of advocacy about Scottish independence. The possibility of Scotland breaking away and forming its own nation, ending the United Kingdom as we know it, was under active consideration.

But, according to the *Daily Mail*, the seriousness of these talks between the prime minister and another very senior leader was secondary compared to the major question of which woman had the better 'pins'. The clearest possible message was being sent that it does not matter what status a woman has attained, or how important her work is, she will be judged on looks.

What was certainly different in 2017 compared with the early 2000s was the social media storm that followed the *Daily Mail*'s 'Legs-it' headline, including clever memes that compared the legs of various male politicians who had been photographed running or on holiday in shorts.

How did Theresa react? Of the *Daily Mail* and today's media she says, '*It is difficult for women, as the media moves to the sensational.*' She recalls in a good-humoured fashion another media moment as follows:

'*There was another occasion when I was going to my husband's birthday party straight after attending a parliamentary debate. I was sitting on the front bench and I had quite a low-cut top on. On the other side of parliament, a female Labour member of parliament also had a low-cut top on, so the headline was about us having a cleavage war.*'

The offender in this case was once again the *Daily Mail*, which contained on 30 November 2007 an article headed 'The Great Cleavage Divide: There's only one real debate at Westminster'. In the piece, journalist Jill Parkin wrote:

'Of course, we should all be interested in what the Shadow Leader of the House of Commons was talking about, but what I want to know is: was she wearing a leopard skin bra? We could almost see, after all, and Theresa May does like a bit of faux fur. Theresa, who once warned the Tories they were in danger of being perceived as the nasty party, now looks as if she wants them to be the naughty party. Her display of cleavage in the Commons on Wednesday looked like a direct challenge to the bold front sometimes displayed by the Home Secretary, Jacqui Smith.'[18]

Theresa does not seem to have let all this sexist silliness get her down. She even points to an upside in the following terms:

'A few years ago, I was in a lift in the House of Commons and there was a young woman, and I commented that she had a nice pair of shoes on, and she said, "Your shoes got me into politics." She saw somebody, me, who she viewed as human, because I am known to like shoes. And that's what got her watching politics. And there she was working in the House of Commons.'

Asked to explore whether a woman who dressed and styled herself as a female version of Boris Johnson could get to the top, Theresa is cautious in her reply, perhaps not wanting to be seen to be reflecting on her successor. She ventures that a man can be judged for what he wears but it tends to be against the standard he has set for himself, saying:

'It may partly go with personality in that there are some men who, if they looked less than smart, people might comment. I am thinking of one or two of my former cabinet colleagues who were always immaculately dressed. And if they turned up looking a bit dishevelled, it would be, "Hang on a minute," that would be commented on. There must be a reason for it. Each of us, as an individual, establishes a sort of style and an expectation in a sense. But then, of course, you have to keep continuing to meet that expectation.'

But thinking about it for a minute more, she concludes that if a woman's style was one where she simply did not care how she looked and frequently looked untidy, then:

'I would guess in the Conservative Party you probably wouldn't get selected in the first place, if you were like that.'

There seems no reason to assume this would only be true for parties at the right of politics.

From the other side of politics, Hillary can and does give a clear overview and historical perspective. She says:

'I came of age at a time when there was an expectation about how you were supposed to dress if you were a woman in public. You didn't go around in sleeveless dresses or wear low-cut ones. Maybe, looking back, it was silly, but we wore skirt suits with white blouses, with little ribbons tied around the neck like it was a phoney little necktie. But that's what you did because you knew that you had to in order to be accepted as a professional. We followed that because we would have been punished otherwise.

I think some of the emphasis on how women look is loosening up a little bit. But there is still an inordinate amount of attention that is paid. Part of the strategy to cope is that you just get a look. In my case I started wearing pantsuits. Same hair most of the time, the same kind of make-up, and then they stop talking about it. They still may quibble about things, "Did you really need to wear that?" or "Look at the colour of that pantsuit," but it became less of an issue. And that's one of the ways you deal with it.'

But even when you have perfected a look, there is still the cost to be paid in time. Hillary has calculated this all out:

'In the presidential election, if you conservatively say I spent an hour a day for hair and make-up, that's an hour that a male candidate didn't have to spend and it added up to twenty-four days. It's absurd! Twenty-four days out of my campaign were spent getting ready to go campaign. A man gets in the shower, shakes his head, puts on his suit, which is pretty much the same as everybody wears, and gets out of the door. So, it does breed a certain amount of resentment where you are, like, "Wait a minute, what am I doing?" It is time-consuming and exhausting.'

The style of Hillary's hair is not the only one that gets

remarked upon. From Norway to New Zealand and beyond, hair has been deemed worthy of discussion. Erna says:

'I became a member of government when I had a two-year-old and a four-year-old. My husband did a lot. But we didn't have any help at home and I was very short on time. I admit my hair was too long, just an easy hairdo, because I didn't have time.

When I was party leader, there were some media commentators who said, "She dresses poorly. She should do something about her make-up." I did cut my hair to a style suggested by my hairdresser, and suddenly I became new in the media's mind. In several newspaper stories, they said, "Look, she's doing better in the opinion polls and look how much better she looks. She must have dieted. She has fresher clothes and she's cut her hair!" It's a funny thing that one or two journalists who were fixated on my clothes and hairdo seemed to think my changing them was responsible for the success of the Conservative Party.'

This echoes *The Times* commentary about Theresa, with a seemingly easy but fundamentally irrational slip from commentary about personal style to political substance.

Jacinda has been thinking about gender issues around dress since her days in high school. She campaigned at Morrinsville College for girls to have the choice to wear shorts like the boys, rather than being stuck with skirts. In her final year at school, her campaign succeeded.[19]

In her life in politics, she has faced her own version of 'it's all about the hair', saying:

'For the first of the televised election debates – keeping in mind it happened not long after I became leader, so there wasn't a lot of time to really prepare – I remember thinking, what can I do so my appearance is not the subject of commentary? I decided to wear

my hair up because then it wouldn't get in my face, it wouldn't distract.

After the debate, all these messages started coming into my office about how much people disliked the fact that I had worn my hair up, and it became a real point of contention. I didn't take the comments personally, but it suddenly occurred to me that in all my billboard photos I had my hair down. I most often wear my hair down and it had been quite jarring for people, so from then on for the televised debates I just wore my hair down.'

At an earlier stage in her career, Jacinda also faced her own version of a 'Legs-it'. As described in chapter 3, in New Zealand's election system voters get two ballot papers: one to elect a local representative and one to give a vote to their preferred political party's candidate list. This double system also means it is possible for a candidate to run for a seat as a local member of parliament at the same time that they are on the party's list. Jacinda did this in the 2011 election. She had been elected to parliament through the party's list in the 2008 election, and she was again in a winnable spot on the ticket. However, she also contended for the marginal seat of Auckland Central against the National Party's Nikki Kaye, who had narrowly taken the seat off a veteran Labour member of parliament in 2008.

This double-up tactic seems odd, but it is done by all sides of politics in New Zealand because taking part in a locally based race is a net positive for a candidate and their political party. If a candidate wins the local seat, then they do not need the party position and that will enable another of the party's listed people to be elected. Even if a candidate loses the contest for the seat, it is likely the additional attention that has been garnered in the local area will bolster the number of people who come and vote for them and their party.

Smart politics, but on this occasion it resulted in manifest sexism. The contest between these two young women was dubbed 'The Battle of the Babes', and the media could not get enough of it. To take one example, the *New Zealand Listener*, a major current affairs magazine, published a feature in which photos of both women appeared, with their outfits described in detail as follows:

'Kaye arrives in an emerald-green dress, belted at the waist; Ardern in a sleek orange and grey number. Both women would prefer to be judged on their performance in the job, but both have made damn sure they look fantastic for the photo. Let there be no doubt: this is a contest.'

The article went on:

'Let's be honest . . . there's one reason we're running this article, studio photos and all. And if you're honest, there's probably one overriding reason that you're reading this article. It's because commentators and political strategists have dubbed the Auckland Central race "The Battle of the Babes".'

And on:

'Nicola Laura Kaye, 31, in the blue corner; Jacinda Kate Laurell Ardern, 31, in the red corner. Poor old Denise Roche from the Greens doesn't fit in the metaphorical wrestling ring. "If this is the Battle of the Babes, I'll be the auntie," laughs Roche, 48. "I don't want to be in the ring." It probably reflects badly on the rest of us that we're more interested in the political equivalent of jelly-wrestling than in debating the ins and outs of the candidates' policies.

(Kaye sighs: "Jelly-wrestling? That must be the hundredth time I've heard that joke.")'

In the article both candidates are good humoured but rejecting of the gendered format they are being forced into.

'Both Ardern and Kaye describe themselves as feminists – albeit a "modern-day feminist" in the latter case. The question, then, is this: how can these two women blithely laugh off the portrayal – by the media, by party strategists, by the public – of this electoral race as a Battle of the Babes? Is it not demeaning? Are they not insulted? . . .

Kaye says: "Obviously I'd prefer it was the Battle of the Policy Wonks, or something. But one of the things I realise about politics is you don't sweat the stuff you can't control. While it was initially a superficial headline, it's actually given us both greater profile around the work we're doing in Parliament . . . It's a talking point."

And on this, too, Ardern agrees. She has worked hard on Labour's [NZ]$250 million youth employment policy package . . . and says the Battle of the Babes profile has allowed her to push issues like pay equity and flexible working. "I always joke that it's a reference to us being youthful. It's not something I get hung up on," she says.

"People do tend to get focused on the fact that we're both young women in a way that they never focus on the fact that we often run middle-aged men against each other. There does still seem to be a bit of novelty around the fact that we're young women in politics. I hope, one day, we get to a place where that isn't a novelty any more."'[20]

Nikki went on to win the seat, though Jacinda's campaign narrowed her margin of victory from 1497 votes to 717. Jacinda returned to parliament through her party list position and tried once again to win the seat in 2011. Again, she was unsuccessful, but she narrowed the margin to 600 votes. And, you guessed it, the 2011 election was also reported as the 'Battle of the Babes'.

Christine also knows what it is like to be the subject of commentary on her appearance. She says it always starts with her hair, too, because she resolved early never to dye it, so the usual description of her is *'white-haired, tall and elegant'*.

Not all of our women leaders are slender and likely to be described so approvingly. Michelle recalls:

'When I was a minister, I had a colleague who was big. He was nicknamed "Panzer", after the tank, to indicate he was a powerful man. But me, I was referred to as fat.'

Erna is a big woman. If she was a political leader in a country prone to mean tabloid media coverage, it is easy to imagine her being lampooned as overweight. Julia describes the sense of irony she felt when, while she was in office, the noted feminist Germaine Greer appeared on Australian national television and said the prime minister had a 'big arse'. Ngozi, ever protective, harrumphs, 'How ridiculous – what arse?' and announces that, in Africa, Julia would be seen as skinny. When the hilarity dies down, Erna, in her no-nonsense way, talks about her own body shape, saying:

'Norway is a small country and if you're a big size, it's not so easy to find full-figured garments. There are only options like large tunics and jeans. So, I had to find some designers and companies that have more sizes, and this helped my style develop more.'

In her country, she says, the media was not cruel about her body shape. Erna describes a more positive approach:

'The media was much more likely to say, "Oh, she has lost weight!" It's done in a positive way because I think in Norway their audience would have reacted if they had used the term fat.'

In this seemingly more benign environment, Erna sees signs of positive change, saying:

'There is a difference in how men and women are treated, but I think there is less focus now. There was a period in Norwegian newspapers fifteen or twenty years ago where, when you went to an

official event, they would give you a score on your dresses and your appearance. We had a wedding for a Norwegian princess and the whole government attended. All female members of the government got ranked on their dress. I probably was the most poorly dressed there, but the guy doing it liked my purse, though he didn't like my shoes. I think there are some magazines that still do this fashion-police thing, but the newspapers no longer do.'

She was amused to see her husband's style critiqued when there was a Nordic Summit meeting with President Obama, including a state dinner in the White House. She recalls:

'My husband was there, so he and the wives all went with Michelle Obama to an art exhibition. He had on a blue suit and he is a redhead, and all that was covered. We had fun with that because, yes, they did cover my dress in the evening, but they also covered his suit.'

Michelle Bachelet has also had run-ins with the fashion police. She recalls that the only time she was reported on as president in a women's magazine that circulated in Latin America, the story said *'something like, "Unbelievable! In the same week she wore the same suit twice!" I was surprised. They could have written about powerful women, but they chose to write about this. But I also knew that if I changed my clothing too much, I would be dismissed as frivolous.'*

Like Erna, Jacinda thinks she benefits from a more benign environment. She says:

'The media here is not nearly as bad as I've seen abroad but, still, I remember very deliberately wanting to neutralise the issue. I didn't want there to be comment about what I wore or how I looked.'

Now that the country is familiar with her and her style, she notes any comments she gets from the general public come *'from a place of kindness. They want to know that I am looking after myself.'*

Joyce talks about being criticised because she continued to wear traditional dress, which in Malawi includes the kanga, a large piece of fabric wound around the body, or two large pieces of fabric sewn together to make a flowing garment, and a traditional headscarf called the duku. In her words:

'When I became prominent, people said, "Are you going to be wearing those kangas? Are you sure? Nobody will respect you globally wearing these tents. You have to buy suits! Don't tell us you are going to be representing us in that duku?" My response was that I hadn't worn Western clothes in so long and I was not going to start now.'

Where Joyce was criticised for this approach, Ellen found wearing traditional dress worked for her. She says:

'I did get a lot of good statements because I dressed well in our traditional clothing. The African clothing was well accepted, even by the men. But I did think about what I wore. If there is one thing I avoided, it was to wear pantsuits. I appreciate the fact that Angela Merkel and Hillary Clinton have broken the mould on that one and people now accept women wearing trousers. I think I would have got some eyes as a woman wearing pantsuits, and certainly churches wouldn't have allowed me in.'

Clearly her words raise a conundrum. It is pleasing to hear Ellen was not judged daily and harshly on the basis of what she wore. But it feels uneasy that this happy result was achieved by conforming to long-held expectations of how a woman should dress. Yet, given the huge benefits men have gained in so many societies by having an accepted uniform, should we really be concerned if staying with one defined dress standard works for a woman leader, in the sense of getting people to focus on what she is saying and doing, not what she looks like?

When we meet with Hillary, she eyes Ngozi's clothing with envy and says to her, '*You've got a great look because you don't have to worry about your hair.*'

Ngozi, who always wears traditional African clothing made of beautiful cotton fabrics and matching headscarves tied in her own unique style, has found, like Ellen, that dressing as who she is, an African woman, is admired and welcomed.

As she says herself, '*I don't have to worry about my hair, I just don my attire, tie my scarf and I'm off.*'

Julia has watched Ngozi quickly tie her scarf with awe and jealousness. Ultimately, Julia did manage to take discussion of her clothes out of the equation by sticking to a few standard looks. But in her early period as prime minister, the focus on her clothing and appearance was overwhelming. For example, after the leaders' debate she had with her male opposition counterpart in the lead-up to the 2010 election, there was commentary and carry-on about the size of her earlobes.

But whether people approve of their clothes and appearances or not, the challenge for our women leaders is getting out the door knowing they will be judged each workday. Worrying about the reception of every single outfit can be frustrating.

However, there was one special moment when being a woman who put on a scarf meant everything.

That came in March 2019, after the horror of the massacre in Christchurch, New Zealand, which targeted Muslims at prayer, killing fifty-one people. Prime Minister Jacinda Ardern met the grieving wearing a headscarf.

Asked about her decision to cover her hair, Jacinda says:

'*I don't even remember making it. When the shootings happened, I was in New Plymouth. I jumped straight on a plane to get to our capital, Wellington. From there I liaised with the police and said that I wanted to go to Christchurch as soon as possible, but I didn't want to get in the way of their operations or make things harder.*

When they said it was okay for me to go, I called a Wellington-based friend and said, "I'm going down to Christchurch tomorrow. Do you have a scarf I can borrow?"

I don't think it was even clear to me at that point the venue we would be in. I knew we wouldn't be at a mosque, but I knew I would be with the community. And for me, there was no decision to be made, it was just a simple sign of respect.

I would be with them in a time of grief – this attack had happened to them. And so it just seemed like a completely natural thing to do. I didn't really reflect on it.

They were wearing their faith in such an open way. And they'd just had their community targeted, so they themselves felt like targets.

When I started getting messages saying my wearing the scarf made them feel safer, then I knew it had absolutely been the right thing.'

The images of Jacinda hugging weeping survivors and relatives of the dead while respectfully adopting a style of dress associated with Muslim women rocketed around the world and became a symbol of love in the face of hate. There was a transcendent power in appearance.

Human beings will always notice and feel a reaction to the way people look. Our hearts will always gladden at the energy and lack of self-consciousness of young children, at the way wisdom can be etched on the faces of the aged. We will see the hipsters, the fashionistas, those who never want to be out of casual clothes, those who abhor being in anything other than the sharpest of suits.

There will always be key moments in a human being's life journey when clothing is part of the ritual: the wedding dress, the funeral outfit.

As Jacinda has shown, sometimes for a leader what you wear matters for all the right reasons.

But, generally, appearance is the least interesting thing about human beings. It tells you nothing about what is in their heads, hearts or souls.

Yet, both the research and the words of our interviewees point us to the same conclusion, which is that women continue to face greater scrutiny than men on this basis. Our women leaders had coping strategies, including creating their own uniform so that interest in their appearance diminished over time. But every one of them was conscious of the issue and thought about how to deal with it.

Their real-world experiences prove our hypothesis that, unfortunately, for women there is still far too much attention paid to how they look rather than what they do. Indeed, in most respects our hypothesis seems to us proven. Women need to take more time to manage issues associated with appearance. Media opportunities that could have focused on substance end up on style.

We would amend one aspect of our hypothesis. It seems that while women can be judged against the one girlish standard of female beauty that Sontag describes, what often happens instead is that the looks of one woman are played off against the looks of another. We also do not find clear evidence that judgements about the woman leader herself are made on how she looks. Really getting to the bottom of that would require a real-time polling study of voters' reactions in various countries to how their female leaders appear. This would need not only resources, but also enough of a cross-section of women leaders in office at any one time to make it doable.

Changing what we have dubbed as it being 'all about the hair' will not be easy. The traditional media should lead by setting new standards. On social media, we can all push back when a vicious, viral cycle starts about a woman leader's appearance. We can all go deep inside and ask ourselves, am I really opening myself up to receive a woman leader as a whole person and evaluating her accordingly, or am I judging the hairstyle, the jacket and the shoes?

In our image-conscious, social-media-whirling world, detoxing ourselves of assessments made on appearances might seem like a hopelessly naive aspiration. Maybe as part of our retraining we need to absorb our political media through listening and reading, not watching. Training ourselves to judge a leader by what they say and do, not what they look like.

The day after Barack Obama departed from his standard look and wore his light-brown suit, there were many media reports explaining what he had actually said while wearing it, because, in the flurry of discussion about his clothing, it seemed many people had missed his message.[21] Between listening and looking, the balance had got out of whack. Maybe we can all play a role in getting the balance between the two right for women leaders.

6

Hypothesis three: Shrill or soft – the style conundrum

Our own experiences and observations of politics and leadership have taught us to loathe the world 'shrill'. In our early discussions about this book, we enjoyed contemplating how millions of dollars could be raised for good causes if there was a global swear jar and a fine was paid every time that word was thrown at a woman. This musing happened as we considered the potential differences in the way conduct by male and female leaders is received. For example, a male leader driven by tragedy to shed a tear would be likely to win plaudits for his compassion, while a female leader would run the risk of being perceived as not coping. A male leader can effectively deploy joking and horsing around to show he's 'just a regular guy', but a woman leader risks being characterised as lacking substance. An angry male leader might be viewed as strong, whereas a female leader would be seen as hysterical or – there is that word again – shrill.

We crunched this thinking down into the two-part hypothesis we explore in this chapter. First, we posit that *Comparable behaviours in male and female leaders elicit different reactions*. However, we wanted to go further, because we were intrigued by the question whether women modify their behaviour knowing that a differential judgement awaits them. Everyone in the public eye, particularly political leaders who need to hold public support, second-guesses their own behaviour. Inevitably there is a dual track in their minds in which thinking about what to say or do next runs alongside considering how saying or doing that will be perceived. The next part of our hypothesis therefore deals with whether gender is an element of that second-guessing, specifically that *In the style they exhibited as leaders, our interviewees were aware of this leadership style–gender conundrum and self-limited their behaviours as a result*. In our mind's eye we were thinking about this intuitive editing as most likely to happen in the very public manifestations of leadership, like the parliamentary performances, the media conferences and the many interactions out on the campaign trail.

Fortunately, there is a rich seam of research evidence relevant to this style conundrum hypothesis. It dates back to 1969, when Virginia Schein broke a glass ceiling by becoming the first woman to receive a doctorate in industrial psychology from New York University. Armed with this impressive qualification, she went to work as a manager in the insurance industry, which employed few women at that level. Inquiring about this phenomenon, she was told women were just not interested.

Dissatisfied with this answer, Virginia began research into gender stereotyping and senior jobs. Her 1973 study gave birth to the 'Think Manager – Think Male' analysis.[1] Virginia showed that when people were asked to describe the attributes a manager needed, and the characteristics they perceived men to have and women to have, men were seen to be the 'natural' fit.

Almost four decades later, in 2011, researchers reviewed the many studies on this theme that had been conducted since Virginia's groundbreaking work.[2] This meta-study concluded that there had been a broadening of views about the qualities required for leadership. Traits more associated with women, like sensitivity, warmth and understanding, were now cited as well as traditional leadership traits, such as being forceful and competitive. However, there had been no reduction in the similarity people saw between traits seen as male and those required for leadership.

The data collected did not identify the cause of the change in perceptions of leadership. Potentially, increased experience with women leaders was having an impact, or the move away from old command-and-control style hierarchies to flatter, more agile management styles might have changed some people's views. A bit of both seems the most likely explanation.

This aspect of the meta-study is good news, but overall the findings do not justify reaching for champagne, balloons and streamers. It concluded that men continued to fit better with people's images of leadership, and the more senior the position, the more male its traits were perceived to be. Think President or Prime Minister – Think Male.

The party paraphernalia also needs to stay packed away given the large numbers of studies that show there is still a generalised gender malaise that causes both men and women to mark female leaders down.

For example, an interactive study of fourteen million entries on the US website Rate My Professor found students were disproportionately likely to rate a male academic as a 'star' or 'genius' whereas female academics were disproportionately described as 'bossy', 'disorganized' or 'ugly'.[3]

A very persuasive study was conducted at North Carolina State University, which had a wholly online course taught to four different classes by a male lecturer and a female lecturer. As a result of the particular way this course was delivered, students never met or saw the teacher. This enabled the male teacher to teach one class disclosing his true identity and the female teacher to teach another class disclosing her true identity. But for classes three and four they effectively switched genders, with the woman teaching the course pretending to be the man and vice versa. When the male teacher's performance was evaluated by students, he was marked down by those who believed him to be a woman compared with those who believed him to be a man. The female teacher scored better with those who believed her to be male compared to those who thought she was a woman.[4] Obviously, the calibre of his and her teaching did not change; the only thing that did was the students' perception of their gender.

Research like this enables us to surface the gender bias. It reveals a worrying automaticity: the very fact of having leadership status, which means having some power over others, is enough to trigger a biased gender response. How the woman acts as a leader is not the causal factor. She is being marked down simply because she is a woman.

Just because this research is scientific in design and the results are presented clinically should not stop us being outraged by the findings. How galling, frustrating and infuriating is it that, in the contemporary world, gender can matter so much, and to the clear disadvantage of women? It makes you want to cry to the heavens, 'What on earth is going on?'

If the heavens were to respond, the answer would be that unconscious bias still exists and impacts how people perceive women in leadership positions.

Against this background, how hard is it for a woman to become a political leader when she is battling this subliminal male stereotype of leadership? As we showed in chapter 3, there is no one pathway to power, and it is impossible to answer whether being a woman made it harder and walking the same road would have been easier for a man. If Ellen Johnson Sirleaf had been a man, would she have been voted in with a bigger majority? Or was a nation heartily sick of warlords, coups and violence more prepared to embrace a woman than a man? If Erna Solberg were a man, would the Conservative Party in Norway be doing better today or worse? What role did being a man play in Donald Trump's election as president?

Politics does not allow for the running of a control test to clearly reveal the impact of gender. Sadly, these fascinating questions all remain unanswerable through objective research. However, once our leaders have arrived and are exercising power, there is research that helps us understand the interaction between gender and assessments of their leadership.

For example, a study of the male-dominated field of engineering shows that a woman leader can be accepted, provided she is not offending against the stereotypes about women that continue to affect our thinking without us even realising it. The researchers found that a confident male engineer would gain influence in his organisation, but for a woman to do the same, confidence alone was not enough. She would need to be seen as competent and caring as well. Presumably being competent needed to be separately proved because it would not just be assumed as it was for the confident man. Then she also needed to be caring so she was not too far away from the female stereotype.[5]

Academic researchers Laurie A. Rudman and Peter Glick conducted experiments on attitudes towards women and men who were presented as agentic – meaning, in this context, having a desire to get to the top even if that meant stepping on the toes of others – compared with those towards women and men with a more cooperative approach. Groups representative of the community were then invited to assess candidates for two sorts of jobs, ones with standard position descriptions and ones that had been 'feminised', in the sense they emphasised the need for social skills.[6]

In an interesting though not happy set of conclusions, the study found even when a firm deliberately feminised a job description, that did not help a go-getter, agentic woman. In fact, agentic men were preferred for the feminised jobs compared with agentic women. In addition, those who most strongly believed women are caring and kind marked agentic women down harder.

The maddening flip side to this discrimination is that a man who is polite and helpful will get a tick, while a woman gets no benefit from the same behaviour. Research has shown that a nice, considerate woman is just conforming to expectations, so her behaviour does not generate a positive reaction, whereas a man will get a good response because he will be seen to have gone above and beyond usual behavioural norms. Indeed, being seen as a helpful colleague has been shown to correlate with employment promotions for men but not women.[7]

Extrapolating these findings into the political world, it is easy to imagine a situation where a section of voters has convinced themselves that men have had their turn and stuffed a lot of things up, and it is time for a more inclusive style of leadership, which they presume women will be better at because they think of them as nicer. Even these very pro-women sounding voters would likely go for a typical male candidate over a woman who failed to balance strong and caring. The potential of them selecting the male candidate may very well be turbocharged if he appeared to be polite, considerate and helpful.

What this kind of research is telling us is that, in order for a woman political leader to be accepted by the voting public, she cannot just exhibit the traits historically associated with leadership. If she does, then there will be a backlash because she is offending against our unconscious gender stereotypes. Instead, she must walk a very particular tightrope, balancing between being seen as 'man' enough to lead, while not being perceived to have shed the expected characteristics of women.

Whether or not they have ever read any of these kinds of studies or thought directly about how to not fall off such a thin line, intuitively women do everything they can to stay on it. This is not just a process of cause and effect, where a woman learns through lived experience and then changes her behaviour. Rather it is a circle, because women, even without personal experience, absorb from their environment that there are issues to do with gender and leadership, and moderate their behaviour in advance to try to avoid hitting a problem.

Researchers Rudman and Glick describe well the likely cost of trying to be the perfect cocktail of male and female traits in the following words:

'The female who displayed agentic competence and communal values was not discriminated against in hiring ratings, irrespective of the job description. This solution, however, is problematic . . . Treading the fine line of appearing competent, ambitious and competitive, but not at the expense of others, is a tall order . . . To the extent that women have to maintain a "bilingual" impression of themselves as both nice and able in order not to be perceived as overbearing and dominant, their situation is more difficult and tenuous in comparison to that of their male counterparts. Further, the need to pay attention to this delicate form of impression management may produce anxieties that, in turn, diminish task performance.'

On the basis of these studies, our style conundrum hypothesis is looking very sound. However, when we put it to our women leaders, they surprised us. We asked them whether they viewed themselves at risk of gender-based characterisations and, if so, did they deliberately check themselves and limit exposing their full emotional range publicly. We also asked what the consequences were of feeling so constrained. In answer, against our expectations, a number of leaders chose not to speak about perceptions by voters but the special hurdle they thought they faced in small but important groups.

Ellen talked of her experiences of grudging respect in her own country and lack of respect beyond. She says, when she was Finance Minister:

'I did get a particular feeling when I went to meetings of the cabinet and everyone else was a man. I had established myself as someone of strength and that is where the term "iron lady" came from, because on fiscal matters I was quite strong. They respected me but they didn't really see me as part of the team. I was the stranger commanding things.'

Many of us would have first come across the descriptor 'iron lady' in reference to Margaret Thatcher when she was prime minister of the United Kingdom. But it has been used a lot since, including for both Ellen and Erna. It reeks of gender stereotyping with its implicit assumption that a lady is too weak to lead, unless she is made of unexpectedly strong stuff.

Ellen further explains how the gender politics of small groups played out. Working in an international organisation, the United

Nations Development Programme (UNDP), she details how she felt underestimated and overlooked.

'*Many times, at meetings, where I would call all the Resident Representatives together, who were mostly men, I said something which was then repeated by a man – maybe not exactly the way I put it, but with the same intent and objective – and then of course all the men would be in full accord.*'

Michelle recalls a similar experience, saying:

'*When I was an advisor to a government minister, sometimes I would outline an idea and the men would look at me and say nothing. Then a male colleague would say exactly the same idea but just change one or two words, and everybody would look at him and say, "Wow! Brilliant! Fantastic!" I even had a man acknowledge that it happens. A male colleague, who was also an advisor to the minister, said to me, "I know that you gave the idea and I just repeated it in another way." It made me think that maybe sometimes women don't know how to package their ideas in a way that is interesting to men. Is it that our narrative is not as successful as other narratives? Or maybe it's just sexist.*'

The answer to Michelle's question is, yes, it is just sexist. Analysis has been conducted into why, in a biotech company, highly qualified female scientists talked less in meetings than men did. It became clear that when the women did speak, if their idea was not perfect then it would be rejected, whereas if a man put forward a flawed position the best bits would get salvaged. The study also showed that women's ideas tended to be ignored until a man restated the same point.[8]

While research is always helpful, women around the world do not need an academic paper to know this truth. Instead, they can just point to their daily lived experience of being underestimated, mansplained to, talked over or having their ideas ignored or pur-loined. Certainly, Julia and Ngozi can relate to that.

But, troublingly, what is verified by the experience of our women leaders is that being viewed as the outsider, the one who is doubted and doubly scrutinised, does not stop when you hold the highest office possible in your nation. Ellen notes that even when she became president, the differential treatment continued.

'*As president I would attend African Union meetings, and even though as head of the Africa Regional Bureau of UNDP I had met with many of these presidents, had gone to their countries and talked to them about development, I was still treated differently. I would notice that at meetings the men would go off in little groups, and if you tried to get in, they would be very pleasant with you but there was this sense that, "We know you are president now, but this is our domain."*

Let's put it this way about my experience in the African Union: when you take the chair to speak, every eye is focused on you, every ear is waiting, maybe to see if you will falter or fail to say something. And then you speak, and if you speak forcibly or knowledgeably with proper information, yes, it is accepted, but the men will never say "Great speech", or anything like that. You will never get that kind of affirmation. But all the eyes go off you, and it's like you've passed a test.'

Hillary raises another dynamic that is verified by research. She says:

'*It's interesting to me that prior to being a candidate myself, when I was an advocate on behalf of other people, I felt much freer. There were still consequences for what you said or people might think you've gone too far, but it wasn't as personally challenging as when you are the person on the front line, standing for election and making the decisions. It becomes incredibly personalised and you are in this conundrum where you're too strong, you're not strong enough, you're too cold, you're too emotional. I mean, you just see the stereotyping and the double standard in full bloom. Some of it is very blatant, you can't miss it, and some of it is much subtler and it's only in retrospect that you see it.'*

Research shows that women negotiating for themselves are likely to be viewed negatively as too pushy, whereas there is no backlash if women are negotiating for others. In fact, women have so thoroughly imbibed these community standards that, when asked to negotiate for others, they will be far more assertive. Harvard University research has shown that women negotiating for others will secure a compensation package that is 18 per cent better than if they are trying to do a deal for themselves.[9] Basically, these women inherently know our societies accept a lioness baring tooth and claw to protect others in the pride, but not roaring and biting to establish herself as the leader.

In the political sphere this meant Hillary was at her most popular at the time she finished serving as President Obama's Secretary of State. All this stereotyping imposes a human cost, as she reflects:

'You're a human being. You're trying to be yourself, which is often not appreciated if you are not fitting into the category of an "acceptable" woman. You are not only being confronted by the double standard, but you're also second-guessing all the time. You're con-stantly trying to calibrate yourself to be as effective as you want to be perceived.'

Asking Hillary if the cost of all this calculation is the risk of being viewed as inauthentic hits a nerve. She says:

'The word "inauthentic" is just another way of saying, "You're not our kind of woman." You're not being appropriately respectful or

subservient or soft-spoken or dressing the way we expect, or whatever it is the bigotry demands.'

Theresa could have a wonderful conversation with Hillary on this topic. In late 2016, John Crace, a sketch writer for the *Guardian* newspaper, christened her 'the Maybot' and even wrote a book entitled *I, Maybot: The rise and fall.*[10] The *New Statesman* published a cartoon of Theresa as a robot next to the headline 'The Maybot malfunctions' on the cover in July 2017.[11] By the end of 2017, Henry Mance of the *Financial Times* decided the word 'Maybot' was the one that best summarised the year.[12] He even offered a definition in the following terms: 'A prime minister so lacking in human features that she soon requires a system reboot.'

Maybot, obviously a portmanteau of Theresa's surname and the word robot, became commonly used to pillory what were said to be her scripted responses and emotionless style. For Julia, all this is eerily familiar. She too was criticised for being robotic.

Theresa is prepared to discuss the Maybot. In her view, the Maybot critique took hold during the election campaign held just less than a year after she became leader. She says:

'In 2017, I called a snap election, so the campaign team kind of dusted down what they had used for David Cameron and I was put into that sort of structure. It was a very set-piece, more formal, behind-the-podium campaign, and it didn't suit me. I'm much more out on the doorsteps, generally meeting people, not the set-piece politician.'

Theresa also recalls the constraints that came with being focused on not making errors during her time at the top of politics.

'I was also very careful with the press. As prime minister, even as Home Secretary before that, you do have to be careful what

you say, because a word in the wrong place here or there can have consequences.'

Of course, male leaders have to watch their words too, but they do not need to balance that kind of carefulness with also coming across as warm or nurturing. Theresa describes the gendered expectations this way:

'People would have assumed a woman leader would be more emotional and empathetic. There's a natural sense that a woman is going to be more like that. So, if you're not, it exacerbates the argument about robotic behaviour, I think. Even maybe subconsciously there's an element of that.'

Once a woman has been defined as machine-like and devoid of emotion, the reaction if she does show any tends to the absurd. Announcing her resignation as prime minister on 24 May 2019, Theresa made a seven-minute statement. Towards the end, and most notably on the final four words, 'the country I love', her voice cracked with emotion. Headlines described this as her crying. For example, *The Times* led with 'Theresa May in tears as she resigns' and *The Sun* with 'PM's teary farewell statement'. A casual reader who had not seen the footage would have assumed she had been openly weeping.

Clearly, Theresa herself felt this was all an overreaction, saying in *The Telegraph* on 11 July 2019, 'If a male Prime Minister's voice had broken up, it would have been said "what great patriotism, they really love their country". But if a female Prime Minister does it, it is "why is she crying?"'[13]

What Theresa reveals now is how focused the media can get on a woman's tears. She recalls her press office constantly being asked about when she had cried. One of her staff members adds that there was even constant questioning about whether she would cry in the future, such as, 'Will you cry when you leave?' Not just wanting to report if Theresa had cried, but wanting predictions of when she might next shed a tear.

Michelle also knows what it is like to be under scrutiny for tears. She says:

'My male predecessor as president was said to be sensitive and that was viewed as fantastic by the people, that they had a president who cared. If I was sensitive it was seen as not coping, not being able to control my feelings. I am not even talking about crying, but my voice changing because of my emotions.'

Her concern about being stereotyped encompassed substance as well as style. Michelle was conscious that if a woman was seen to talk only about women's issues she would soon be dismissed. She says she would counsel women in her political party to speak out on broader issues like international affairs and economics. Her advice was:

'Of course, you must speak with a gender perspective, but you shouldn't only talk about women's issues otherwise we don't get everybody on board.'

When campaigning herself, she said she talked about programs such as eliminating inequalities and improving health and education, which mattered so much to women, but she did not frame her campaign as one on gender.

Joyce was in a very different position, having come into politics as a result of being a noted campaigner for women's rights. In describing her pathway to power, she speaks of her first cabinet meeting in the midst of the crisis after the death of the former president. In those circumstances a human, warm approach to the grief and loss worked for her. She proudly describes her leadership style as open-door and inclusive, and is not afraid to use the word 'love' about the relationship a president should have with the people of their nation. She describes in chapter 7 a hard-hitting gendered characterisation she faced as president, but she does not speak of limiting or second-guessing herself.

Christine also talks of emotion and shedding a tear. She says:

'I am a weeper. When something is moving, I cry. I have often said in meetings or in ceremonies that it is okay to cry, it will make you feel good. I want to give people that space because it is healthy. I never put mascara on my bottom lashes so I can cry and not look like I've had a hangover.'

Erna is convinced it depends on what you are crying about.

'Depending on where you are, being moved is an okay thing. I mean, I shed a tear when I see children singing. I shed tears even at memorials for things that happened ten years ago. But if it's a reaction to something happening to you, for example if you lose a vote in parliament and sit down crying, then people will say things.

Norway is different. Our politics has less testosterone. A man who starts shouting is not going to be considered a very good politician in Norway anyway.'

Like Erna, Jacinda also views her home political environment as more benign on gender than many other places in the world. But even so, she has been conscious of the need to *'not display too much emotion in your voice. Just always being seen to be stoic. I thought that was something that I would be judged on, if I wasn't able to sustain that.*

I remember very early on as a new politician asking one of the male members of parliament, who I thought was probably the most stoic of all, the toughest, the one who never seemed flappable, "How do you do that, because I feel things quite deeply."

And he was almost offended by the question. He thought he was a person who felt things really deeply too. He said to me, "Never ever try to stop feeling emotion, because the moment you do that you lose your empathy and you will just fail as a politician." And I thought, that's true, we shouldn't neutralise all of our emotion. Actually, that's what we're there for, we're there to feel empathy, we're there to reflect on what it would be like to walk in others' shoes, and if we try to cauterise that, what kind of politicians would we be?

So that was a really important moment for me. However, there have been a couple of times where I haven't been particularly good at hiding that I've felt moved by an issue or a moment. And I've often reflected on those moments and worried about the way that they would be interpreted, the way it would reflect on me. So, it's still something I worry about.'

We ask Jacinda about how she so perfectly captured the need for healing in the community in the days after the Christchurch massacre. She says:

'We just had to focus on looking after people. And so, because that was the focus, it meant that I just did exactly what felt like the right thing to do at the time. And it was made easier by the fact that New Zealanders were particularly unified. There was a huge out-pouring of grief on behalf of the Muslim community. At that point I felt I was the mouthpiece for a whole nation's grief.'

The image of her embracing the grieving while wearing a headscarf was balanced by a pitch-perfect sense of strength. Jacinda says:

'I was angry. I was particularly angry at the idea that the perpetrator would use our justice system as a platform. It was so clear in the way that everything about this attack was about his notoriety – the fact he emailed his manifesto to me and others, broadcast it

live – the attack was all about notoriety. And I thought, that's one thing I can at least try to deprive you of.'

In the most tragic of circumstances, going with her instincts, not stopping to think about gender stereotyping, was exactly right.

The world's reaction was embracing of the people of New Zealand and of Jacinda's leadership. We ask whether being so praised – in fact, placed on a pedestal – now sharpens in some ways the consequences of getting something wrong in the future. Julia and Ngozi share with Jacinda that we have been discussing our concern that the problem with pedestals is that there is such a long way to fall from them, and women who have been placed on them tend to come off not because they have done something bad, but simply as a result of being human and consequently imperfect.

Jacinda says she is grateful that we are worrying for her, but that:

'New Zealanders are very grounded. Domestically, we are never ones for putting people on pedestals. We will acknowledge that some-one's done a good job but then normal transmission resumes and you just get judged on the same criteria you always have been.'

Jacinda responds thoughtfully about the extra scrutiny women leaders face, saying:

'From the moment I became leader there was an expectation that I would bring a tidal wave of young people into the election and cause this "youth quake". They called that "Jacindamania". I really pushed back on that. I just didn't want that, because I'm absolutely fallible. I would often say that I am going to make mistakes. And so, I've felt that pressure the entire time.'

Theresa also had to respond in times of terrorist crisis both as Home Secretary and prime minister. She encapsulates the dilemma she and Jacinda each faced in the following words:

'*When we had terrorist attacks, you had to show strength, so people felt that somebody is actually gripping the situation and knows what to do. People can feel safe and secure under that. But on the other hand, they want you to show empathy and sympathy, naturally enough, for the victims. And you need to get the balance right so that you can show that natural concern that you have for the victims but at the same time show you've got the strength to be able to take the country through.*'

Is the pressure of gendered expectations getting better or worse? Given her unique experience of being president of Chile, then having some time away, then successfully being elected again, Michelle is well placed to proffer a view about whether things are improving or worsening. She says:

'*You know, I thought it was better, but I later realised it was the same or worse. I think politics is getting more complicated these days and more vicious. There is less respect. It's more personalised now.*'

Given the tightrope they need to walk, this more personalised politics is likely to be even tougher for women. Then there is evidence that gendered expectations are growing, not diminishing.

A study of attitudes in sixteen opinion polls in the United States found that, in a 1946 poll, only 35 per cent of respondents answered that women and men could be equally intelligent. By 2018, that had risen to 86 per cent, and some in the remaining 14 per cent asserted women were smarter than men.

But the same polling also showed that expectations that women would behave in a more cooperative way have grown. In 1946, 54 per cent of respondents indicated that women are more communal than men; 83 per cent did so in a 1989 poll and 97 per cent in 2018.[14] This means women who do not meet this expectation are jarring more people's beliefs about what women are like.

It is interesting to speculate whether advocacy for women is in some ways playing into the increased perceptions that we are the kinder, more empathetic ones. Women and girls' empowerment events will often be premised on a narrative about us being as strong and smart as men but also more inclusive and caring than them. Much of the management literature that advocates for diversity at work is couched in the benefits that come from having the more team- and people-orientated approach that women bring.

For example, a meta-study of transformational versus transactional leadership concluded that women are better at the former.[15] In this context, transformational leadership means the ability to set goals, develop plans to achieve them, innovate, and mentor and empower team members. Transactional leadership was seen as a more narrowly defined approach in which specific objectives for subordinates are set and the leader monitors compliance with the tasks, rewarding or correcting subordinates as necessary. The researchers also defined a third style of leadership, which was characterised by the holding of rank but failing to act as a leader. This was styled as a laissez-faire approach.

Both male and female leaders were found to have mixed and matched various aspects of these approaches. However, female leaders were shown to be somewhat more transformational than male leaders, particularly in the sense of being supportive and encouraging to those they managed.

Women were also seen to engage in the rewarding behaviour associated with the transactional leadership model when a subordinate achieved a set objective. Men were more likely than women to engage in the compliance side of transactional leadership, correcting and disciplining team members who had failed to deliver. Men were also more likely than women to be laissez-faire leaders.

Based on this type of analysis, women are said to show the kind of leadership that management theory identifies as the most effective in today's world.

There is a seduction in this conclusion, but is it really helping? After all, this theorising has not led to a revolution in which women are showered with leadership positions, but it does reinforce gender stereotypes.

Over the years since 1946, has an increasing burden been laid at women's feet about being the communal ones, without putting any extra expectations on men? There is much to think about here, and we return to this question in chapter 12.

Looking at our hypothesis, it seems, like everything else to do with gender, there are nuances. Not every tear is seen as female weakness. Not every criticism of a female leader arises because of her gender.

But our women leaders have felt a gender lens colouring the judgement of their leadership compared to that of men. Even inside smaller groups, the extra scrutiny is felt.

Our women leaders do self-limit because of this kind of bias. Not every leader, every time, but it is a feature of how our leaders think through their engagement with the world. Simply because they are women, extra energy is expended in second-guessing the gender dynamic about how their conduct is going to be received.

Our women leaders' experiences and the many academic studies buttress each other. This hypothesis is proven. However, in the face of it, we want to suggest adoption of Christine Lagarde's fighting words:

'*When people reject me or are dismissive because I am a woman, I say, "Sod off! I am not working with you. If you don't like me because I am a woman, or you won't work in partnership with me because I am a woman, I'm off! I will find better."*'

7

Hypothesis four:
She's a bit of a bitch

'What's resting bitch face?' Ngozi asks.

The short answer is that it is something that's only ever said about a woman. The longer answer is it is one of those ideas that flashes around the world and takes hold. In May 2013, a production company called Broken People uploaded a short video to the Funny or Die humour website.[1] Formatted to mimic a public service announcement, it warned about a phenomenon where a woman who is not a bitch looks like one when her face is at rest.

While the comedians also explored a male equivalent, dubbed 'resting arsehole face', all the subsequent attention was on the bitch bit. With almost eight million views, the video has triggered a lot of laughs.

But the idea has not stayed where it began in the comedy arena. Instead, scientists have discovered what causes it,[2] while plastic surgeons have offered to fix it.[3]

Ngozi asks this question as we walk away from our Brussels meeting with Erna Solberg, who said:

'One of the things I've learnt is, when you grow older, everything falls down a little bit. Recently I learnt from my communications officer that this is referred to as "resting bitch face". Even before I knew those words, I worked out years ago to always smile a little bit, so everyone says I'm always in a good mood. You have to combat resting bitch face because it is used to undermine women and portray them as sour, hard and aggressive.'

Intuitively, Erna has been trying to out-smile our fourth hypothesis. In chapter 3 we discussed the difficulties of women owning ambition. In the previous chapter we broke down the way women censor their behaviour to combat or conform with gender stereotypes.

In this chapter we drill a little deeper into the problem of women being seen as unlikeable, as 'a bit of a bitch'. We are conscious that even using the word 'bitch' might be offensive to some, for which we apologise. But we decided to stick with it because it does capture a commonly held sentiment about women leaders. If we are all really honest with ourselves, we can probably remember a moment when that word sprang into our minds about a woman with power and authority. Indeed, at one point we contemplated calling this whole book *'She's a Bit of a Bitch'*, but we decided the full sweep of what we wanted to explore was more complex than that.

The hypothesis of this chapter is, *As a result of unconscious bias, it is generally assumed that women with power are unlikeable, or in the vernacular, bitchy.* Have researchers developed a gender nastiness index? Not quite, but a relevant study comes from the Harvard Business School. There, students were asked to read a case study about a businessperson and then select ratings associated with their likeableness. Half the students read a case study in which the businessperson was a woman. The other half read about a man. In all respects other than gender the case studies were identical, yet the students scored the woman as less likeable than the man.

This result was not about what an individual woman's face looks like. The students were given text, not photographs. What was being revealed is that among the other unconscious biases in our brains there appears to be one that whispers to us that a woman leader is probably 'a bit of a bitch'.

For women political leaders, this is obviously unpleasant and unfair. But the real impacts are deeper than that. Psychological research shows the gendered assumption that a woman who wants or has power is 'a bit of a bitch' can cost votes. Yale University conducted an experiment in which reactions to male and female political candidates who expressed different levels of ambition were measured. The researchers concluded that 'voting preferences for female candidates were negatively influenced by her power-seeking intentions (actual or perceived) but that preferences for male candidates were unaffected by power-seeking intentions.'[4] It is worth pausing for a moment just to feel the weight of this finding. It is not startling given it fits with the body of work about agentic women discussed in the last chapter, but it is shocking that in the twenty-first century something as vital as a vote in a democracy could be solely driven by sexism.

This study and many others make it crystal clear that when it comes to women and leadership, people have prescriptive stereotypes in their heads, not just descriptive ones.

A descriptive stereotype is best defined as something that is regularly assumed about a particular group. Imagine a new colleague joins your workplace. She is Chinese. At a welcome morning tea in the staff room, the discussion turns to food and she contributes by saying that she hates rice and never eats it. A common reaction in the staff room would be surprise and interest. Your new workmate has fallen outside a descriptive stereotype about Chinese people.

However, in this example, no prescriptive stereotype comes into play. You would not like her any less having heard she does not eat rice. That happens when people assume a group has a certain characteristic and they also view it as right that they should have it.

Expecting women to put others first and act communally, rather than being individually power hungry, has been shown to be such a prescriptive stereotype. We do not just associate that character trait with women; research shows we mark them down in our regard if they do not exhibit it. In the words of the Yale study, 'the presence of moral-emotional and avoidant reactions – moral outrage reactions of contempt, disdain, anger, irritation, disapproval, disgust, and revulsion – suggest that the power-seeking aspirations of the female politician were not just unexpected but also "wrong".'[5]

That list of reactions is worth reading twice: contempt, disgust, revulsion are mind-bogglingly strong words.

For Julia, reading this study was a light-bulb moment given the sustained and highly negative reactions by many to her successfully challenging a man for the prime ministership. To give just one example of the gendered references to her actions, in the days that followed Julia taking the top job, leading Australian political journalist Michelle Grattan wrote a comment piece that started with these words:

'Nice girls don't carry knives. So Julia Gillard, who has arrived in the prime ministership with the image of the clean, fair player, knows she has to be persuasive in explaining how she came to plunge one into [former prime minister] Kevin's neck.'

It ended: 'But Gillard does do [spin] with panache and that disarming girlish laugh.'[6]

That the academic research shows such toxicity in the feelings towards women who are ambitious is concerning, as is the fact that prescriptive stereotypes are not shifted by exposure to more people who do not fit the standard. If, following the hypothetical morning tea described above, the next twenty Chinese people that joined the workplace all said they did not like rice, then the descriptive stereotype held by the people who worked there would start to give way in face of this new information. A prescriptive stereotype about what is right and wrong, on the other hand, does not just disappear because more people are seen to offend against it.

Earlier we discussed the Think President or Prime Minister – Think Male analysis. Here our hypothesis can be summarised as Think Woman Leader – Think Bitch.

In exploring this hypothesis with our women leaders, we briefly explained the research and then asked whether they felt this characterisation, and if so, how have they coped with it? In asking that second question we are conscious that women adapt to sexism so profoundly throughout their lives that the line between 'This is me' and 'This is what I do in response to gender stereotyping' is impossible to draw. To take one example, research has shown that women are more likely than men to be participative, collaborative leaders.[7] How much of this happens because women are intuitively trying to project authority without receiving the backlash of being seen to be nasty cannot be calculated.

Erna makes sure she smiles, but generally she is not too worried about being labelled unlikeable or a bitch. Personally, she notes:

'One of the things people often say about me is that I'm always calm. Naturally, I am calm as a person, but I've also had to learn to be so. If a woman becomes too aggressive, too agitated, then I think people react to it.'

These words echo the self-limiting behaviour discussed in the previous chapter. Erna is an optimist about her own nation and gender, however, saying:

'I think that's where our society is very different. There is a bigger focus on personal issues for female politicians than male politicians. People ask me, "What about your family? How do you run your home?" I mean, you can get irritated with these questions because you would like to be asked about foreign policy or the new NATO strategic concept or something. But there is a positive aspect for women in that it increases our likeability. In our culture, being likeable is also about people being able to think, I can identify with you because you can understand my problems. It brings you closer to people.'

For Erna, her perceived normalcy, in coming from an ordinary family background and being able to share mum-style worries about whether her children remembered to take their sports kit to school, has been a bulwark against problems with perceived likeableness.

Michelle says she never felt the 'she's a bit of a bitch' problem at all, but the fact she was viewed as pleasant created another dynamic. She says:

'People thought I was very nice and likeable. So much so that, at the end of my first term, when I was going to Congress for the ceremony for the new president, a woman said to me, "Let me recommend something to you, don't ever get involved in politics again because politics is a bad thing and you are a good woman!"

In fact, people were so fond of me they would call me "Mummy". Originally, I felt this was a negative, but I came to understand the point they were making. They were saying, "She's our mother because she protects us, she wants to support us, she wants to incentivise us, she wants us to get out of poverty." So in that sense it was not a bad thing.'

Michelle managed to balance on the tightrope discussed in the previous chapter. However, through bitter experience, she was especially inoculated against falling off and being viewed either as a bit of a bitch or a bit of flake. As a torture survivor who had fled fascism in Chile, she was not someone whose history put her at risk of being stereotyped as too soft.

Christine quickly agrees with our hypothesis when it is put to her but volunteers that she thinks, in the face of it, women *'over-prepare, we over-rehearse, and we are more conscientious'*. In this view, women put their efforts towards winning respect in their field in the hope that this proves more important than being liked.

Joyce indicates part of her struggle was about something more basic than whether she was viewed as nice. Instead, some people in the opposition parties sought to encourage an outright rejection of female presidential leadership. She says:

'In Malawi, there is a saying that a bull goes to the farm to pull a cart, a cow is kept at home for milk. So, people in the opposition said, "How unlucky are we to end up with a cow pulling our cart?" It was vicious and cruel and could only be used because the person at the end of the insult is a woman.'

Ugly words indeed.

Theresa faced the Maybot characterisation, which had embedded in it a lack of likeableness. But looking more broadly, she says:

'The first speech I did when I became PM was about reaching out to people who were just about managing, recognising the struggle that many had day to day. That really tapped into something for a lot of people. In a sense, I think that might have overcome anything that was about, "Well, you're a woman in a leadership position, therefore you can't be likeable."'

The leader with the greatest lived experience of our hypothesis is Hillary. In order to come to terms with the election result in 2016, she studied and thought about this issue. Like us, she is no stranger to the psychological research. She says:

'Everybody has a different personality, a different temperament, a different public persona, so you can like or dislike people for whatever reason. But women are much more likely to be judged unlikeable if they are assertive, if they are strong, if they are willing to stand up and speak out. I saw it over and over and over again in my campaign. People would say, "There's something about her I don't like." Then, when pressed on what it was, they could not provide any more detail. They would say, "I don't know. It's just something, I don't know."'

Hillary sees two dimensions to this reaction. She believes this was a genuine response from people and they were not refusing to give further details, they just could not:

'A lot of what they were feeling was deeply rooted and they could have passed a lie detector test.'

But she also believes that this sense of concern by sections of the community was seized upon and accelerated.

'I got accused of every crime you can imagine. There was a negative campaign that was used to undermine me. I came to the presidential election with a very high favourability, likeability and acceptability numbers in our political system. There was an effort to

take me down by just making stuff up and hurling accusations, until even people who were supporting me couldn't help but be somehow in the zone of, "I like her but a lot of people don't." "Why not?" "Well, you know, I saw it on the internet." So, it was very artfully, effectively done to undermine me.'

There are three layers being described here, and it is important to pick them apart. First, there is a gender-based predisposition to think women who seek or hold power are not likeable, even bitchy. That would have been in play in relation to general perceptions of Hillary. Second, it would have specifically fed into and exacerbated any underlying unease about her based on factors other than her gender. Third, there was then a deliberate effort to magnify and exploit these doubts about Hillary, the first woman to have a real shot at being president of the United States.

About it all, she generously sums up by saying:

'You can't expect one hundred per cent of people to like you, so that's not what your goal is, but you would like to be judged fairly and on an equal basis with your male counterparts.'

At the time of our interview, Hillary could already see the unlikeable word being used against female contenders for the 2020 Democratic primaries. Depressingly, but not surprisingly, President Trump's first round of criticism of vice-presidential candidate Kamala Harris centred on her being 'very, very nasty,' 'horrible' and the 'meanest.' He went so far as to say that 'Nobody likes her. She could never be the first woman president. . . . That would be an insult to our country.'[8] Media commentators interpreted this remark as a calculated dog whistle on race, given Kamala is of Jamaican and Indian descent.[9]

Our hypothesis does not seem to ring true in any way for Jacinda, whose image is based on being compassionate and kind.

In opinion polls, she is more popular than the political party she leads, which is a reminder, given governments win or lose depending on the number of votes for the party, that being seen as likeable is better than the alternative but no guarantee of continued electoral success.[10] Asked about the usual correlation of unlikeability and leadership for women, Jacinda is quick to point out that her context is different, in the sense that her nation is a much smaller one with a gentler political culture than the United States. She is also the third woman to be prime minister of her country. Referring to Julia's experience in Australia, she says:

'I saw what you went through and that was just brutal. I wonder sometimes if our environment was the same as Australia, would I have stuck it out as long.'

No doubt Jacinda's reference is to things like people standing at rallies referring to Julia as a witch or bitch. Or the vulgarity of a menu at a conservative party fundraiser reading 'Julia Gillard Kentucky Fried Quail – Small Breasts, Huge Thighs & A Big Red Box'. A shock jock popularised referring to her as JU-LIAR, a play on her name to work in an allegation of dishonesty. The same radio personality also said her father had died of the shame he felt about his daughter.

In contrast, describing the New Zealand environment, Jacinda says:

'It's not perfect, but the things that I can recall will probably seem insignificant in comparison. That's how I feel as well when I look at the election for Hillary.

I don't really recall many stand-outs during my election that were particularly about gender. There were moments that you could say could have been taken as an attack on my perceived inexperience and age, and maybe gender in combination with that.

The prime minister at the time called me "stardust". Some politicians called me "snowflake". The leader of one party said I was a hamburger without the meat patty. And then there were things like, there was a photo that was widely circulated of a sign at a protest calling me a "pretty little communist". Things like that, but relatively speaking, I consider it to have been pretty minor.'

Ellen accepts our hypothesis but challenges its implications. She certainly sees a gender dynamic to leadership, saying:

'As a woman leader and particularly as president, you find yourself so lonely at many times. You don't have much of a social life. What you say, what you do, how you dress, how you talk is always under the microscope. You have to be very careful. Whether it is your colleagues out there who are either presidents or other leaders, whether it is your peer group in your country, people are always looking for someplace where they can say you messed up and then use that to say women should not meddle in politics.'

But she also believes women have a special attribute when it comes to leadership, which is that they are less motivated by popularity. She says:

'But facing certain decisions is where a woman has strength. There are times when you don't back down because it might make you unpopular, or because the crowd might like you less.

Yes, women are expected to be more compassionate, and they are, but because they are women they are not expected to take those strong decisions that will bring them under question. Yet it is men who actually do not make those decisions, they find a way around it. Women are the ones who make those decisions as they see it, and in making those decisions, women are not sensitive to what it means for their own image.'

Ellen relates her experience with fighting the West African Ebola outbreak in 2014 as an example of doing what is right and not caring about image. She says:

'*The World Health Organization came out with a prediction that two hundred thousand people were going to die a day, and millions of people would die. After the WHO statement, I took to the air and told our people, we will not die, we are going to take this on ourselves, we will save ourselves and our livelihoods. Community leaders take charge! We will give you the support you need."*

And then I got on the road. I went to places where they had Ebola patients being treated and I spoke with health workers, and that also calmed people down. But I had to do something about burials. The Ebola dead are also able to spread the disease, so there was only one solution: we had to cremate. And, of course, everybody said, "No, you can't do that. People have the right to be able to bury their dead."

But I stood firm and announced cremation.'

A horrific disease requiring courageous decision-making. But is there a gender dynamic at play here, or would a male president in his second term and ineligible to stand for re-election have acted the same way? That is impossible to know, but Ellen is convinced that the fact women leaders do not tend to be viewed as likeable is a benefit, not a burden. It means they are more likely to do what is right rather than care about burnishing their image.

It is also impossible to know from Ellen's account how she was perceived by the population as a result of her preparedness to make this hard decision. Was she judged more harshly because she was a woman?

Where does that leave us with this hypothesis?

Undoubtedly, on the basis of the research, we can declare our hypothesis proven. The lived experience of our women leaders is nowhere near as conclusive. All our women leaders agreed there is a problem in general but views varied about whether and how it applied to them. Hillary saw the hypothesis come to life in her election campaign. Christine thought hard work was somewhat of an antidote. Ellen had a unique take on how the hypothesis related to courage in leadership. Joyce pointed to her struggles with an even more unpleasant display of sexism. Erna, Jacinda, Michelle and Theresa did not feel the force of the hypothesis in their own lives.

We can add to these viewpoints Julia's own experiences. She understands what it is like to do media appearances and interact with the public while opinion polls record low favourability ratings and damning commentary is everywhere. It would be impossible to get out the door and do your job if the dominant thought in your mind was *Everyone hates me*. Keeping that kind of thought at bay is made easier because there is a dissonance between that negativity and your day-to-day interactions. When meeting a president or prime minister face to face, most people are hard-wired to be respectful and pleasant. In fact, Julia can count on one hand the number of times, across her entire fifteen-year political career, a member of the public was actually in her face spitting insults. Whatever might be in their heads, people prefer easygoing interactions to confrontations.

Weighing our women leaders' words and Julia's experiences, the variation between the research and their perception might in part be explained by the fact that, in the real world, there is no reliable feedback loop about what people are muttering to themselves in the back of their minds. Even pollsters might find it hard to dig deep enough to work out whether people think 'she's a bitch'. Commonly done favourability rankings can capture measures of likeableness, but many elements would be in people's minds as they participate in those surveys, not just gender.

Second, and more importantly, the laboratory-style research is generic in the sense that people are being asked to judge the likeableness of a woman leader from the one engagement the researchers present, whereas in normal life people have far more rounded experiences to judge their leaders on.

Our best conclusion is that there is force in the research, and it is taking us to an important truth that would be hard to mine out of observations of community perception about women political leaders. There is a predisposition for people to view a woman wielding power as unlikeable, a bit of a bitch. However, on the basis of our women leaders' experiences, we do think this negative assumption can be knocked down depending on the context and the conduct of the woman leader, with context trumping conduct. By that we mean a woman in a hard political environment would not be able to out-smile the bitch characterisation. Hillary's experience is a demonstration of this, and also shows that once an idea about a lack of likeableness is raised and becomes a pervasive view about a woman leader, it becomes impossible to stop the perception, especially because opponents can weaponise it against her.

The happier news is that women can break through. Like Jacinda, Erna has polled a higher favourability rate than her political party.[11] Both are leaders in more gender-equal societies that have had women at the top before. In these environments they seem to have had the opportunity to overcome the predisposition that women leaders are not likeable. An interesting point to muse upon is whether being mothers and leaders at the same time helped both of them bolster how nice they are seen to be. Erna certainly pointed to her openness about her family life being one of the keys to the public's view of her. Is the flip side of the coin that it is harder for women who have never had children to be viewed as likeable? We will return to these considerations in the next chapter.

What can be done to halt the feedback cycle of women leaders being perceived as unlikeable? Just talking about it really matters. In saying that, we are making the optimistic assumption that in everyday life the 'she's a bit of a bitch' stereotype is more a descriptive one than a prescriptive one, meaning it can be overcome by reason and more frequent experience of women leaders. Roll on the day when, on a political talk show, if someone says the problem with a candidate is, 'She's just not very likeable,' the others on the panel respond by saying, 'Hang on, is that true or is that gender bias?' If the issue can be surfaced routinely, then ultimately it might become commonplace for the voting public to take a second look rather than react instinctively, fuelled by unconscious bias.

Let's end with two snapshots, one about a potential future and one of where we are now. Jacinda says:

'I've started this exercise with people, particularly when I go into schools. I ask in classrooms for the children to close their eyes and think of a politician and then name for me what they see, to describe the physical and character traits. And it's exactly as you'd expect. They say the person in their mind's eye is male, of a particular age, confident, aggressive, sometimes people would say selfish. They might use the word liar. I mean, it's never particularly flattering.'

She worries that if this is the image then people who want to go into politics will feel the need to conform themselves to that stereotype. Jacinda thinks that these political aspirants might conclude, *'Even if I don't particularly like any of those things, that's what you need to succeed.'*

Early in her career, Jacinda thought about this herself and decided:

'*Actually, I'm willing to hand my political career over to fate. My stark choice is either to adopt these traits and therefore be seen as a more successful politician, or just be myself. I made that very deliberate decision. I even remember points where that was tested and thinking, no, I'm just not going to change who I am.*'

This has left her hungry for discussions of leadership to be more attuned to individual characteristics than stereotypes. For example, if a woman had an aggressive political style, Jacinda believes she should not feel the need to change that to avoid revving up the critique that she's bitchy. She says:

'*We should just be able to be who we are, regardless of whether it's considered likeable or not. We have to start trying to demonstrate different traits – leadership traits – and show that they can be accepted as a norm. We have to be willing to break the mould and show that you could survive by being your own person.*'

Political professional Nick Merrill has worked for Hillary for a long time. Asked about the differential treatment of women leaders today, he says:

'I could go on for days, but my favourite story about this is when the campaign started we had all these Obama people come on board, and they were all very happy to be there, but they all wondered at the beginning when we would say, "Just wait, wait until you see what the press does to this woman." And they would say, "It's a campaign now, we know how to handle this." And two months in, it was like this chorus of people, all who'd never experienced this before, who had been at the highest levels – they had worked for [former US senator] John Edwards through all of his scandals, they had worked for Obama through eight years – and they all would say, "My god, I just assumed everybody was full of it when they said they would treat her differently, but they treat her differently." These were seasoned political veterans who had worked for men on presidential campaigns before. The reason is you don't get the benefit of the doubt, you don't get any assumption of trust.'

It is pleasing to see that this kind of unfair treatment of women is now subject to more scrutiny and challenge. In the 2020 United States election, the #WeHaveHerBack campaign raised and pushed back against an array of gendered media coverage and campaign insults in real time. These included reports focussing on appearance, the use of political barbs laden with sexist stereotypes and disrespectful commentary about candidates' backgrounds.

Nick's words reinforce just how much we need to change to get to a world where every individual gets to be themselves and encounters no prejudice as a barrier to their leadership capabilities. Daunting, yes, but we are up for the challenge.

8

Hypothesis five:
Who's minding the kids?

'*I believe that you can be both empathetic and strong, that you can be a leader and also be kind. I always thought that the notion of "mother of the nation" also has that same implication.*'

These are the words of Prime Minister Jacinda Ardern as she comments on the fact that some New Zealanders use the terminology 'mother of the nation' to refer to her.

But the world's fascination with motherhood and Jacinda has not arisen because of such a metaphor. It is the result of her actually becoming a mother while in office, the second woman to ever do so. The first was Benazir Bhutto, the prime minister of Pakistan, back in 1990.

The circumstances of the two pregnancies could not have been more different. Prime Minister Bhutto hid her pregnancy from her colleagues and the nation. At the same time as having her child she was at the centre of a political storm, which resulted in a no-confidence vote and the eventual dismissal of her government by the president.

In today's era, when any woman of child-bearing age in the public eye is likely to see headlines that scream 'baby bump' if she so much as eats an extra sandwich at lunch, secrecy was never going to be an option for Jacinda. On 19 January 2018, less than three months after being sworn in as prime minister, Jacinda announced she was expecting a baby with her partner, Clarke Gayford. Baby Neve was born on 21 June. Jacinda became the first prime minister ever to take maternity leave.

It is an extraordinary story and an ordinary one all wrapped together.

A couple in their early thirties falls in love. They decide that they want to have children but experience difficulties falling pregnant. The woman then gets an amazing promotion at work, and not long after falls pregnant. This could well be the story of your sister, your next-door neighbour, a colleague at work.

What is extraordinary is that Jacinda has experienced this under a white-hot global spotlight, which has thrown into stark relief all the practical and perceived issues of combining mother-hood and leadership.

Male leaders who are the fathers of small children are likely to be viewed as in touch with everyday life. Specifically, a father can use his status to demonstrate he understands the pressures on voters as they struggle to make a good life for their children.

For female leaders, the perception of family is more mixed. As discussed in the last chapter, a woman with young children may be seen as approachable and caring. However, there is a risk that voters will worry about her ability to acquit the rigours of political life because of her caring responsibilities. For men, such questions tend not to be raised because it is assumed that wives are under-taking the principal caring role.

Julia saw this first-hand during her political career. She served with women and men who were combining having a family with being in parliament. Only her female colleagues reported being asked at community meetings about who would be minding the kids.

Our fifth hypothesis draws on these experiences and breaks down into two parts. First, that *Having children and being a leader plays out differently for women than it does for men*. We think one evidence point for this hypothesis is that, to date, the women who have made it to the top echelons of political leadership disproportionately did not have children or their children were adults at the time of their political career.

The second string to our hypothesis is that *While being childless means a woman leader has not had to face the challenges of combining work and family life, it brings other issues*. We explore this through the experiences of Theresa and Julia.

To gather information from our women leaders for this hypothesis we asked how they weighed up and made their choices about whether to marry, when to marry, whether to have children and when to have children. We also inquired whether they faced community or media questioning about their family life, including their life partner and caring for their children, that were not routinely asked of male politicians. We invited them to tell us about the practical reality of managing their multiple roles as a spouse and mother with their political career. Our final question was how their families felt about the way politics impacted their lives.

To hear the answers, let us go first to the women leaders who directly combined leadership and child-raising, Jacinda and Erna.

How does Jacinda see all this?

First, she felt anxious about announcing her pregnancy, with her worries accelerated by the backstory, which started in August 2016 when Jacinda was serving as a member of parliament under then Labour leader Andrew Little. In a profile piece in the *New Zealand Herald*, she was asked about her ambitions for leadership and loyally supported Andrew.

Her response as to what would happen if Andrew was no longer leader was reported in the following way: 'the next leader won't be her. She doesn't want to work the ridiculous hours, she doesn't want the acute spotlight of media scrutiny and having recently moved in with her partner, Auckland media personality Clarke Gayford, she wants to have kids. She can have these things as an MP but not as the leader of a party. Sure as heck not as Prime Minister. It's a very human answer.'[1]

As history now records. Andrew Little exited the Labour leadership in August 2017 and the party turned to Jacinda. Within seven hours of being elected leader, Jacinda was interviewed on television about her plans regarding having children. She responded that she faced the same dilemma on motherhood and career that was faced by other women.

The next day in a radio interview she bristled when an interviewer asserted that employers had a right to know whether a woman was thinking of becoming pregnant, so voters should be aware of her plans. Not just on her own behalf, but for women generally, Jacinda emphasised that it was both illegal and viewed as unacceptable to question a female potential employee about whether she would be likely to want maternity leave, and had been for a long time. Understandably, Jacinda also pointed out that such questions were not asked of men.

She says about announcing her pregnancy:

'I was worried about the whole country's reaction. I thought, what if they think that I haven't taken my role seriously? But I didn't want to have to give all the backstory to the timing of the pregnancy to help people understand, because it was so private.'

Her fears were natural, but the reaction of the New Zealand people seems to have been positive, even joyous, at the news. Ngozi shares her own story about how the reaction to announcing a pregnancy plays on women's minds, saying:

'When I first started work at the World Bank it was exactly the same. The week after I started, as a young professional, I found out I was pregnant. Totally unplanned, and actually I was terrified. When I spoke to a few people they said, "Oh my god, you've ruined your career. In this place, nobody gets pregnant." I didn't know what to do. I hesitated and hesitated to tell anyone in authority, and when I finally did their reaction was so positive.'

The role-modelling impact of her own experience is moving for Jacinda. She recalls getting a beautiful long letter from a woman who explained that:

'She had fallen pregnant not long after me and was so nervous about telling her boss. She thought it would ruin her career and she was really worried that would be the end of her employment. She said when she told him she absolutely knows the fact that I was pregnant had made a difference to the way that he responded. It was really lovely, and I think, gosh, if all this has made a difference for just a handful of people, that matters.'

Given the background to the birth of Neve, Jacinda finds it hard to respond when she is asked publicly about the choices she has made in her life. She says:

'The word "choices"; it's a very loose use of the word. There's lots about where I've ended up that I don't feel as though there

were choices per se. I don't regret that. I think, actually, I needed to have those choices removed because otherwise I wouldn't have taken on both the work and family opportunities. It's all about life being life.'

Another word Jacinda finds tricky is 'balance', when asked about combining work and being a mother. She says:

'I don't think I particularly balance anything. I just make it work. I'm really religious about this; I don't think women should feel as if they have to do it all and make it look easy, because it's not easy and we shouldn't have to try to do everything, and I don't. We must not pretend we're superhuman, because that sets a false expectation and it also leaves the impression that we shouldn't need support.'

On how she makes it work, Jacinda describes:

'Clarke works making a fishing television show, and so about ten weeks of the year he is away filming. When that happens, my parents help. But otherwise Clarke is our primary caregiver. He cooks all the meals, he manages the logistics of living in two places, our home in Auckland and the official residence in Wellington. I'm very open about that, because I don't want women to think they should do absolutely everything.'

The example also changes views about who should do what in a family. Jacinda says:

'When we announced that Clarke would be the primary caregiver, many women got in contact to explain that their husbands or partners had done the same thing. We haven't talked often enough about that reversal of perceived roles. Why shouldn't we? Because these roles are for the men as well. There should be no stigma attached to a man being the primary caregiver.'

But even with all this, Jacinda is clear that it is not emotionally easy. She says:

'I don't think there is such a thing as balance because women always feel guilty. Even if you do something fifty-fifty, you split your time and your life so that you're giving your time in equal amounts to family and work – we are high-guilt creatures. I mean, we feel guilty no matter what. And so, I don't think there ever is this thing called balance because we'll always feel as if we should be giving more of ourselves to everything. It's just a matter of making it work.'

Asked if men feel that guilt too, Jacinda muses:

'I can't really speak on their behalf. I just see that we women carry it, whether it's guilt around how much time we spend without our children or siblings or caring for our parents or being present. We feel that guilt quite acutely.'

In a world seemingly filled with Instagram and Facebook posts that jumble together envy about how quickly some women regain their pre-pregnancy bodies with a rejection of the very concept that anyone should feel any pressure to do so, we ask Jacinda how she thought about her physical shape and health. She says she did not feel any public pressure about this, but she did impose some on herself. She remembers:

'I came out of hospital and then put on weight after having the baby, probably because my mother was around and she kept feeding me lactation cookies, which were really just cookies. And so, I felt as if I needed to get my energy back.

Looking back on that period, those first four months, I think I was probably ignoring how hard they were. I kept breastfeeding and the logistics of life – it was so difficult. I was so focused on just making everything work, and being seen to do everything as well as I could, there was no time to even pick up on any sense of pressure from anyone else. It was all self-imposed.

I needed to be on top of my game. I just needed to be quick in every sense: to feel agile, to get my quick thinking back, to feel physically well. For a long time, I didn't feel like that. I needed to hide that because I did not ever want to leave the impression that I dropped the ball on something because I was a new mum.'

That is a hell of a lot of pressure, and it was combined with an additional burden around the entitlements of office. In thinking about how leaders travel, including overseas, there is no real precedent for a breastfeeding mother and what that necessitates in terms of extra arrangements. Jacinda says:

'I was very aware of never wanting to create any sort of set of circumstances where people felt as though me having a child in office would come at a cost to the public. I didn't want that to be a debate because I didn't want to create an environment where it was hard for any other woman in parliament. So, I felt a real duty to make sure that was never a story.'

As noted elsewhere in this book, New Zealand is a high achiever on international rankings for gender equality. It also seems open-minded on family arrangements, with no real negative commentary on the fact that Jacinda and Clarke were not married when Neve was born. Jacinda says, *'People asked out of curiosity if we were going to get married but not out of judgement.'*

At the time of our interview, she went on to joke that the most incessant commentary on the topic came from her family, and given how much celebration there had been on Twitter about the absence of discrimination in New Zealand against an unmarried prime ministerial mother, she felt she would be letting people down if she got married. However, she must have decided the Twitterverse would understand, because Clarke has since proposed and Jacinda accepted.

Ellen, who married at seventeen and is the mother of four, has a story from a far harder place. In telling it to us, Ellen effectively uses the words of our hypothesis. She tells us the general reaction to the blockbuster speeches she delivered throughout her career was positive but also says:

'The bar talk was, "Why doesn't this woman take care of her children, instead of meddling in things that aren't her business?"'

In the context of Ellen's story and the obstacles she faced, these words have truly caustic bite because her accomplishments came at a dreadful price in terms of her family. She explains:

'When my husband, who already had a college degree from Wisconsin University, was given a scholarship to go back for a master's degree, that gave me an opportunity. We went to the US together and I went to Madison Business College.

In keeping with our system, we left the children at home in Liberia. Two with one grandmother, two with the other grandmother. One faces certain decisions in life that can make a big difference in what happens to you. When we left, my youngest son was only a year old. One year old. And the decision was . . . can I do that? The opportunity for schooling had come and it would not come again. Yet my son was only one year old. So that was one of the hardest things to do. But I did that because in the end . . . well . . . to this day I still have a heavy conscience about that.'

To the ears of those from richer, more opportunity-laden parts of the world, this may sound an inconceivable sacrifice. Yet, for many millions of women, such wrenching decisions are unavoidable. Ngozi has her own family story and shares:

'You know, my parents left me with my grandmother in the village when I was a year old and went abroad to Germany to study on a scholarship. It still bothers my mother. So, I understand.'

Ellen responds:

'*But, you know, the bad part about that is that I left before he could be baptised, and in baptism your friends become the godparents of the child, so he doesn't have any godparents. I mean, later on people came in, but . . .*'

Her voice trails off.

This is not the only family sacrifice Ellen's life has brought her. As described in chapter 3, leaving her violent husband meant three of her four sons no longer lived with her.

In her autobiography, *This Child Will Be Great*, Ellen acknowledges that family separation has consequences, but she writes too of forgiveness and success:

'it would have been easy for any one of [my sons] to have slipped into drinking or drugs or gone bad in some other way. Instead, they have all become professionals in their careers and wonderful men in their personal lives, and today we are, all of us, very, very close. Even Adamah, who for many years, I believe, felt I should not have left him when he was only one year old – I think even Adamah has forgiven me now.'[2]

Compared to Ellen, Erna, coming from Norway, would be the first to acknowledge that she has walked a far easier path. She is very clear about the importance she places on family, saying:

'*If I'd had to choose between having a family and being in politics, I would have left politics.*'

Of course, she never faced Ellen's choice of staying with her children at the cost of losing the chance to learn and lift herself out of poverty and dependency on a violent man. Even as she clearly states her highest priority, Erna celebrates that in Norway there are support systems that aim to prevent people being forced to choose, saying:

'Most Norwegian women want to have both; we want to be mothers and have our career, and so it's taken for granted. Norwegians all have access to affordable child care and long maternity leaves.

Political life is quite flexible when you're in parliament. There is great understanding. If you have to leave a meeting because you have to pick up your kids from kindergarten, it's okay. Recently there was a small debate about whether this was really okay. A few people said, "What about the rest of us who have to stay and sit there and do things?" But that view was rejected.'

For Erna, this meant she benefitted from a break in the parliamentary day between 3 pm and 6 pm. During that time, parliamentarians could attend to duties outside the chamber. Erna found this system to be a godsend. She describes:

'As a mother, this break made it easy. I could go fetch my children from the kindergarten, drive home, make dinner, and I could go back by six o'clock and my husband could take over.'

As she moved up in politics and her workload became heavier, managing work and family life became more difficult. Erna reflects on this period in the following terms:

'But when I became a minister, much more of the family work ended up on my husband. As minister, I had a wide range of responsibilities and I could be required to be on the radio or television nearly every day.

It was very difficult to plan, so my husband said that he would take the planning responsibility for our children and he would give me notice if I really had to be there. He had a system going, if there was something serious at his work, I would be there for the family. But we didn't have to negotiate every week. I had the freedom to opt in to the very important events, and he took the responsibility of organising things.'

Erna is very appreciative of the way her husband shared and, at times, disproportionately shouldered the family responsibilities. But she does smile wryly as she says that, even in Norway, *'there are more expectations for women than there are for men. My husband was given prizes like "Man of the Year" for being so supportive of his wife, and I heard some of the wives say, "Well, what does he do that we haven't done?" That's very true. But the way my husband behaved was more special and surprising because it's not what would happen in every family.'*

Erna has some wonderful memories of the ways she found to combine being there for her children while thriving in politics. She describes Norway as a 'bandy' country, by which she means it is mad about the sport of bandy – a kind of ice hockey played with a ball instead of a puck, by more players on a larger area. By definition, games are played outside in the cold with lots of gear, including skates. Erna recalls:

'I was sitting in my car while my son was practising bandy in minus-ten degrees Celsius. I was on the phone participating in a debate on the radio. I looked around and saw that the person I was debating was also in a car in the same parking lot. He was the father of my son's teammate and Minister of Social Affairs at that time.'

While Erna and her husband found a way to make it all work, she is clear that young women need to think carefully and discuss frankly with their partners how they will manage family life. She says:

'You have to discuss and understand that sometimes there is a priority on one partner's career. It's very difficult to have a double career where both parents are equally as busy.'

Ngozi emphasises this need for honest conversation. In her view, one important part of coping is talking seriously with your spouse or partner ahead of having children about how you would both share the burden so that each person's career is respected and supported along the way. Doing this after the child or children arrive creates stress.

There is an African proverb that says 'It takes a village to raise a child'. Hillary popularised this expression internationally when she used it as the title of her first book, which was published in 1996. In her own way, Erna has discovered the wisdom of these words.

'It's great to have very nice grandparents. Our parents live in different cities to us. For my sister's children, my mother has been an extremely important person because they have gone home to her after school and all of those things. But my husband and I were in a different part of the country, so we had to work with neighbours and friends. We were very good at getting to know the whole neighbourhood's age group of potential babysitters, and we paid the best to ensure they would come back.'

Interestingly, because Norway gives families more options than many other countries, Erna says there is less sympathy for those who complain work is getting in the way of family life. She recalls:

'I was at the theatre once. I had been asked to play an official role as prime minister and I said no because I just wanted to enjoy myself. The leader of the opposition said yes to the formal role and when speaking said something like, "Oh, of course I would love to have more time with my children," and there was an immediate response of, "It's your choice!" from someone in the audience. I think that's the Norwegian culture.'

Like Erna, Christine also has some advice for young women about combining work and family life. She says:

'I was lucky because it was France and because I had enough money to afford a nanny. And when they were young, from eight in the morning until I came home, the nanny would stay. I spent more

than half my earnings on the nanny, but, you know, she was a friend and she spent ten years with me.'

While this made the logistics of life work, Christine was worried about what this would ultimately mean for her bond with her children. She shares those feelings in the following words:

'My fear was that the nanny would become a surrogate mother, but my fear did not come true. In some ways it is a mystery to me how it all works, but I know an enduring bond formed between me and my children. So young mothers should really appreciate and understand this.

I have seen some of my friends picking very uneducated or underqualified nannies because of this kind of fear. They wanted to ensure their relationship with their children was of higher value or the nanny wouldn't warrant attachment.

My tip is to pick the best nanny you can, because then you feel confident and rely on that person and you know the children will be okay. And never assume that person is going to steal your children away from you.'

Christine's other tip is harder to hear. She says her life has worked because of *'Short sleep! That's a big one.'*

She is conscious of the public exposure and its impact on her children. She says:

'I consulted with my children before I took high-profile jobs. They always supported me, and they are proud of me, though they suffered as a result. One of them had to leave France and finish his schooling and university in the US, where he was more anonymous. And one of them still doesn't want me to go to his restaurant during opening hours.'

Both Michelle and Joyce are also conscious of the impact of their choices on their children, confirming that there was much about the public attention that was hard to tolerate, even though their children were not young when they were each at the apex of their political leadership, serving as presidents. Michelle does echo Christine's sentiments that, despite it all, family love and connection pull through. She says:

'I tried to balance, and of course it's not a balance because my children believe that I left them alone too much because of my choices. But we have a good relationship.'

Hillary also did not combine the days of her own political leadership as a senator, Secretary of State and a presidential candidate with child rearing. Chelsea, her daughter, was already an adult by the time she pursued these roles.

But Hillary recalls something that beautifully sums up our hypothesis. She says:

'When I was a young lawyer, and Chelsea was a year or two old, I read a very well-known advice column in the local newspaper. The question to this man who gave advice about work life was, "I've been promoted. I'm going to have my own office for the first time. How should I decorate it?" So, the guy's response was, "You've signed with initials so I can't tell if you're a man or a woman. If you're a man and you have a family, fill your office with pictures of them because people will think you're reliable, and you're a good family man and therefore a good employee. If you are a woman, do not have any pictures of your family because people will think you can't keep your mind on your work." I will never forget reading that and I thought, wow, what a terrible burden to impose on young women who are working as hard as they can and are being told you cannot be seen as both a mom and a good worker.'

Obviously, this is a memory from decades ago, but Hillary also shares a very up-to-date experience, telling us:

'The other night I went to support a new group which is raising money to help women with children run for office. It was started by a woman who had two young children and ran for office herself. She saw how hard it was and that there really is a bias against women with children. There's always the question of, "Why are you not home with your children? Why are you doing this? Why are you subjecting yourself to it?"

If there were one single formula for managing work and family, we would all be promoting it for everybody. But it is so dependent on your financial circumstances, your partner's attitude, whether you have help that is reliable. I mean, there are just so many different variations on how women cope with having children and having a job. But there's no doubt that women with children are penalised and a lot of it is silent, implicit bias.'

Tony Blair and David Cameron both 'did a Jacinda' and welcomed a new family member while holding the office of UK prime minister. Current Prime Minister Boris Johnson joined this dads' club on 29 April 2020. Blair's memoirs and the reporting at the time of the birth of Cameron's daughter record public interest, even excitement at a new baby in 10 Downing Street, the official prime ministerial residence.[3] The media coverage of the latest Downing Street baby has principally focused on the tumultuous lead-up to the birth, in which Boris was gravely ill with Covid-19 and his fiancée, Carrie Symonds, also suffered a bout of the virus, albeit much milder.[4] But none of these male prime ministers have been subject to any suggestion that becoming a father again would hinder them in the performance of their official duties. There is just none of the sense of pressure that is experienced by our women leaders.

This comparative, as well as the words of our interviewees, make the case for our hypothesis, that the personal reality and political perceptions around caring for children are still more fraught for mothers who lead.

But what about women without children? As detailed in chapter 3, Theresa and her husband, Philip, wanted children but were unable to have them. May has been publicly candid about this matter. For example, she said while campaigning in 2016 to be selected by the Tory party as the prime minister to replace David Cameron, that:

'Of course, we were both affected by it. You see friends who now have grown-up children, but you accept the hand that life deals you. Sometimes things you wish had happened don't . . . There are other couples in a similar position.'[5]

A few days after Theresa spoke these words, her remaining opponent for the position of prime minister, Andrea Leadsom, who has three children, was quoted in an interview with *The Times*, saying:

'I have children who are going to have children who will be a part of what happens next.' She added, 'Genuinely I feel that being a mum means you have a real stake in the future of our country, a tangible stake.'

Asked to detail the differences between her and Theresa, Andrea said, 'I see myself as one, an optimist, and two, a member of a huge family and that's important to me. My kids are a huge part of my life.'[6]

Reaction to this interview was overwhelmingly negative, with the statement seen as playing Theresa's childlessness against her and implying she would be a less effective leader because of it. Andrea initially described the article as 'gutter journalism', but after *The Times* released audio and transcripts of the interview, she apologised to Theresa.[7] While her campaign manager described it 'as the establishment trying to get Andrea' and asked rhetorically, 'Since when has it been a crime to be proud about your children?', leading Tories described the remarks as 'vile' and indicative of Andrea 'not being PM material'. The social media reaction was very condemnatory.

Two days after the interview was published, Andrea withdrew from the leadership contest. In doing so, she made a statement, which did not refer to the interview or reaction to it. Instead, it spoke about the need for unity. However, there can be no doubt the interview was profoundly damaging to her leadership campaign.

How does Theresa see all this? She says:

'From time to time I have been asked about not having children but, actually, by and large, the journalists here have kept off that subject.'

She notes, in an understated way, that there was *'quite a sort of reaction'* to the Leadsom comments. She speaks admiringly of a number of her colleagues who have managed being in politics while having small children, including Caroline Spelman, who was rejected by twenty-seven constituencies for preselection before a local Tory party decided to give her the opportunity to run for election as a working mother with three small children.

Julia is intrigued about the fact Theresa feels she was generally treated respectfully in the press about being childless. In Australia, her experience was different. As deputy leader of the opposition in 2017, Julia was chided by a senior conservative senator for being 'deliberately barren', and then had to stomach reading follow-up pieces like the one entitled 'Barren Behaviour' in *The Australian* newspaper:

'At the Junee abattoir, manager Heath Newton knows what happens in the bush to a barren cow. "It's just a case where if they're infertile they get sent to the vet to get checked and then killed as hamburger mince," he says . . . In the Kimberley region, near Broome, where [the conservative senator] issued his public apology for his remarks, the barren cows even have a name: killers. It's the ultimate fate of an animal that can't breed.'[8]

She also recalls the meltdown that occurred when she was photographed in the kitchen of her suburban home on the day she arrived back from an overseas trip. The fact the kitchen was clean and there was no fruit in a bowl on the table was nationally discussed as a symbol of her childlessness and remoteness from ordinary life. No amount of pleading about the bowl being a decorative one, with the pattern only visible if it was empty, made any difference.

Of course, there were voices of protest and complaint about these moments. One of Julia's favourite memories is being on a street near her home when a woman who had children in the back of her car pulled over and yelled out the window, in a joking manner, 'If you need kids, you can take mine.' She was not the only community member horrified by the carry-on. Ultimately the conservative senator apologised after public outrage was expressed around the country. While some media commentators have publicly stated they found the fruit furore ridiculous, it was still cited on the list of explanations for Julia's downfall as prime minister on one of Australia's top news websites. The fact the photo was taken more than eight years prior to her finishing her time as prime minister was not allowed to get in the way of a silly story.[9]

It certainly does seem the reaction to Julia's childlessness was more acerbic than the one Theresa faced. Is this a cultural variation between the United Kingdom and Australia? Perhaps. But another likely explanation could be that a woman who wanted children but could not have them elicits a respectful reaction, but a woman who simply chose not to have children does not. In being seen to offend against female stereotypes, is there anything bigger than not becoming a mother by choice?

How would the world view a male leader who chose not to have children? Perhaps with interest, but it certainly does not seem to be a dominant feature of the coverage of leaders like President Emmanuel Macron of France, or Prime Minister Mark Rutte of Holland, or Prime Minister Stefan Löfven of Sweden, or former Prime Minister Paolo Gentiloni of Italy.

At this stage, on a case study of one – Julia – we are not prepared to call this part of the hypothesis proven or disproven. But given the proportion of women not having children by choice is going up, this discussion will and must continue.

9

Hypothesis six: A special place in hell – do women really support women?

Thinking of taking up cross-stitch? If you are, grab the decorative pattern with the words 'There is a special place in hell for women who don't support other women' at the centre. Julia, who has been known to knit, is a particular fan of feminist subversion of traditional women's crafts and will applaud your efforts.

This aphorism of fire and brimstone is most often attributed to the first female US Secretary of State, Madeleine Albright. In addition to being cross-stitched, it has appeared on Starbucks coffee cups, T-shirts and bumper stickers.

In this chapter we ask ourselves, if Madeleine is right, how crowded is that special place in hell going to be? Do women really support other women, or is there a tendency for women to compete rather than cohere?

If you are shaking your head at this point and saying that will not do, because a hypothesis has to be a definitive statement, not a bet each way, then please put this book down for a moment and take a bow. When we began to discuss what we wanted to examine in this chapter, our aim was to boldly state the proposition that women support women, but we found ourselves giving each other examples of times they did not. Hence the equivocation, but below we do detail a firm two-part hypothesis to test.

In our defence, in recognising that there are complexities to female solidarity we feel in good company, given even the wonderful and iconic Madeleine herself has run into difficulties. In February 2016, she quoted the saying in a speech urging support for Hillary Clinton against Bernie Sanders and was briefly subjected to a backlash from those who thought she was prepared to condemn women unless they always voted for women solely because of their gender. In an opinion piece a few days later, Madeleine apologised for generating this misunderstanding, saying she had inadvertently used one of her favourite phrases at the wrong time and in the wrong context.[1]

No one is really saying that, no matter the circumstances, women always have to vote for, work with or provide uncritical allegiance to other women. There will be elections when the political party that best represents your values is not the one led by a woman. Or when the best candidate for the job is a man. Or times when a woman leader has made a mistake and it needs to be pointed out and corrected. However, there is a form of solidarity among women that matters.

To explain that phenomenon, we were attracted to the wise words of the incredible US elite sportswoman Abby Wambach, who is a two-time Olympic gold medal winner and the highest scoring professional soccer player – male or female – of all time. In a much-noted commencement address she delivered to students at Barnard College, an all-women's university in New York City, Abby said:

'During every . . . match there are a few magical moments when the ball actually hits the back of the net and a goal is scored . . . What happens next on the field is what transforms a bunch of individual women into a team. Teammates from all over the field rush toward the goal scorer. It appears that we're celebrating her, but what we're really celebrating is every player, every coach, every practice, every sprint, every doubt, and every failure that this one single goal represents.

You will not always be the goal scorer. And when you are not, you better be rushing toward her.

Women must champion each other. This can be difficult for us. Women have been pitted against each other since the beginning of time for that one seat at the table. Scarcity has been planted inside of us and among us. This scarcity is not our fault. But it is our problem.'[2]

Contemplating these powerful words made us ask ourselves how many times we have succumbed, even fleetingly, to a feeling of mean-spirited envy when a woman broke through a barrier or was being celebrated. Though we champion the cause of all women, about a particular woman's achievement we might sometimes feel a marauding sense that she, as an individual, did not deserve it. In Abby's words, while we may have congratulated and applauded her, in our heart of hearts we were not really 'rushing toward her'.

Does this begrudging inner-monologue really matter? Many would say that what counts are not our feelings but our actions and collective impact; that the measures of feminist achievement are to be found in the real world and in hard numbers: more girls going to school, maternal mortality rates dropping, women getting to make their own choices about whether and when to partner or have children, rates of sexual violence going down, more women leading communities, businesses and nations, and so on.

Ngozi and Julia are practical people and spend much of their time studying these kinds of statistics and trying to figure out faster and more effective ways to achieve sustainable development and equality for women. Yet we find that in this case the old feminist slogan 'The personal is political' remains instructive.

One strand of the second wave of feminism, which swept through much of the world in the 1960s and 1970s, was women coming together in consciousness-raising groups to think their way through and out of the sense that we must compete against other women to be the prettiest or best dressed or most attracting of male attention. That war still is not won, and new fields of competition have opened up. Quotas, targets and community pressure have created a wave of positive change around securing seats for women on corporate boards, spots on judicial benches and ministerial positions in government.

Of course, all that campaigning is aimed at equality of representation. But the mechanics of formal quotas have often been to set a target of less than 50 per cent and then meet it through pitting women against women for the designated spots. Think of how many progressive political parties have adopted quotas like one third or 40 per cent of parliamentary seats, and then used schemes like all-women shortlists to select candidates and deliver the 'right' number of women.

Even when no formal target is set, research tells us that an informal benchmark becomes persuasive. The term 'twokenism' was coined in one study to explain the significant clustering around having two women on the boards of companies on the Standard & Poor's 1500 index.[3] Basically, there was an accepted norm that if a board only had one woman on it, then it was at risk of being publicly derided for tokenism. The accepted safe strategy was therefore to appoint two women. The study went on to show that there is a clear predisposition when making further appointments to not select another woman if the social norm number has been reached. This means that effectively there is a men's track and a narrower women's track to appointment, with the women really in competition with each other.

Now, none of that means activism, including arguing for quotas to get more women into positions of power, is misconceived. Without that pressure, we would be seeing even less change. But this evidence does reinforce the need for our advocacy to be focused on reaching nothing less than half, and genuinely fair competition between women and men.

It also highlights how right Abby's analysis is of the politics of scarcity. Fighting against other women for a limited number of seats at the table undermines our solidarity and takes our attention away from the more profound task of completely changing the rules of the rigged game that currently ensures men take a disproportionate share.

Even how we talk about what we are trying to achieve matters. A study at the University of Newcastle, Australia, assessed how willing women and men were to take collective action after hearing two very different messages.[4] The first stated:

'While gender inequality continues to be a significant social and economic issue, those women who are in senior management roles show that it is possible to move up the leadership ladder by working hard, "leaning in," and making sacrifices. These women demonstrate that all individuals can succeed in the workplace irrespective of their gender – as long as they are prepared to invest the time, energy, and significant effort needed for such advancement. Indeed, in the business world, those who apply themselves and make sacrifices along the way reap the rewards, because business – and society more broadly – has always rewarded hard work.'

The alternate stated:

'While gender inequality continues to be a significant social and economic issue, it is now an issue that matters to both men and women. However, our report shows that progress toward this common goal has stalled, which is why it's important that both parties are engaged and committed to tackling this issue together. Admittedly, while there is no "silver bullet," we know that men and boys working together with women and girls to promote gender equality contributes to achieving a host of health and developmental outcomes, not just those within the business world.'

The results showed that while the framing of the message did not make a difference for men, it made a significant difference for women, who were more likely to want to work with others to create change after having heard the more inclusive, less individualistic pitch.

This research reinforces that every effort to bring women together matters. The wrong words corrode our capacity for collective action. Every breakthrough is more than, and must be seen as more than, an individual achievement. Not sincerely celebrating each other's wins also undermines our shared sense of victory and enthusiasm for making the next advance. And, let's face it, nothing gives more heart to those who want to stymy gender progress than the spectre of women squabbling among themselves.

What does the research say about whether women support women? Here the findings may surprise you given the commonly held stereotype that the woman who does break through so revels in her status as the lone achiever that she does not help other women. This image has been with us since as long ago as 1973, when the term "Queen Bees" was coined to describe a woman in a position of authority in a male-dominated environment – for example being the only female executive in a company – who treats other women badly and does not want any of them to reach her level.[5] Are Queens Bees fact or really just another manifestation of the 'she's a bit of a bitch' stereotyping we discussed in chapter 7?

The Australian study we cite above looked directly at this question, and it shows that it is group norms that hold women back, not the behaviour of women who have got to the top. Further evidence on this point comes from a study of senior management in the Standard & Poor's 1500, as opposed to board appointments.[6] This study discovered that when one woman reached senior management, it was 51 per cent less likely that a second woman would make it. At this point you may well be thinking this evidence supports the Queen Bee theory, that women who have achieved success in their career do not like to be surrounded by female competitors. But the study also found that the block in the path of the second woman was not the conduct of the first woman but rather general acceptance of the view that having one woman was enough. Advocacy around gender diversity and other forms of diversity in senior management is now commonplace, but in general, that campaign started later than the efforts about women on boards. That might help explain the lower target number, which does not even reach twokenism.

Hearteningly, the study finds that when a woman is made chief executive, the chances of other women joining the senior ranks improves. Further research has shown that increasing the numbers of women on company boards leads to the businesses appointing more women managers.[7]

There is also some evidence from politics that women leaders have a positive effect on establishing a better gender balance in ministries. A 2013 study of the impact of female presidents in Latin America found they appointed an increased number of women as ministers compared with earlier male-led governments, but only if they were in a society that generally had better attitudes to gender equality. Or, put another way, if a nation had a history of very rarely having women ministers, then the breakthrough of electing a woman as president did not make a difference.[8]

A later European study of nations where women served as prime ministers or led the largest party in a governing coalition showed female leadership meant the number of women ministers went backwards.[9] But more light was shed by research released in 2019, which broke down the data to a party level, given that a leader in a coalition government has the most direct influence on the appointment of ministers from her own political group.[10] The conclusion of this analysis was women leaders do make a positive difference to the number of women appointed as ministers.

This means we can give ourselves a little collective pat on the back, but it would be going too far to conclude we have overcome in our hearts and heads the emotions and behaviours that are brought about when women are forced to compete for limited positions.

Obviously, the leadership level we are examining in this book is about being 'the one'. There is only ever one president or prime minister at a time, and politics is a competitive arena. Inevitably, come election time, there are winners and losers. That means in developing our specific hypothesis for this chapter we had to take the concept of women supporting women and see how it plays out for a single position.

The first leg of our hypothesis is that, *On their pathway to power, our women leaders felt generally supported by women, but the higher they climbed the more they saw the animosity the politics of scarcity can engender.*

The second leg is about role models, mentors or sponsors. In many discussions these terms would be used interchangeably, but we mean different things by them here. A role model can be any person who is looked up to and whose character traits and achievements are admired, including historical figures or people on the world stage. Billions of people of all genders and races would cite Nelson Mandela as a role model whose life story taught them lessons about fortitude and forgiveness. However, role models are also found closer to home and many people tend to seek out someone in their circle of contacts who is likely to have faced challenges similar to their own.

Mentoring is a personal relationship between a more-experienced, usually older, person and a less-experienced, usually younger, person. The standard example would be a senior manager mentoring a more junior employee who is considered talented and a potential leader of the future. The discussions between a mentor and a mentee tend to span giving advice, encouragement and personal support.

The relationship is not just a one-way street from mentor to mentee. Many mentors speak about how much they gain from exposure to new ideas and perspectives, as well as the enjoyment that comes with feeling they are helping someone. Indeed, in some businesses it is now increasingly common to strike 'reverse mentoring' arrangements where a senior manager is the mentee of a junior employee in order to get a sense of what it is like to see the world through their eyes.

Interestingly, the literature on the impact of mentorship shows that while women usually feel they get something out of these kinds of relationships, it does not make a difference to the mentee's career outcomes.[11]

The relationship of sponsorship has more grunt. It may include all of the elements associated with mentorship or it may not, but being a sponsor does require the preparedness to utilise your power networks and reputation in service of the other person. At critical junctures, that means going into bat for them and pushing hard for them to get the next opportunity or promotion. The risk for the sponsor is that it will reflect on their judgement if they effectively lend their 'brand' to an individual who then does not perform well. No one thanks you if you strongly recommend a person for a job and they turn out to be hopeless at it. But, in accordance with the general life rule that the higher the risk, the higher the reward, the literature shows sponsorship is more effective in changing career outcomes.[12]

In politics, role-modelling, mentorship and sponsorship matter. Every woman leader hears story after story about how girls and young women followed her career and that doing so sparked interest, engagement and political aspirations. Many potential or young politicians seek out formal or informal mentoring from someone more senior. In addition, in the competitive world of politics, having people prepared to put themselves on the line to provide support is a key part of the system.

For our women leaders and more generally, given political leadership is still overwhelmingly the preserve of men, it is inevitable that men will be among the role models, mentors and sponsors. But in the second leg of our hypothesis, we wanted to test the proposition that *Female role-modelling, mentorship and sponsorship had less and less relevance as our women rose through the ranks.* We thought this likely to be true because, given how few women have gone before, it is less likely that there would have been a female mentor or sponsor available with direct experience or huge political pull.

In testing our hypothesis, we first sought to find out how our women leaders did or did not experience role-modelling, mentoring or sponsorship during their careers. Having canvassed early influences in chapter 4, however, we do not detail here role models from the family home or school. We also directly asked whether our women leaders could reflect on the comparative role men and women played in supporting them. Each was invited to describe whether women were generally more supportive and if women's empowerment networks existed and helped.

Theresa explains she never really had a role model or mentor. She says:

'That's not how I operate. There have been people who from time to time have given me a bit of help, but not a mentor. Not somebody I've looked up to and said to myself, "Right, I want to sit down with that person, find out how they did it."'

Christine clearly describes the woman who ran the Paris office of the law firm where she started her career as a mentor. She is also full of praise for the people who have worked for her, including many women, and the support they have provided. But other than this one legal leader, mentorship and sponsorship have not played a role in her career.

Erna is somewhat sceptical of the way a lot of role-modelling and mentoring is presented for women. She says:

'I think you should learn from different people. I don't think there is a single person who you should model your life after, or that you can learn just from the wisdom of one person. You can learn a little bit here and a little bit there. You can admire someone's abilities in one area, but not all. And you can learn from that.

Of course, getting somebody who knows your business, knows the politics and can try to give you guidance along the way is good. But you should not use them as a mentor, but rather take their advice as an input.'

However, as described in chapter 3, she did benefit enormously from sponsorship by a woman, specifically the woman who pushed for her to be selected for a parliamentary seat by her political party. In addition, seeing a young female Conservative role model on television when Erna was a teenager helped her imagine a life in politics.

Jacinda also benefitted from preselection support, in her case by a man, Grant Robertson, who stood aside to enable her to be selected for a winnable seat and enter parliament. Even earlier, her aunt facilitated the link that started Jacinda campaigning for and being noticed by the New Zealand Labour Party.

Unlike Erna, for Jacinda mentorship is something she has valued and sought out from the start of her career. She recalls when she was making the decision about whether or not to run for parliament, *'I took a train out to see someone called Marian Hobbs. She was an ex-MP and minister, and she's a person that I would call on for advice.'*

Jacinda says she and Marian now laugh about the fact that her mentor's advice was, *'Don't go into parliament single, you'll stay single.'*

Obviously this advice was given out of love and concern, but fortunately it was not heeded by Jacinda.

Michelle had male sponsors in the sense that her political party's powerbrokers, the male 'Barons', offered their support to her to become the candidate for president. She also points to the importance of early male political role models in her life, saying:

'I decided to join the Socialist Youth movement because I heard its representatives speak at an assembly at university on different issues. I thought to myself, I like the way these guys articulate their ideas and I like their proposals.

So, I went up to two of them and said, "My name is Michelle Bachelet and I want to belong to your youth organisation." And they looked at me and said, "Are you sure?" It was very difficult to get them to believe me, but I joined.'

Hillary describes how she has benefited from male and female mentorship in the following words:

'My most important mentor in college was a man, a professor of mine, who was incredibly helpful. But in my law school years it was a woman who made a big impression on me. That was Marian Wright Edelman, who gave me a summer job working for the Children's Defense Fund, and she became a role model for me. It was a mix, and I can look at the individuals at different points in my life and think about the role that each played.'

Ellen does not point to any role model outside of her family. But she speaks movingly about the impact of women's support for her at pivotal times. As she tells her life story, time and again the risks that her sister, Jennie, and friend Clave took to support her stand out. Because Ellen's life has been a mosaic of periods of exile and time in jail, those women who chose to stand next to her risked sharing this fate.

More broadly, she explains how the women of Liberia campaigned for her to be released from behind bars when she was facing ten years of hard labour. More than ten thousand women signed a petition that specified they were prepared to demonstrate to secure her release. She also describes the special role women played when she ran for president, saying, '*The women all rallied around me and said, "This time we can win, and we can win with Ellen."*'

She recounts how, as president, she repaid this trust by prioritising education for women and better conditions for rural women. She speaks with a sense of pride about the Sirleaf Market Women's Fund, which was established by the women whose stalls had kept food and supplies flowing in spite of enormous challenges during civil war. Ellen's government proudly partnered with this organisation, which still exists today.

But Ellen does express a sense of disappointment about encountering a real-world example of a limited number of women being seen as enough. She says:

'*I did appoint women to strategic posts in my government, and I did help increase local female leadership, with more women serving as mayors and paramount chiefs. But some battles you just have to give up on, and one of those for me was the battle against men around the number of women in parliament. Their position was, "You are president, you have all the power as president. That should be enough for you women."*'

Joyce also experienced grassroots support from women as the community rallied around her. In describing her pathway to power she explained how both men and women wore T-shirts emblazoned with the words 'Friends of Joyce Banda' to show their support for her when she was being pressed to resign as vice-president. In addition, she stresses, over the seventy-two-hour period in which it was so unclear whether Joyce would become the president, '*Ordinary men and women came from everywhere in Malawi to demand that I be sworn in.*'

Like Ellen, as president, Joyce appointed women to important roles. She believes:

'*These women, like me, wanted to prove that they could do better. One thing that is true is that women work harder because they don't want to let their fellow women down, and they also don't want to appear weak.*'

But she sadly recounts that she was also undermined by women, saying:

'*I was shocked because I found that men had no problem working with me and respecting me. I don't remember a scenario where I felt as if a man was undermining me, but that happened with women. A typical example is when I gave my most famous speech, at Nelson Mandela's funeral, a speech everyone says is my best speech ever.*

On the Friday, the day before my daughter's wedding, the South Africans called and said, "You must come and speak." I was honoured but explained that I could not miss this important family event.

It was agreed that they would send a plane for me on the evening of my daughter's wedding, so I would arrive in South Africa the next morning. On the plane, I scribbled out the speech. The whole world praised that speech, except two women in Malawi, who wrote in the newspapers that this was a terrible speech.

I think with women sometimes there's a sense of, "Why is it you and not me?" I have never been able to understand whether this is driven by jealousy or spite. I still don't understand, but this is something that pains me greatly.'

Ngozi can relate to this. She notes the active support of many women throughout her career, with three in particular standing out who helped her at critical periods. But she has been equally surprised by the undermining and direct attacks by other women, especially some she helped in their own careers. She says, '*People told me at some stage these women felt, "Why is she there and not me? What's so special about her?" So, they attacked.*' In fact, men have been more instrumental in her career than women. At some stages when she was competing for top posts, men seemed more comfortable speaking up for her than women, even women in high positions.

For Joyce, this lack of support from professional women has continued in her post-presidential political life. She says:

'*It is my male friends who call me and ask how I am doing. Some women do too, but if I had to count there are maybe three women to seven men. Even when the current president threatened me with arrest if I returned to Malawi, I was better supported by local men than women. Globally, women mobilised themselves to support me and say enough is enough. They wanted ten Malawian women to sign their petition. Instead, they found ten men. Eventually they did find the women, but these were young people who all looked up to me as a role model. My colleagues, who I had actually assisted and promoted, refused to get involved. I've also learned on my journey that sometimes it is men against women through other women.*

I think fear plays a part in all this; if they stuck their necks out for me, they thought they would lose their jobs. I am talking about professional women who I had placed in their positions. Grassroots women supported me immensely, and even during these hard times gathered to wait for me on my return home. I returned to a hero's welcome. Thousands of ordinary men and women welcomed me at the airport.'

The experiences of lack of support from women detailed by our other leaders are nowhere near as dramatic.

Both Michelle and Theresa talk of women journalists treating them differently compared to male leaders.

Theresa says, '*I've always found female journos will say to you, "We need more women in politics." But they almost have to prove themselves when they're reporting on women by being harsher about them than they are about the men. It's quite interesting. You would think there was a sort of sisterhood – we want to promote women in politics – but there's none of that.*'

In her first run for president, Michelle remembers:

'*One female journalist asked me how I was going to cope without a husband. In response, I asked her, "Excuse me, would you have asked a question like this of a male candidate?" And then she immediately realised what she had done. But it was very strange that, being a woman, she thought, in a very sexist way, I wouldn't cope if I didn't have a shoulder to cry on at home.*'

But Michelle also recalls women supporting each other, saying:

'*When I was a minister there were five of us and we would go out and have dinner together. When somebody was having a bad time, we would call and say, "How can I help you?" There was a lot of solidarity and connections among the women.*

I also think all of them were very good professionals. They did their jobs as best as they could and, of course, many of them included the gender perspective in all their policies. This was the same during my time as president.'

With these words, Michelle is recalling the relationship that existed between women on the same side of politics and serving in the same administration. Hillary reflects on how political partisanship can change things in the following words:

'*I didn't really run into any problems with other women until I became a politician myself. When I was advocating for education improvements, better health care access and all the other issues that I worked on before I got into public life, I was pretty much surrounded by people who were like-minded. And then when I got closer to the top, or even earlier, when Bill was president and I was First Lady, that was when I began to engender opposition and hostility from women largely divided along partisan lines. You know, it is something that is very complicated, because I never quite knew whether they opposed me simply because I'm a woman, or because I'm outspoken and I don't meet their definition of what a woman should be and behave like, or because I'm a Democrat.'*

Christine takes a very middle road on whether women have helped her or blocked her. She says:

'I don't think I had obstacles or barriers from other women, but I didn't get particular support either. For sure, not many women have supported me, but I don't blame them because they also had so much to prove professionally, as well as raising their children, having a spousal life and looking after lots of other people who generally depend on women. It is just unbelievably heavy. When the time comes, so many of them don't even have time to support their friends. So, I wouldn't say I felt blocked, but I felt delayed sometimes by lack of female support.'

Christine is very understanding of these pressures and indicates she, too, is time-constrained, saying:

'You know, I often receive lengthy letters from young women asking if I can be their mentor. And I have to tell them I'm terribly sorry, but I can't. I am happy to talk to them for half an hour of my time, and I suggest the best time for that is if they are at a juncture and really need help. But I would not have the time to check on and guide them as a mentor. I do try to accept speaking engagements where I can talk to a large group, but to have those individual relationships? I'm sorry, but I don't have time now. I will when I retire.'

With these words, Christine is pointing to a problem many prominent women feel. Julia can certainly recall dozens and dozens of times young women have rushed up to her at a public function and asked her to be their mentor. So can Ngozi, and in her case it is even more pointed because women of colour have an even harder time finding role models and mentors. Both Julia and Ngozi, like Christine, lack the time and feel the guilt that comes with saying no to a full mentoring arrangement, while still sharing as much as they can. Indeed, this book is an endeavour to share insights with as many women and supportive men as possible.

Julia's work at the Global Institute for Women's Leadership is about dismantling the big barriers, but it also enables her to reach women in their thousands through speaking at events and exploring the personal stories of great female role models on her podcast, *A Podcast of One's Own*. Through the Global Partnership for Education and CAMFED, the Campaign for Female Education, Julia tries to contribute to improving the education and life chances of some of the poorest girls in the world. In her work on private company boards, Julia always tries to introduce a gender analysis and push for change. But none of that alleviates the discomfort in having to say no to mentoring requests.

Ngozi has a similar story. In virtually all the work she does she tries to figure out how to include girls and women, especially finding practical ways to uplift their lives. She is very active on gender issues, and pushed for inclusion of girls and women in World Bank programs and analysis during her tenure there. She built partnerships with organisations like the Nike Foundation and their Girl Effect program, and she served on the World Bank's Gender Advisory Council for years. When there were very few African women at the World Bank in the 1980s, she founded a peer support group with four other African women. The group still exists thirty-six years later, with well over two hundred members in 2020.

As Finance Minister in Nigeria, she introduced gender-based budgeting to strengthen economic empowerment and agricultural, health and technology services for girls and women. With her team she started a Youth Enterprise With Innovation program (YOUWIN) that supported thousands of women entrepreneurs in Nigeria. In her current work at Gavi, Ngozi pays a great deal of attention to ensuring equal access to life-saving vaccines for girls. Chief among these is the HPV vaccine, which prevents cervical cancer, one of the leading causes of death among women. Ngozi mentors up to ten young women and men at any given time but still sees her efforts as inadequate in view of the tremendous demand. Like everything else that women face, this continues to be a balancing act.

Christine does convey to us an experience about role-modelling and what she has learnt from it. She recalls:

'I was interviewing as a young lawyer with a specific law firm and the only woman partner in that firm told me, "You will not make partnership unless you have gone through the hell that I have gone through." And I thought to myself, oh, great, I'm out of here!

Sometimes young women are miserable in their workplaces and they are trying like mad to get through the misery and to push, and sometimes I tell them, "Just pack up! Don't stay! Don't feel miserable and awful and beaten up. Go and try something else in another firm, or life. There are some doors that you shouldn't exhaust yourself pushing! It is useless."'

What can we glean about our hypothesis from all these experiences?

No prime minister or president talked about having a mentor while in office.

It is interesting that the youngest of our leaders, Jacinda, is the only one who talks about deliberately seeking out political mentorship on her pathway to power. Intuitively, this leads to the conclusion that her generation is more open to the benefits of such arrangements than those who have gone before. But even Jacinda does not speak about someone acting as a mentor to her while she is prime minister.

In our hypothesis, we identified as a likely constraint on female mentoring or sponsorship of our leaders, as they neared or reached the top, the simple lack of women who had the leadership experience to really be a useful mentor or the political pull to be a sponsor. Having heard from our women leaders, we would add two other factors. First, most of our women leaders did not feel that, once they had reached a certain level, mentoring or sponsorship was relevant. Second, to reverse-engineer Christine's remarks, the real pressure of time constraints is a barrier. As leaders, finding time to be mentored or be a mentor to others seems close to impossible.

How big a problem is this lack of time, space and availability? Julia recalls how refreshing it was to get an outsider's perspective on the way being a woman was impacting her prime ministership through meeting Laura Liswood, the Secretary General of the Council of Women World Leaders. This group, formed in 1996, is a global network of current and former women prime ministers and presidents. Laura's main message was that Julia was not alone. Aspects of the way she was being reported on in the media and some of the lines of attack being used against her were common to women leaders. What was at play was sexist stereotyping. In her overburdened diary, Julia remembers the discussion as an analytical one that was so eye-opening it was well worth an hour of her time. She also recalls how consoling she found it to get a line of sight from her own experiences to those of others. While the impact of the meeting was powerful, Julia still finds it difficult to imagine having been able to set aside regular diary slots for truly meaningful and regular mentoring sessions.

Every woman leader will make different choices, but our advice is to find, at the very least, enough time to step out of the day-to-day and get a new view on gender. It can be hard to see the sexism and the stereotypes when a leader is in the middle of them. Fresh eyes can make a real difference, and it could take as little as an hour every six months.

To help meet and manage the demands made on leaders to act as mentors, a task that could go on our collective to-do list is having clear ways of referring aspiring mentees to other women who have both leadership experience and more time to assist.

On the other leg of our hypothesis, about the politics of scarcity leading to women viewing each other with suspicious eyes, we do not find enough evidence to answer with a definite yes or no. Some of our leaders are clear about experiencing on-the-ground support from women, but undermining behaviour when they were at the top. Our leaders do speak of women being their harsher critics, of women journalists being tougher than they would have been about a male leader, of the women who succumbed to fear of reprisal or partisanship in a greater way than the men. Yet the causal factors of all this are too elusive to capture and hold up to the light.

Your authors are nowhere near certain enough to cast anyone into a special place in hell. We think the better approach is for all of us to think about the politics of scarcity and our own conduct, past and future. For each of us, it is worth asking the question, 'Was there ever a time I deserved a turn in the fiery pits?' If the answer is yes, it reinforces that we are all human and we can do better in the future.

We see three ways of improving. First, women must have deeper discussions about the fact that, as Abby Wambach says, 'scarcity is not our fault. But it is our problem.' As women, how are we going to address this issue? Like all complex problems, talking openly about it is the first step to resolution.

These discussions should be frank and recognise that women are not always going to like each other or agree. It is naive to expect no sense of competition or even animosity to arise between women on opposing sides. The fact that happens is not the problem. Whether we let it undermine any ability to act together on agreed feminist agendas for change is the issue.

Second, and it almost seems silly to have to say it, we have to remember every woman in the world is a mix of strengths and weaknesses. The vacuousness of the 'all women are superheroes' brand of feminism peddled by some celebrities, social media influencers and razzamatazz women's conferences is not doing us any favours. It reinforces a sense that the support of other women should be reserved for perfect golden girls. Like unicorns, these women are mythical, not real. Our challenge is to support each other in a way that makes space for the inevitable imperfections.

Third, even if you do not have the ability to help another woman because of the complexities and stresses of your own life, you can make sure you never block the next woman's progress. If you do have the ability to help, get to it.

10

Hypothesis seven: Modern-day Salem

Witches are everywhere. Or so many believed during what has come to be known as the witch craze of the sixteenth and seventeenth centuries.

Across time and cultures, suspicions have always abounded about individuals having a connection with the devil, but this phenomenon reached a fevered height in Europe for about a century, with whole communities racked by suspicion, trials, torture and death. It is estimated that in regions of modern-day Germany, the epicentre of the witch craze, twenty-five thousand so-called witches were executed. France killed five thousand, Switzerland four thousand, the states that today form Italy two and half thousand, and Britain one and half thousand. While some men were accused of being witches, the targets were disproportionately women. Indeed, women made up around 80 per cent of those put to death.

The craze was exported to the New World, as it was then

known, specifically to the town of Salem in Massachusetts, which was roiled by accusations.

Now historians can look back dispassionately at this era of anti-witch mass hysteria and try to come to grips with the underlying causes, including the societal tensions arising from the Protestant Reformation and its challenge to the Catholic Church. Yet looking at this period leaves a lingering sense of deep unease about the apparent ability of human beings to suspend reason, practise cruelty, use community panic to settle old scores, and show cowardice in going with the flow rather than taking the risk of standing up against it.

At this point, you may well be wondering what on earth this has to do with a contemporary analysis of women and leadership. A quick, glib answer could be that women leaders often get referred to as witches. During Julia's prime ministership, people stood at rallies holding up signs that described her as a witch. When a bombastic Australian radio personality called for her to be 'put in a . . . bag and dropped out to sea', Julia grimly joked that clearly he was failing to understand that you cannot drown a witch. This was a reference to the 'ordeal by water', a test that was thought to identify witches during the craze. Bound and dunked in a river or lake, a woman was supposedly a witch if she could float. Those who sank below the water were said to be innocent, but that was very cold comfort indeed if they were not pulled out before they drowned.

A deeper approach to the question would be to ask whether, all these years after the witch craze, we still see wrongdoing through the prism of gender, and what this would mean when applied to women leaders.

Every leader will make errors. Inevitably, at some point in their career, a political leader will be accused of breaking promises to their constituents, misusing benefits or entitlements, covering up information voters should have had, or some other misdemeanour. Sometimes arguments about political conduct morph into quasi or actual legal proceedings, such as impeachment hearings or corruption trials.

Indeed, not only will accusations be made, but sometimes the leaders in question may very well have done something wrong that needs to be exposed and criticised. This is true of male and female leaders. No one is perfect and politicians are rarely saints.

But, is any of this exacerbated by gender? Do women pay a greater price if they commit a political sin?

To explore these issues, we decided to test a three-part hypothesis. First, that *Male leaders benefit from greater grace and forgiveness in the event of wrongdoing, whereas women are punished more harshly.* Second, that *In times of political trouble, the language and imagery surrounding an embattled woman leader becomes more gendered.* Third, that *Women leaders are disproportionately likely to become ensnared in legal proceedings rather than having scandals remain in the world of politics.*

To unpack these issues, we turn to two principal sources: the existing research in this area, and then expert analysis of the impeachment of President Dilma Rousseff, the first woman to lead Brazil. Unlike the testing of our other seven hypotheses, because of her recent, directly relevant and dramatic experience, we examine here the life story of a woman leader we were not able to interview.

Let us tell you first about a very clever experiment conducted in the United States, which analysed how a randomised sample of people viewed men and women leaders and their mistakes. Different scenarios were played through in relation to the actions of the president of a women's college and a police chief. Both needed to make a decision about how many police officers were required to supervise a campus or community protest. In the first scenario, each of them got the judgement call right and the protests proceeded without causing problems. In the second scenario, they erred and deployed too few officers, and the protests got out of control.[1]

Of course, you would expect anyone judging these scenarios to score the college president or police chief more negatively on competence if they made the mistake of underreacting. The purpose of this experiment was not to demonstrate that obvious conclusion, however, but to work out whether the president or police chief were marked down more for the error if the gender of the person holding those roles was not what you would stereotypically expect. Generally, people would expect the president of the women's college to be a woman and a police chief to be a man. What if that was changed?

The result of this experiment was clear. Gender mattered, or, more precisely, gender incongruence mattered, meaning if a job was held by someone of the opposite gender than the usual norm, they were marked down more for the same error. A female police chief scored worse in the error scenario than a male police chief, and a male president of a women's college scored worse than a female president.

For good measure, the researchers repeated the exercise with scenarios involving a woman as CEO of an aerospace engineering firm and a woman chief judge.

At one level this is bad news for both men and women, showing as it does that an extra penalty is paid if a person steps outside their societally defined roles. But it is especially bad for women leaders because, as we have explored elsewhere in this book, the Think Manager – Think Male paradigm still holds sway. In becoming leaders, women are almost always stepping outside their societally defined roles and holding positions that are thought to be the domain of men.

The gender experiment cited above falls into a broader slipstream of research that shows similar conclusions when the variable is race. For example, studies have shown that when a black person holds a job that has historically been held by a white person, if they are absolutely fantastic at the job then very high evaluations will follow, but once errors are made they will pay a greater price.[2]

Looking at the life and times of Dilma Rousseff enables us to study the question of whether an extra price is paid by women leaders through a real-world lens. We are very conscious as we work through this example that reasonable people, without being motivated by any form of bias, can come to different conclusions on substantive political questions like impeachments. Should Bill Clinton have been impeached for lying about his inappropriate conduct with Monica Lewinsky? Should Donald Trump have been removed from office over his approach to the Ukraine?

People around the world have argued both sides of these questions and will continue to do so. Unsurprisingly, the same is true of Dilma's impeachment. Views differ sharply. The Brazilian people are still processing this experience, including through the work of artists and creatives, such as Petra Costa's documentary *The Edge of Democracy*, which was nominated for an Academy Award in 2020.

We are not trying to tell you what to think about the impeachment, but we are trying to tease out the gender threads that showed at the end of the presidency of Dilma Rousseff. In doing so, it is important to realise that Dilma was different to those who had held the office before in more ways than solely because she was the first woman.

Dilma became president having never before run for any elected office. That broke the mould in and of itself. Instead, her pathway to power was via being the chief of staff to outgoing president Luiz Inácio Lula da Silva, known widely as Lula.

A former trade union official and one of the founders of the Workers' Party, Lula served two terms as president. In 2009, President Barack Obama famously referred to him at a G20 summit as 'the most popular politician on earth'.[3] Towards the end of his time in office, Lula had approval ratings above 80 per cent, and presided over a nation in which the economy was growing strongly, with the poor sharing in this new prosperity, including through more of their children being able to go to university.

Given all this, it is very likely that Lula would have been re-elected easily if he was eligible to stand in the 2010 election. However, Brazil has a limit that prevents a president from running for a consecutive third term. As a result, he instead used his political authority to nominate and campaign for his chosen successor. It was a major surprise when the person he selected was Dilma.

Up until that point, Dilma had been viewed as a highly capable back room person. She was seen as strong, having been part of a movement that fought against the military dictatorship that governed Brazil from 1964 to 1985. Imprisoned and tortured in 1970, at the age of twenty-two, Dilma is acknowledged as a person who did not break. Speaking about this period, she has said, 'all of us are terrified of feeling pain. And it's a terrible thing, that makes people lose their dignity. That is the component of psychological pain. They want you to lose your dignity, make you betray your convictions, make you let go of what you think . . . This process of destroying someone makes people become living dead. What will a person do after they betray what they think, betray themselves? . . . I think we can only endure torture if we trick ourselves. You say you can take five, two minutes. "Now I can take another three minutes." Because you can't fathom enduring a whole day, that's an eternity. So you trick yourself. That's what you do.'[4]

With Lula's support, Dilma secured the Workers' Party nomination and triumphed in the election with 56 per cent of the vote. Dilma invited other women who had been tortured under the dictatorship to attend her inauguration on 1 January 2011.

During her first term as president, the economy of Brazil softened considerably, causing hardship for many people. Super-high global prices for Brazil's major exports had enabled the economic boom experienced under Lula's presidency. Just as Dilma took office in 2011, these prices started to tumble, cutting Brazil's economic growth abruptly to 1.9 per cent by 2012. Foreign finance fled in 2013 after the US Federal Reserve announced it would stop buying Brazil's government bonds. The good years had ended.

In June 2013, huge street demonstrations, initially provoked by an increase in bus fares, broke out around the country. A frustrated populace was showing its acute dissatisfaction with the inadequate services available to the community and diminishing economic opportunities. Many of those protesting were young people who had escaped poverty and gained a university education only to find themselves unemployed or underemployed. Their dreams of a better future had turned to bitter anger.

With an election due in October 2014, any president facing these circumstances would be at risk of a jaded electorate lashing out politically. For Dilma, things were even more fraught. Many had assumed that her presidency was a placeholder and that Lula would re-emerge as the Workers' Party candidate. This would have been possible at this point, because the legal bar was only against running for three terms in a row. As a result, there was some disappointment when it became clear Dilma intended to run again.

Brazil hosted the football World Cup in mid-2014 and was preparing to hold the Olympics in 2016. In more buoyant economic times, both might well have been a source of national pride. However, in this environment, resentment grew about the large expenditure on the necessary venues and associated infrastructure. This feeling was compounded when the Brazilian World Cup team underperformed against expectations and did not make it to the final. Adding humiliation to disappointment, the team's 7–1 knockout defeat by Germany was the worst-scoring loss ever experienced by a World Cup host nation.

Ultimately Dilma narrowly won the election, but the campaign was divisive, unpredictable and hard fought. The opposition effectively refused to concede defeat and publicly questioned the result.

Also in the lead-up to the election, a major corruption inquiry had begun, and rumours were everywhere about who would be implicated. Almost immediately after Dilma's re-election, arrests started to be made as a result of the increasingly high-profile investigation. Initially its focus was on kickbacks from Petrobras, the national oil company, to political figures. Prior to becoming Lula's chief of staff, Dilma had served as chair of the board of directors of Petrobras. While she was cleared of benefitting directly, she was criticised on the basis that she must have known what was going on.

Into this volatile mix, Dilma implemented budget cuts, backflipping from arguing against austerity measures prior to the election. The community was outraged. On top of that, Dilma was accused of various manipulations in the run-up to the election to make the government budget look better than it was in reality. All of these things added to a sense of illegitimacy around her continuing presidency. The economy also continued to stagger.

Arrests, including of leading politicians and advisors to Dilma, continued throughout 2015. The media was always tipped off to be there to get footage of the arrests. Community opprobrium followed and calls for Dilma to be impeached grew.

In the first week of March 2016, Lula himself was taken in for questioning, grabbed at his home early in the morning. Every moment was captured by television cameras, and it made for sensational viewing. This was a crisis for Dilma too, given how tightly bound to Lula she was in the public's mind.

However, things were still to get worse, as Dilma moved from being implicated in corruption by association to being implicated by her actions. The transcript of a tapped phone call between Lula and Dilma was released, in which they discussed Lula being appointed as Dilma's chief of staff. In Brazil, the chief of staff position is of ministerial rank, and this provides immunity from prosecution. The public was disgusted. The Supreme Court struck down the appointment.

The stage was therefore set for the successful impeachment proceedings, which had begun in December 2015. In April 2016 the lower house of Congress voted to impeach. In late August, the impeachment was finalised when the Senate voted in favour of it. As a result, Vice-President Michel Temer stepped up to be president.

The grounds for impeachment were narrow; Dilma was found to have delayed repaying state-controlled banks from the government's budget without parliamentary authority, with the aim of making the budget look better before the election.

By the time she was impeached it was a popular move with the electorate. Indeed, at one point 3.6 million people took to the streets, calling for Dilma's removal.

It is a dramatic story. But what role, if any, did gender play? To try to get to the bottom of that complex question, we turned to Malu A. C. Gatto, Assistant Professor of Latin American Politics at UCL, who was born in Brazil but now lives and works in London. Her field of expertise is in gender and politics.

Malu has met Dilma and is quick to debunk some of the stereotypes about her that were bandied around in the media. She says:

'There was one magazine that published a picture of Dilma watching Brazil play at the World Cup. She was up on her feet, yelling, like fans do. But they made the photo look like she was in an everyday setting, rather than at the football. The headline talked about her "rage".

This is just one example, but throughout her presidency there was a lot of talk about how Dilma's personality was in itself unfit for the role of president. From the moment that she became a candidate to the time she left office, the media would constantly pick on her and display her as not smart, not eloquent. They would ask her questions about books and then they would make a huge thing out of parodying her answers. During a lot of her speeches, the media would cut to people saying, "She's not eloquent, she can't explain what she's saying."

And yet, when you meet her, she is not like that. If you ask her about a government program, even one too minor to really expect the president would know the details, she will draw graphs in the air to explain the government budget expenditure on that program and how it has evolved over time. I have heard her talk about French philosophers and cite them in French. She is clearly really well read. And she is funny. She cracks jokes on the spot. Sometimes when things happen, she will spontaneously respond in a ridiculously funny way.'

All this sounds disturbingly familiar. As we have already seen, many women leaders are portrayed as angry, shrill or robotic. What Malu says next harks back to other women's experiences around the theme of authenticity.

'When Lula first ran as president, a really famous political adviser was hired and Lula changed his image completely, including changing his teeth and his hair. He dressed and spoke differently. And the same thing happened with Dilma. They completely changed her image, the way that she dressed, her haircut. I don't know what it was like every time she would come up to speak as a president – I wasn't there, and I don't know what people were telling her to do. But I think she was trying to essentially fit into a box and deliver in a way that wasn't natural to her, and it came across a bit weird.'

While Malu is clear that the image consultancy was not done just for Dilma, it is interesting to speculate how much more constraining it was for her, given those providing the advice had never worked with a female president before and would have had male role models as their guide. As we have seen throughout this book, the style conundrum and the 'she's a bit of a bitch' problem loom large in crafting ways of presenting women leaders so they are perceived as authoritative and engaging.

Around the world, the art of politics involves drawing people to you, getting them to work with you to deliver your agenda. Politics in Brazil seems to have its own special take on why and how a president does that. There are around thirty-five political parties in Brazil and many of them successfully get at least one representative elected into the national parliament. As a result, in Brazil's post-dictatorship political history, at most a quarter of congressional representatives have been in the same political party as the president.[5] That means to get legislation passed, a president must weld together a significant coalition. Doing so tends to require a combination of force of personality and preparedness to do deals, including those that reward individuals with positions and electorate benefits.

Anthony Pereira, Director of the Brazil Institute at King's College London, compares how Lula and Dilma acted in this environment in the following way:

'Lula loved physical contact with people. He would come onto the floor of the lower house of Congress and he would be hugging everybody, and everybody had his telephone number. Before he became president, he used to say that when he got to the presidential palace, he was going to have barbecues, play football, drink, do all the things that regular Brazilians like to do. The public embraced this style and it worked to bring politicians to Lula and to forge a coalition he could make work.

Dilma didn't do any of those things. She didn't host barbecues, few people had her telephone number, and she didn't like to back-slap. In fact, Lula said Dilma never would have been impeached if she had asked him over every weekend and invited people from Congress over.'

The question remains open as to whether, even if Dilma was a real party-going extrovert, she could have replicated this political style. Only around 10 per cent of the Congress was women. Could she really have bought political goodwill by drinking and carousing with the boys? Or would that kind of conduct have been viewed pejoratively if undertaken by a woman?

In Anthony's view, Dilma's difficulties extended beyond a lack of a general goodwill from elected representatives, to her specifically rejecting deals that could have saved her. He says:

'Michel Temer was picked by Lula in 2010 to be Dilma's vice-president, and he ran again with her in 2014. He was from a different political party, one that needed to be relied upon to form a working coalition. He had been in parliament for thirty years, knew all the people in Congress, and a lot of them owed him.

It has been reported that Dilma said to him, as impeachment loomed, "You be my representative, my liaison with Congress." And the story is that he went and did deals and came back and she said, "How dare you do this? I'm not accepting that, go away."

Whether one accepts that version or not, it is clear that ultimately Temer did actively work with and support those seeking impeachment. This is conjecture, but I don't think he would've behaved that way if she had been a man. There would have been more of a sense of obligation, of loyalty.'

It is a matter of public record that Dilma also rejected a deal, which Lula urged her to accept, that may have saved her from impeachment.[6] Eduardo Cunha, the speaker of the lower house, was facing corruption allegations and offered to prevent any impeachment vote coming to the floor for decision if Dilma protected him from any criminal charges. She refused.

In May 2016, another taped telephone conversation was given to the media. This time the source was not the corruption inquiry but the recipient of the call. In the conversation, the then Minister of Planning, Budget and Management, Romero Jucá, who was a close ally of Temer, appears to say that impeachment would 'stop everything' and 'staunch the bleeding'.[7] At that stage, the tentacles of the corruption inquiry seemed to be about to ensnare hundreds of serving and former politicians. On the basis of this call and Dilma's rejection of the deal offered by Cunha, some in Brazil contend that she became the sacrificial lamb whose spilt political blood was used to satiate and stop further action by the howling media and furious public.

Whatever one makes of this argument, no one could reasonably contend that every parliamentarian voting for impeachment did so based on a dispassionate assessment of the evidence. Nor that all those involved had clean hands themselves. Eduardo Cunha, who oversaw the impeachment process in the lower house, was sentenced to more than fifteen years in prison for corruption in March 2017.[8] Michel Temer has been in and out of jail as he has faced corruption and money-laundering charges involving hundreds of millions of dollars.

Lula was behind bars for 580 days as a result of a charge relating to the potential purchase of a waterfront apartment. He was originally sentenced to twelve years in prison but, along with thousands of other prisoners, he benefitted from a Supreme Court decision that all appeals had to be exhausted before people could be incarcerated. He was released in November 2019 but will face further proceedings. [9]

This saga contains many twists and turns, but for us the critical question remains: if the circumstances were exactly the same, but instead of Dilma, the president had been a man, would he too have been impeached?

Malu answers:

'I think that a man in the exact same conditions as Dilma would also be impeached. But I think that the process of the impeachment would have been different; the rhetoric around it would have been different. In terms of how she was characterised by the media, the level of incompetence that was attributed to her individually and the types of words that were used to describe her. It was about her being hysterical and therefore not being able to communicate with other people in politics, it was about her not being able to maintain her cool.'

Anthony views it a bit differently. He specifically points to an edge to the anger that a man would not have faced. He says:

'I think an analogy with Hillary Clinton's treatment is useful, in the sense that if a male candidate with Clinton's policies had presented at that election against Trump, I can't imagine people would have been chanting "Lock him up".'

Whether, for Dilma, that extra force behind the anger was the difference between being impeached or not, he cannot say with any confidence, but he thinks it might have been.

Malu and Anthony are in clear agreement, though, on the gendered nature of the discourse around Dilma's impeachment. While voting to impeach, legislators held up signs that said 'Tchau querida'. There is not an easy translation that captures the spirit of these words. In English, it would equate to saying something like 'Bye-bye baby' in a dismissive and callous way when breaking up with a girlfriend. Anthony says:

'There's definitely a pejorative and nasty edge to it. A combination of "Get out of here, bugger off, silly girl."'

Malu tries to capture the flavour of the words as follows:

'It means something like "Goodbye dear," but not in a nice way – in a disrespectful, dismissive way. It would never be said to a man.'

Both also spoke about stickers that were widely circulated within Brazil. These stickers, showing Dilma with her legs spread, were designed to be plastered around the door to the fuel tanks on cars. When filling up the car, the pump nozzle would look like it was penetrating the image of Dilma. A vivid reminder that, for women leaders, recourse is readily made to threats and images of rape.

Coming back to our hypothesis, it is obvious that the second part relating to the gendered imagery around women leaders who have made errors is proven. The sticker of Dilma is a revolting example.

What about the first part: do women leaders pay a greater price for errors than men? The research base says yes. Simply because women leaders are in gender-incongruent roles, in positions historically held by men, a greater backlash awaits when an error is made.

Unpacking Dilma's example yields complications and layers to the clear picture that emerges from the research. The first is around patronage. Many leaders, male and female, get to their leadership position because of the sponsorship and support of an earlier, still powerful leader. Inherently, because of the gender skew in who has held leadership positions in the past, the patron is highly likely to be a man. Is it harder for women to grow as leaders, free from the shadow cast by a patron? Do we more easily accept that a sponsored man grows into being a leader in his own right, whereas we see a woman as continuing to be the subordinate partner in the relationship, even when she holds the highest office?

These questions certainly swirled around Dilma. Of course, they arose from more than just the gender dynamic. It is true to say that Dilma would never have become president without Lula. After all, she was not even an elected politician prior to being handpicked by him. But did she stay more shackled to him in the minds of voters and political colleagues than a man would have? It is hard to say, but a tentative yes feels right.

Then, because the rituals and bonding rites of politics have been forged by men over generations, should we conclude it is more difficult for women to grow the deep web of connections with colleagues, which yield immense loyalty when times get tough?

The coalition-building culture of Brazil is an extreme example. But, in a different context, President Obama was routinely criticised for not doing enough schmoozing with congressional members to build the rapport necessary to secure his legislative agendas. Critics would urge that he should be inviting key figures to play golf with him – quite a different activity from a boozy barbecue but still an inherently male bonding ritual.

Julia intellectually feels that there is merit in this argument in general, though circumstances vary. In her own political career, she experienced immense support during even the worst of times from a core group of allies. The safest conclusion seems to be that until we reach a stage where all of the rhythms and rituals of politics are forged to suit a diverse array of parliamentarians, not just the stereotypical male, there are additional risks that support for women leaders will not become ingrained.

What about the third arm of our hypothesis: that, for women leaders, what should be political disputes spill over into legal ones? Dilma's case is not directly probative of that proposition, given the impeachment mechanism is an inherently political one, though it is supposed to be about making a judgement on whether wrongdoing sufficiently grievous to warrant removal from office has occurred.

Neither is Hillary's experience with the House of Representatives Select Committee inquiry into the 2012 tragedy in Benghazi,

Libya, when a diplomatic post was attacked by terrorists. Four Americans, including Ambassador J. Christopher Stevens, died. One would hope a probe into a matter such as this would put politics aside. That certainly did not occur in this case and, in general, congressional inquiries are political, though in format they mimic aspects of judicial proceedings, including taking evidence and issuing findings. At a public hearing, Hillary was grilled for eleven hours about her conduct as Secretary of State at the time of the incident. About this experience, she says:

'There still is an expectation that women have to be better, more honest, more public-minded. What the propagandists – particularly on the right, but it's not exclusively on the right – know is that a steady stream of attacks on a woman candidate have much greater negative impact than on a male candidate. I remember on the Benghazi hearings, which were a total political attack, the guy who was the second-ranking Republican in the House was basically asked, why do you keep these hearings up? Everybody has concluded, Republicans and Democrats alike, that it was a terrible tragedy, but nothing happened that you can pin on anybody and she didn't do anything wrong. And in reply he effectively says, just look at her numbers. We've been driving her numbers down. So the longer we keep attacking her, the more people will think there must be something wrong, even if they don't know what it is. Whereas with a lot of men it's kind of like the background noise. "You know what, I'm not perfect. I make mistakes, but that's how it is. That's how it goes." So you don't have the lasting damage. I do think attacks in a political, public context are much more successful against women candidates than against men, and it doesn't take as much to impact them.'

After thirty-three hearings and an estimated cost of US$7 million, the committee ultimately released an eight-hundred-page report in June 2016, when the campaign for the election in November was well underway. There were no findings that placed blame directly on Hillary.[10]

The chant of 'Lock her up' aimed at Hillary throughout the 2016 election campaign and since seems to show that her most ardent haters will never be satisfied just by an electoral defeat. Instead, they want to see her arrested, charged, prosecuted and behind bars.

Dilma's and Hillary's experiences do not extend to actual legal proceedings. Julia has experience to share that does. She is the only Australian prime minister ever forced to face a royal commission, which is a form of politically initiated inquiry that has special legal powers, into her personal conduct. The inquiry was held after she had left politics and had nothing to do with her actions in office. Instead, it related to matters that occurred years before she was elected to parliament. The fact she was exonerated of any legal wrongdoing has not stopped hardcore haters saying she too should be locked up.

Christine also faced an unusual legal proceeding after she left office. It was in relation to a government payment made during her time as Finance Minister in France. There was never any allegation of misappropriation or personal benefits acquired by her with respect to this payment. Yet, she was brought before a special tribunal, which has only ever met on four other occasions and combines judges with political representatives. While this body found her guilty of negligence, no conviction was recorded and no punishment was ordered. Even the chief French prosecutor in the trial, Jean-Claude Marin, described the evidence against her as 'very weak'.[11]

Throughout this politically charged period in France, Christine carried on her duties at the International Monetary

Fund assiduously. She had the respect and support of her peers in the international community, who admired her graceful handling of the tough situation in which she found herself.

These two examples are probably not a big enough corpus of evidence to declare the third arm of our hypothesis proven. But it does seem right to say that women leaders should be on the lookout for opponents grasping for ways to do extra harm, beyond the usual machinations of politics. Hillary's theory about women being held to a higher standard and so being more easily tarnished does fit well with what we have learnt through examining the style conundrum.

Looking at our hypothesis as a whole, our conclusion is that we might not be living in modern-day Salem, but it is too soon to be forgetting that history.

And, in case you are wondering what happened next in Brazil: in 2018 Jair Bolsonaro, a former military officer on the political far right, was elected president. Prior to his election he had been a member of parliament. When he cast his vote in favour of Dilma's impeachment, he dedicated his act to Carlos Brilhante Ustra, an army colonel who, during the days of the dictatorship and Dilma's own imprisonment, was the head of a torture unit.[12]

11

Hypothesis eight:
The role-modelling riddle

Writing this book, we had in our minds the simple and, we hoped, potent idea that reading about the real lives of our leaders would inspire women to walk their own pathways to power. In keeping with the approach of the book, we thought our shared belief should be subject to scrutiny and testing. It is the final hypothesis we present to you and can be pithily summarised by the saying, 'You can't be it if you can't see it'; that is, that *Exposure to women in leadership roles enables women and girls to see the door is open and encourages them to step through it.* There are two different but equally important aspects of this hypothesis, namely that role models both lift ambition and change behaviour.

Perhaps at this point we should be writing 'spoiler alert' because, fortunately, we find this hypothesis, which is so foundational to this book, proven, especially for young women. Having digested that fact, now please imagine your authors high-fiving and saying 'phew' to each other.

Given we are talking about gender, though, which is so complex and nuanced, the more we thought and worked, the more we came to see that the result of role-modelling is not simple and linear. It is not as predictable as saying that if a woman or girl sees a role model, then she experiences increased ambition or acts differently.

In this chapter, we dive into some of the factors that give role-modelling its power, and some that detract from its potential impact. This exposes what we see as a riddle about how to be the best role model, which we try to solve.

Before delving into the knotty and vexed parts, let us prove the hypothesis to you. We start with a unique study of the role-modelling effect of women leading villages in India.[1] We briefly mentioned this research in chapter 2, but it is so important we now want to work through its details.

As we have remarked elsewhere in this book, one of the frustrations of research into gender biases is that it is nearly impossible to do a control test. When analysing new pharmaceuticals, scientists undertake randomised trials in which some patients get the new drug while others get a placebo with no active ingredients. This process enables conclusions to be reached with some precision about the efficacy of the new product. If the patients taking it experience improved health and those taking the placebo do not, then it is safe to conclude that the pill or potion works.

Life does not provide us with these kinds of laboratory conditions. We are always left wondering whether things would have played out the same if a man was in the same set of circumstances as a woman leader. Thankfully, a 1993 decision by the Indian government created a real-world control trial. A law was enacted that meant at each election cycle in a randomly selected group of villages only women would be able to nominate for election as the local leader. As a result, villages that had never had a woman in charge could be compared to those in which a woman had served as leader once. Both could then be compared to villages that had been required in two elections to elect a woman leader. This enabled conclusions to be drawn about the 'dose' effect, whether having a woman leader more than once made more of a difference.

By surveying the attitudes of parents and children, this body of work showed that in villages that had a woman leader, the aspirations of girls themselves and parents for their daughters increased. Interestingly, there was a significant jump in the number of fathers who thought their daughters could become a leader after experiencing their village being led by a woman.

Seeing and being subject to female leadership, adolescent girls changed both their perspectives and their behaviour. The changed outlook on their aspirations for their own lives included an increased predisposition to say they wanted to get an education and choose their own job, rather than being a housewife or having their future in-laws pick their occupation for them, which was a common feature of community life. In addition, the girls were more likely to say that they did not want to marry until after the age of eighteen.

Rising ambition was linked to changed behaviours. As a result of envisaging more of a future for themselves, the value the girls put on study changed. In the villages that had had two women leaders, the gender gap in classroom results between boys and girls was either erased or reversed. The dose effect was very clear here. More than one woman leader was required to change educational outcomes.

Apart from the randomised control trial standard, other notable features of this research are how direct and close the role model was to the girls. The woman leader was like them and near them because she came from the same village.

What happens if we broaden the frame and look at role models who are not so closely connected? Fortunately, there is a great deal of research on the power of female role-modelling in politics to help us answer that question.

The backdrop to much of the research is the comparative lack of interest in politics by women compared to men. For example, studies have shown that women score lower in political knowledge quizzes than men, are less interested in campaigns and are less likely to discuss politics with their family and friends.[2]

Understandably, that has prompted academics and others to ask the question, does seeing more female role models in politics lift engagement levels by women? Overwhelmingly the answer has been yes. For example, a cross-national study of twenty-three countries, including European nations, the United States and Australia, found 'Women of all ages are more likely to discuss politics, and younger women become more politically active when there are more women in parliament.'[3] Similar results have been shown in sub-Saharan Africa and in Latin America.[4][5]

We need to be aware of the links in the chain that are being revealed to us by these studies. The first link is interest in politics. Obviously this matters because no one is going to say to themselves, 'Gee, I want to become president or prime minister' if, up until that point in their lives, they had little interest in politics.

The second link is getting active. If men disproportionately take that step and women do not, then that skew will likely have an effect on all the other links in the chain: who steps forward to be selected as a candidate, who gets elected and who gets to the top.

The research is telling us that the increased presence of role models impacts the initial link in the chain for women generally, and the first two links in the chain, being interested and getting active, for younger women.

All of this probably sits easily with your intuitive feelings. Ordinary life experience demonstrates that it is often easier for women to both imagine themselves doing something and then to actually get out and do it if they have had the benefit of seeing a woman role model.

Even small children respond to role-modelling gender cues. A cute study that illustrates this is the classic social science experiment of getting children to draw scientists. As more women have gone into science and learning materials have been more careful about not reinforcing gender stereotypes, more of the artwork depicts female scientists, with girls being more likely to draw women.[6]

Based on all this research and analysis, we are prepared to declare our hypothesis proven but with the nuance that the effect of role-modelling on behaviours is greatest for younger women. That does not mean that older women cannot change their lives and embrace activism, politics and leadership for the first time. However, it makes sense that an older woman with no previous history of involvement and a life full of existing obligations is less likely to choose to do so.

If, like your authors, you have several decades of life experience already behind you, do not be downhearted as a result of these words. As we wrote this book, Nancy Pelosi, the Speaker of the US House of Representatives, was very frequently a prominent figure in global news reports at eighty years old. She commenced her initial term as Speaker in January 2007, when she was sixty-six years old, having first been elected into Congress in her late forties.

Nancy's formidable presence feels like a rebuke to any idea that aspiring to be or becoming a leader is only for the young. Her example shows that women can kick political butt at any age.

At this stage you may be thinking this whole role-modelling thing is easy. In recent years, we have seen some improvement in the gender diversity of politics, so doesn't it follow that with more women stepping in to parliament, more women will go on to become leading political figures? Then, girls and young women will see more female role models, get more interested in politics and become active, which means they are more likely to run themselves, and then there will be even more women in politics. A few turns through this virtuous cycle and job done, right?

To that, we have two 'if only'-style caveats. First, as we have shown throughout this book, women who get interested, get involved and then choose a career in politics can face barriers that prevent them getting a start or rising through the ranks once there. Whether it is work and family life dilemmas, being seen as 'a bit of a bitch' or getting trapped in the style conundrum, there is a glass labyrinth between being a political aspirant and getting to the top.

Second, while we hate to break it you, role-modelling is not quite that simple. There is a riddle at the centre of it and, unfortunately, it is not the kind that produces giggles. In this chapter we reveal this unfunny problem by working our way through the various limitations of role-modelling.

Let's get started by discussing the first constraint on the power of role-modelling, which is a time-based one. As we have seen, the presence of more women on the political stage matters. What is true of increased numbers of female legislators is also true of even more high-profile women, like presidents and prime ministers. But what happens when a leading woman is gone? Unfortunately, it appears that the extra interest dies away.

Ian McAllister, a researcher at the Australian National University, produced a fascinating study on precisely this point.[7] He had available to him a clear dataset for comparison because the political knowledge of voters, male and female, has been tested across many national elections in Australia. That meant Ian was able to zero in on the difference Julia's prime ministership made to the political knowledge of women voters.

His study looks at the national elections in 2007, 2013 and 2016, in which both the prime minister and the primary contender to take that top spot, the leader of the opposition, were men. The political knowledge of women and men at the time of those elections was then compared with the 2010 election, in which Julia as prime minister was pitted against a male opposition leader. Ian's study found that the gap in knowledge between men and women was reduced to 'statistical insignificance' in the 2010 election, whereas in all the other elections men outscored women on this measure.

In addition, 2010 was the only time when women and men were on par in expressing the view that they were paying a 'great deal' of attention to the election. In all other elections, it was men who disproportionately said that they were closely following the campaign.

What is different about this study is the ability to get such a clear chronological progression, looking both before a woman stood on centrestage and after she has exited. The results show that having a woman break the glass ceiling does matter to the first link in the chain – women's interest in politics – but the gains are not sustained if the system then goes back to looking like it is male-led business as usual.

To really see sustained changes, politics has to deliver more and more prominence to women over time, or at least not reduce their presence. This observation is not put forward in order to advocate that every leader should be a woman so that there is no risk of backsliding on women's interest in politics. Rather, it is offered as evidence about what degree of change should be viewed as enough to make a difference. If there is only one woman, or the occasional woman leader, it is unsurprising that that does not really change the alienation caused by the perception that political leadership is basically the domain of men.

Similarly, if the number of women in parliament increases, but then it gets stuck at a number like a quarter or a third, it would be cavalier to assume ever-rising levels of interest in politics from young women. Much more likely, a plateau would be reached with interest levels that are still lower than those of men, even though there would have been an increase from the earlier baseline when there were fewer women in politics.

A second constraint arises from the fact that watching a role model means seeing her whole experience, not just the good bits. Unfortunately, what happens to women in politics is not always a great advertisement for getting involved. When a woman political leader is seen to have been badly treated on gender grounds, that message is heard loud and clear.

To take one example, in Julia's hometown of Adelaide, the University of Adelaide and the local Young Women's Christian Association (YWCA), which in its modern iteration pursues feminist issues, conducted an online survey about young women's political aspirations. The results were released in early 2014 and showed that the gendered treatment of Julia as prime minister had been so disillusioning that two-thirds of those who had previously expressed an interest in going into politics now said they were less likely to want to do so.[8]

Undoubtedly, those answering in this small survey group were not a representative sample of the whole community. Instead, these young women were already interested in feminism and overwhelmingly held progressive personal politics. But that does not make the result any less disheartening, given one would have hoped that it is exactly this kind of young woman who would be most inspired by witnessing a female leader from Australia's centre-left party. Sadly, respondents saw Julia's treatment by the media as unfair and demeaning, and this drove them away.

From these two constraints we can learn two lessons. It seems that for role-modelling to really work, it needs not only to be sustained over time, but the experience of the role models cannot be too negatively gendered. Our women leaders are conscious of this, with Theresa specifically denying that her removal from the leadership of her political party was a sexist act. She says:

'I'm pleased that there are young women who look positively on having had a female prime minister, and who say that is spurring them on in whatever it is that they're doing. I'm disappointed about what they saw at the end, and I know there are those who say it was all the boys and so forth. But it wasn't about gender. Overall, I hope there's a sense among a cohort of girls that there is no limit to what they can do.'

Jacinda prospectively puts forward a similar message. She says:

'My goal is for young people in the future to be able to look back at my time in politics and see that you can be yourself and survive, comfortable in your own skin.'

Of course, she knows that the rules of representative democracy mean she will finish being prime minister at some point, and she expresses the hope that, when her time in office ultimately comes to an end, it is viewed as '*normal to politics*', with gender not a factor.

A further constraint is that the outcome of role-modelling seems, in part, to depend on the relatability of the woman leader. A field of study called social identity theory tries to get to grips with when a person will put someone in the same category as themselves, relate to them and be inspired to emulate their achievements, as opposed to seeing them as different.

Turning to politics, being of the same gender is one characteristic that helps women relate to a leader, but it is not the only one. There are class, race and other dynamics. A girl from a disadvantaged background may feel no real connection to a woman leader who comes from a wealthy, upper crust family. If women in politics are all of one race, or all heterosexual, or all able-bodied, then a girl with characteristics other than those may not find them relatable. Indeed, what may well happen is not positive role-modelling but alienation. The message heard and received could be that girls like you do not make it.

One outlier piece of research on role-modelling from those cited above is focused on East and South-East Asia.[9] It shows an inverse relationship between both female and male interest in politics and greater numbers of women entering parliament. Without further work it is impossible to say whether this result is pointing to cultural differences or varies because, unlike many other studies, it includes systems of government that are not democracies.

It may also be that images of female leadership in the region are not seen as relatable, given most of the prominent women leaders who have served to date had family connections to a leading man. For example, both President Megawati Sukarnoputri of Indonesia and President Park Geun-hye of South Korea are the daughters of former presidents. President Corazon Aquino of the Philippines became leader of the opposition after the assassination of her husband, Senator Benigno Aquino Jr. President Yingluck Shinawatra of Thailand came to office after her brother, who also served as president, was ousted in a military coup and exiled. Perhaps this has sent a message that politics is the preserve of a particular kind of person, not the overall population.

Shared personal characteristics are not the only factors that feed into relatability, though. There is a line between seeing a high achiever and believing you can emulate her, and concluding she is so extraordinary that it is impossible you could ever do what she has done. At one level, this proposition is just common sense and we can feel it at work in our own lives. For example, we might well watch a gold-medal-winning woman athlete with admiration, but the vast majority of us are not going to try out for the next Olympic Games.

However, this line manifests itself even when the high achievers are in the same field of endeavour and there are no objective reasons others cannot do what she has done. Evidence from a number of studies shows that, even in these circumstances, role models can fail to inspire if women conclude their achievements are unattainable. This will happen if the high achiever is perceived as having characteristics that are well outside the norm, like being super-intelligent or hyper-energetic.[10]

Which side of that line a potential role model falls is always up for grabs. In politics, every woman leader is likely to have heard both 'I want to do what you have done' and 'I could never be like you.'

The women leaders in this book are undoubtedly aware of

this line and through their leadership have wanted to include and inspire, rather than alienate by painting an image of themselves as extraordinary. Each has strived to be as encouraging as possible to the next generation of up-and-comers; to not put their success down to something unique to them, but instead present it as a future that can be realised by other women. In part, this flows from their preparedness to be candid about the highs and lows, stresses and strains, doubts and triumphs.

Yet, ironically, this is the core of the issues with role-modelling. If a leader makes it sound as if it has been easy for her, women analysing her achievements are very likely to conclude she is a special kind of human being. That is excluding, not inspiring, because women will not see themselves as like her. But research also shows that candid conversations about how difficult it all can be may put women off.

For example, a field experiment in Switzerland traced the result of women members of parliament having open discussions about what the job is really like with young, interested university students.[11] The topics included things like the difficulties of getting work and family life to fit together, with one woman detailing the problems she faced when she was first elected. At the time she was the only woman in the legislature, lived far from the capital and had young children.

The result of all this honesty was that the young women were put off considering a political career. The researchers do point out that there are special features of the Swiss system, including the fact that being in parliament is not usually a full-time job. Rather, elected representatives have jobs and attend to their political duties outside of normal working hours. Obviously, for a working mother, this exacerbates challenges like accessing child care.

On the other hand, it would seem too dismissive to say this research has no relevance outside of the nation in which it was conducted. As the study itself says, 'Nevertheless, the issue of work–life balance is not specific to the Swiss case. Political careers are extremely demanding on politicians' private lives.'

While calling for more research, the paper on this role-modelling experiment concludes:

'One hypothesis arising from this study is that role models can fail to motivate women to pursue a political career if they discuss their experience bluntly instead of following a motivational script.'

Where does that leave us? Apparently, superwoman is an alienating role model and so is the super-honest woman who speaks frankly about the problems she has encountered. That is our role-modelling riddle.

In light of it, should women leaders engage in spin or follow, as suggested above, a 'motivational script'? How would that read? Something like:

'I am human, just like you, and some days feel harder than others. But politics is a terrific profession through which you can change the world, and any issues about being a woman in politics can be worked through. I know because I have done it, and you can too.'

These are fine words, and we thoroughly endorse the sentiment. But are these words too glib? Will they hold up when women ask their role models for more specifics about the challenges faced? Will they sound hollow when the real world comes calling?

A clear contemporary example of the kind of problem that cannot be hidden by spin is the toxic nature of much of the online environment for women. This is the subject of ongoing reporting, but it came into particular focus in late 2019 in the run-up to the

UK general election. A number of very high-profile Conservative Party women announced they would not be standing for re-election and pointed to abuse online as a factor in their decision.

A collateral debate broke out about whether the number of women retiring was unusual or not. Statistics circulated saying that nineteen out of the fifty-nine members of parliament standing down were female, equalling 32 per cent. It was said this result was to be expected given that 32 per cent of all elected representatives were women.

However, on a second glance, it became clear that, particularly among the governing Tory party, the resignations were disproportionately coming from women who were viewed to be on the up in their political career, not at the natural end. This was a different pattern compared with men who were leaving. The *Guardian* published a piece saying the women were on average ten years younger and had spent a decade less in parliament.[12]

The rollcall of those leaving did include well known cabinet ministers and women seen as having leadership potential. A number of them directly referenced abuse, including on social media, among their list of reasons for exiting politics. Caroline Spelman, who was leaving at the end of a long career, summed this up on behalf of others by saying:

'Sexually charged rhetoric has been prevalent in the online abuse for female MPs, with threats to rape us and referring to us by our genitalia . . . Myself, my family and my staff have borne an enormous brunt of abuse and I think quite frankly we've had enough.'[13]

This election was being held three years after the Brexit referendum. During the campaigning around the referendum, a Labour Party member of parliament, Jo Cox, was murdered while out on the hustings. That hideous act of violence showed that the ugliness is not just confined to the virtual world. Caroline Spelman referred to wearing a panic alarm around her neck.[14]

Exploring the reasons for the resignation of so many promising women prior to the election, Sky News reporter Beth Rigby wrote:

'I have been told that one female MP is standing down at the behest of her child, who is racked by anxiety that her mother will be harmed at work. Another MP, who said she was quitting because of intolerable levels of abuse, has been stalked by a local man who was subsequently jailed for harassment.'[15]

Labour's Diane Abbott, who was the first black woman elected to the UK Parliament, did recontest in 2019 and continues to serve as a politician. She faces the double whammy of sexist and racist abuse online. An Amnesty International report about the 2017 UK election showed Twitter abuse was disproportionately directed at women, with the five parliamentary members who received the most abuse all women. Stunningly, it showed that Diane 'was the target of almost a third (31.61%) of all abusive tweets we analysed. She received even more abuse in the six weeks leading up to 2017's snap general election, when 45.14% of abusive tweets were aimed at her.

This amounts to an average 51 abusive tweets per day over the 158 day study.

The type of abuse she receives often focuses on her gender and race, and includes threats of sexual violence.'[16]

Diane took leave towards the end of the campaign and spoke of her experience in the following terms:

'It's the volume of it which makes it so debilitating, so corrosive, and so upsetting. It's the sheer volume. And the sheer level of hatred that people are showing . . . It's highly racialised and it's also gendered because people talk about rape and they talk about my physical appearance in a way they wouldn't talk about a man. I'm abused as a female politician and I'm abused as a black politician.'[17]

In the lead-up to the 2019 election campaign, she described her strategy to cope as 'putting one foot in front of the other.'[18]

Diane's words are a reminder to us all about the importance of recognising intersectionality, which is a long and cumbersome word for the simple concept that discrimination compounds. Sexism is not the only form of bias. Racism and prejudices based on sexuality, gender identity, disability and health status – especially mental ill health – are all too real. That means for millions and millions of women, negotiating their way through each and every day entails confronting more than one form of discrimination.

Among our leaders, none of them reached the top in a nation where the majority of the population did not share their skin colour. We are conscious that this means that our book does not thoroughly explore intersectionality.

Ellen, Joyce and Ngozi are black women but their periods of political leadership were in their home African nations. In her novel *Americanah*, Chimamanda Ngozi Adichie puts beautifully the difference between being black in Africa compared with being black in a society that identifies itself as white:

'I came from a country where race was not an issue: I did not think of myself as black and I only became black when I came to America.'[19]

Michelle, in the various periods she lived in the United States, would have been labelled Hispanic, but in her own country she did not face racist prejudice.

That does not mean that our women leaders have zero experience of encountering the combination of sexism and racism during the times they have lived and worked outside their own nations.

For example, Ellen recalls:

'At UNDP, I was the first African woman to lead [as Assistant Secretary General overseeing the Africa Regional Bureau of the United Nations Development Programme] and some of those in the organisation were rebellious about that. There was this idea of, "How can she run this thing? She's a woman from some poor African country where she was Finance Minister, there's not much to that." You can see that type of thing in their eyes.'

Ngozi also recalls earlier in her career at the World Bank when she was the task team leader for a project in Thailand. In this role she led a three-week supervision mission in that country. All her team members were older male engineers, agriculturists and other specialists. Each time the group met government officials or village elders, remarks were addressed to the oldest man on the team even after Ngozi had been introduced as the team leader. Ngozi says:

'I could see doubt and a question in their eyes: how can a young black woman be the leader of this important team? Not possible.'

Kamala Harris had to confront both sexism and racism within her nation during a sharply partisan election campaign. TIME'S UP Now provided statistical analysis of the gendered and racist nature of commentary, including finding that, in the two weeks following the announcement of Kamala as a vice presidential candidate, there were more than 11,000 online news articles about her using biased language. Twenty-one million people actively engaged with this content by liking, sharing or commenting on it.

Despite these kinds of findings and the seemingly perpetual onslaught of abuse on social media and its interrelationships with gender and race, interestingly and hearteningly, more women, including women of colour, ran for election in the US House of Representatives in 2020 than ever before. Progress, but nowhere near equality, given that as of September 2020 women supported by major parties made up 35.6 per cent of all US House nominees and 30.8 per cent of US Senate nominees.[20]

Similarly, in the United Kingdom, in 2019 more women were elected to the House of Commons than ever before, with the number now at 34 per cent.[21] This total includes a record number of women from BAME backgrounds, which is a term used in the UK to refer to people from black, Asian or minority ethnic groups.[22] Progress, but nowhere near equality.

It may be that, with eyes wide open, women will continue to choose to stand anyway. However, we feel that more time needs to go by before we can truly analyse how the treatment of candidates like Kamala and the social media landscape of abuse against women ultimately comes to influence women's willingness to consider political careers.

Theresa recontested the 2019 election as a member of parliament and is clearly concerned about the changing nature of politics, including social media. She says:

'In the past few decades we've been through difficult policy issues, but in the context of a relatively benign political environment, including an expectation about how politics will be conducted. In general, not always, there has been respect and willingness to argue things. Now we've got into a quite different scenario, and the natural fallout of that is that women are more likely to be put off by it.'

With these words, Theresa is pointing to a broader problem about the political temper of the times, of which social media abuse is a symptom.

Against this exploration of a pressing, visible, real-world gender problem, we return to consideration of our role-modelling riddle. In our view, the reality means that there is no way women leaders can sanitise the experience when they are talking about life in politics. No motivational script could ever be enough to completely conceal from women who are potential political aspirants the facts and challenges so squarely in front of their faces.

Even if it somehow could, there would be a profound lack of honesty and authenticity at the heart of such an endeavour. Women leaders would likely feel disingenuous doing anything other than telling it like it really is. In addition, papering over gender issues by trying to ignore or diminish them is not a strategy for long-term change. Our world can only eradicate the gender bias in politics, and leadership generally, if it is identified, discussed, studied and challenged, and evidence-based change strategies are implemented. A 'this is fine, nothing to see here' approach is anathema to working our way through that process.

When we met with Hillary, she suggested we call this book 'Conundrums', and we were quite attracted to that idea, though we ultimately picked a different title. But Hillary's word really applies in this context. Considering how to be an honest, inspiring, inclusive role model for women and girls requires working through conundrums, trying to solve the vexing problems we have exposed and explored.

There is no simple answer. But, for us, a key message has been that women leaders who are being asked to speak as role models always need to start with why it is wonderful to be a leader. After all, what better use of one's lifetime can there be than steering and shaping the future?

Being a leader brings moments of great joy that should never be underestimated. When speaking to women and girls, it can be easy to assume that they are already keen to lead, and therefore to jump over pointing out the many amazing aspects in favour of giving 'how-to' tips on facing the gender challenges. As a result, women leaders might dive right in to discussing the hard bits. We definitely believe role models should be frank about the kinds of issues we have examined in this book. But the framing of that conversation matters. Skipping over exploring why it is wonderful and worthwhile to be a leader risks putting women off, rather than having them step forward.

A great mentor for Julia was Joan Kirner, the first woman to ever lead the government of the state of Victoria as premier. Joan was subject to dreadful sexist abuse while in office and, seared by that, dedicated much of her time post-politics to creating a better political world for women. She was the leader of the campaign within the Australian Labor Party for the affirmative action target, and pivotal to the creation of Emily's List, a body that funds and supports women candidates. It would have been easy for Joan to harp on about negative experiences. After all, she had her own scars and would have heard more horror stories every day from the many women candidates and politicians she nurtured. Julia's recollection, though, is that Joan always reinforced the 'why'. She emphasised why politics is important, why being on that public policy front line mattered. In her talks with aspiring young women today, Julia endeavours to do the same, and advises that not only should you be clear about the sense of purpose that drives you, it should be written down and carried with you day by day. Julia did this herself as prime minister and found having a touchstone within easy reach was steadying and uplifting.

Let's always share the power of the positive first and find ways to carry it with us.

12

The stand-out lessons from eight lives and eight hypotheses

For aspiring leaders – Be aware, not beware

Initially, we intended to call this section 'The stand-out lessons for young women'. However, as discussed in the previous chapter, while writing this book we have become far more vehement about rejecting ageism and embracing ambition for all women.

Why the words 'Be aware, not beware'? The answer flows from the analysis of role-modelling canvassed in the previous chapter. It is an insult to the intelligence of women and girls to try to delude them by ignoring or minimising the challenges. We want aspiring leaders to be aware of the gender dimensions.

That being said, we do not want anything we write to put off even a single woman or girl from aiming to be a leader. Our message is the exact opposite of beware. Rather, it is *GO FOR IT!* And yes, we are *SHOUTING*. That's how strongly we feel about the need for women, in all their diversity and in record numbers, to aim to be leaders in every field.

In this concluding chapter, we want to distil the lessons our leaders have shared and offer some other general insights on achieving equality in leadership.

First, we want to speak personally and directly to the women and girls who look at the seat at the head of the top table and aspire to it. We offer for your consideration the following ten lessons. Eight of these we believe can be learnt from the words of our women leaders. Two we offer to you from our own experiences.

Given this book has focused on women and political leadership, we have tended to express these lessons in terms that are most relevant to those considering a future as a parliamentarian, a minister, a political appointee, a prime minister or a president. We are convinced that these lessons, which have resonance in the white-hot spotlight of political leadership, are also worthwhile for women seeking to be leaders in business, the law, news media, technology, local communities and countless other meaningful pursuits.

As you walk your pathway to power, we hope you feel better informed and equipped as a result of the contents of this book, and these lessons in particular. But it is not our job to preach. Ultimately, whether you accept and how you apply these findings is up to you. Please view this as a buffet from which to select the most appealing items. Obviously, we would love it if you took big servings.

Lesson One – Leadership actually isn't 'all about the hair', but sadly judgements about women are still based more on their appearance than is true for men. Knowing this does not necessarily mean you should do anything, let alone change your style in any way. We are not recommending a wardrobe consultant and a make-up artist. But we also do not want you to be surprised or discomfited when there is commentary about how you look. Expect it.

One strategy our leaders have employed to try to minimise discussion about how they appear is to develop a standard look, including outfit, hairstyle and make-up. A bit like a uniform. People may have opinions about whether they like the chosen uniform or not, but the lack of variation means there is no point in having that chat each and every day.

For some of you, this approach may seem sensible, even a relief. Like Barack Obama, you may be grateful to not need to ask yourself every day, 'What should I wear?' For others who enjoy fashion this might sound like a living death, a stifling of one of your preferred creative outlets. But it need not be. Ngozi deployed her flair to develop a certain African look that has become her unique brand. In the end, it is all up to you, but when you make your choices, do so understanding that while it is very unfair, they will have consequences.

Often political parties will access styling services for both women and men. This can be a useful process because there are some things these experts can tell you, including very practical guidance, like which spectacle frames throw too much light for television or which clothing patterns cause strobing on camera.

We suggest that you be wary of any gendered advice in this process. For example, Julia recalls that when she was first a candidate, the team taking the campaign photographs always advised men to wear suits and women to wear bright block colours. Julia is quite happy to wear the occasional coloured jacket. She did wonder, however, for the central image that would be used on all election material, whether anyone had thought through the potential for popping, pretty hues to lead some voters to the conclusion that the women should be taken less seriously. As she remarked at the time, photographs of Winston Churchill giving his renowned speeches as he led the United Kingdom in World War II do not show him wearing canary yellow.

Lesson Two – There is no right way to be a woman leader. Your style of leadership is precisely that – uniquely your own, not someone else's.

That is true of our women leaders, yet each of them honestly described how they did self-limit their behaviour in some way because of what we label in this book the style conundrum. Women leaders need to walk a tightrope between being seen to have authority while not being seen to lack empathy and nurturing skills.

In the face of this knowledge, which has been shared by our women leaders and backed up by the research, what should you do? The answer to that might well be nothing. As a future genera-tion of leaders, you may decide to push the current boundaries of the acceptable range of conduct for women in the public eye. Be aware that will be noticed and commented on.

You may also take the view that you want your leadership energy to go elsewhere and that you are prepared to think through the style conundrum in order to minimise distractions from your key messages and actions. Once again, the choice is up to you.

A subset of this debate is how visibly you want to be seen to own your ambition. There is nothing wrong with a proud declar-ation that you are aiming for the top, you have what it takes, you are ready to be a great leader. If that is the way you feel, you may choose to plainly state it. We would applaud that because we feel an itchy frustration with the gendered problems around squarely claiming leadership ambitions. But we know those words will be weighed differently coming from a woman than a man and that this is a decision with consequences.

There are still issues to think through for women who choose to express their ambition to lead as arising because they wish to be of service, stress how lots of luck has brought them opportunities, or emphasise the way they have been supported by others. As we have discussed in this book, all this is the safer course. However, there is a judgement call to be made between giving a response that may be well received by the audience but is not too self-effacing or passive.

Lesson Three – Erna talked about trying to out-smile the problem of being seen as 'a bit of a bitch'. Can this work? Maybe, and many of you might think it is worth a try. Who doesn't like to smile, and if it solves a problem at the same time, all the better.

It should be noted that whether our women leaders felt the 'she's a bit of a bitch' hypothesis applied to them was very context-specific. Hillary shared her experience of negative electoral campaigning and Joyce recounted being compared to a cow. Taking leadership from a man, appearing in adversarial environments and being in the centre of highly polarised political campaigns all seemed to enhance the likelihood of this criticism.

Political leaders or aspirants for leadership never get to control the whole context, but you can be analytical of it. It is worth asking yourself from time to time, is the current climate one in which the 'she's a bit of a bitch' summation is likely to come to the foreground? If it is, then knowing that and thinking about strategies to minimise its impact seem to us to be important. Should you try to forestall the problem by sparking a debate on gender, leadership and these kinds of characterisations? A secondary question is whether you should lead this debate or ask others to do so. It is always hard to be received as genuine about wanting an open discussion if you are seen to have personal stakes in the outcome, or 'skin in the game'.

Alternatively, should your public positioning strategy be deliberately calibrated to counter this critique, and include activities and messages that show your caring, sharing attributes, rather than allowing others to reduce you without contest to the caricature of 'a bitch'? All decisions for you, but certainly an issue to be thoughtful about. As we have detailed, once this characterisation takes hold, it can be impossible to shift.

Lesson Four – Our women leaders do not point to the one best way to manage work and family life, including children. There is obviously no handbook or set of rules that will work for everyone. One clear message from our women leaders is the need to work through with your partner what the rigours of leadership, in politics or any other field of endeavour, will mean for your family. Doing this early can make it more manageable to strike an arrangement that works later.

Another lesson from our leaders is that there will be some guilt. Expect it and think in advance about how you will cope with it. The message in this book should reassure you. Our women leaders are clear that it is survivable. They continue to enjoy strong relationships with their children despite the most dramatic sacrifices of family time having been made during their careers.

A related dimension to consider is that leadership is not forever. While there will be some in the coming generation of politicians who go into parliament and remain there for several decades, like in other fields of endeavour, the norm seems to be changing and it is likely that being in politics will be one career among many held over a lifetime of work. At the ultimate level of being prime minister or president, between political cycles and term limits, the time period of service is normally measured in a few years, not long decades.

For these reasons, in planning your life, whether your aim is politics or leadership in any other field, you can think about it in periods – years when you will step fully forward into the world, and years when you will step back and be more intensively in the family domain. We suggest not framing the decision to enter politics or have any other career or leadership position as an all-or-nothing proposition: 'If I do it then it will take me away from my family forever.' It won't.

The discussion by our leaders also reminds us that there is a shared interest by women and men in pushing politics to be more inclusive of family life. The next generation of male leaders is less likely than previous ones to have family structures that include a wife who does not work. Men too will want to be able to combine politics with being present parents. In the cause of improving this aspect of politics, our advice is it is never too early to start, and everyone should be active. Even before you have children, even if you are not going to have children or your offspring are all grown up, you can be involved in advocating for change.

As part of the campaign, look at good examples from around the world. The Australian Parliament House has a childcare centre. The House of Commons in the United Kingdom has granted a woman politician the ability to appoint a locum who can manage her electorate work while she is on maternity leave. Erna talked about the special features of the Norwegian system. Sparking a global race to have the best conditions, not only in politics but in all workplaces, would be a terrific outcome for both women and men.

So too would exhibiting thoughtfulness about family choices, including if a woman makes a decision to not have children. As we have discussed in this book, women and men can use that to criticise and diminish a childless woman as out of touch. We can and should be better than that.

Lesson Five – The politics of scarcity will tear women as a collective apart if we let it. As you climb towards higher and higher levels of leadership, there will be more competition. That is really how it should be. To bolster the vibrancy of our democracies, we want many people to aspire to lead, rather than turning away.

These contests will sometimes pit you against men, sometimes against women, sometimes against both. If the contest is structured as between you and another woman or other women, we suggest taking a moment to stop and think. Ask yourself, is this fair or is this a set-up? Are the women being forced to knock each other out in a contest on a narrow track to a limited number of leadership spots while, as the women fight it out, men scoop up the bigger share of the positions?

If you conclude yes, it is unfair; that does not necessarily mean you should refuse to put yourself forward in the contest. After all, as supporters of gender equality, as part of an interim strategy we may prefer to see some women getting through than none at all. To take an example from the business world, we would rather see 30 per cent of directorships on a corporate board going to women than nothing.

However, the fact that women are involving themselves in contests for the limited number of opportunities available should not detract from the need to put our energies into the deeper agenda of sweeping away the rigged rules of the game. At an individual level, that means do not get so carried away with the fight for the spot you want that you ignore the vital structural reforms needed. If you do not get the role and another woman does, do not undermine her in a gendered way. That would deserve a special place in hell.

Turning squarely to politics, we believe it is important to recognise that the current era is one of enhanced tribalism. This can be seen in the predispositions of political supporters, the frenzied and often ugly exchanges on Twitter, and the ever-harder-hitting and more personal tone of political debates. As women, we should be conscious that all these forces mean it can be harder to support other women in politics. To take one example: if a woman from another political party is being criticised in a sexist way, the partisanship of politics can make it harder to live up to Abby Wambach's sentiments and rush towards her.

This is a problem worth thinking about in advance, before the heat of the moment and the need to make a split-second judgement call. Hopefully, we can all commit to finding ways to be better supporters of other women, even in divisive environments.

In addition, there is continuing work to do on developing networks and organisations that assist women to get into politics, and thrive and achieve once there. Inevitably, much of the advice under this subheading has been framed around individual women and choices. It is important to recognise though that all the big advances for women have been made because of collective action, so the structures that bring women activists together are vital.

There are practical constraints on time and energy to consider. We are not suggesting that you are failing unless, every day, on top of your huge workload, you add the extra activity of getting out and supporting other women. As our women interviewees have said themselves, sometimes on top of being a leader and caring for family, picking up more work can be all too much. Yet even on those days when you cannot positively lean in to help another woman, you can make sure you are not doing anything to block her. You can share the occasional kind and encouraging word. Even if you cannot be as active as you would like within women's organisations, you can endorse their work.

Overall, we suggest taking a life-cycle approach. You may not be able to assist, mentor and sponsor women or attend feminist meetings every day, but there will be periods in your life when you have the time and space to make a real difference. We urge you to use them to maximum advantage to pay it forward or as your way of paying back the women who have gone before and made space for you.

Lesson Six – Imagine yourself in the heated final week of an election campaign. Opinion polling shows that it is possible your party will win, but a boost in the last few days before voting would help. Getting elected will create the opportunity to implement a huge array of policies that matter for gender equality. A scandal breaks out around misuse of parliamentary travel entitlements by a leading woman in another political party. It is clear that she has taken a taxpayer-funded flight when she should not have. Usually such matters cause a bit of political embarrassment and repayment of the monies improperly claimed. This time, your party's campaign team quickly develops a damning advertisement that depicts her as a thief and promises she will be prosecuted. Test groups of undecided voters who are shown the commercial are so influenced in their views they say they will now vote for your political party. It is your decision. Do you put the advertisement to air? After all, you could tell yourself that this is not about gender – your party is just setting a new and higher standard about how poor conduct should be punished.

A pretty tough dilemma, right? We outline it to help illustrate the themes we discovered in looking at Modern-day Salem. There are times when women in politics will do the wrong thing and should face sanctions. Fine judgement is then required about what is equal treatment, so the process and opprobrium are not different to what a man would face. Given the partisanship, heat and fury of politics, it is especially difficult to keep it fair.

Here, we think being aware of the problem is an important step one. The second vital step is talking about it. The more discussion of this phenomenon of holding women to a higher standard and punishing them more severely if they slip, the easier it will be for people to see the bias next time round.

Third, Jacinda talked compellingly about considering early on in her career how she would hold true to her essential self in politics. We think that is wise practice and one to be emulated. Doing it will help you know more about who you are and the lines in the sand you will draw for yourself.

Lesson Seven – Think now about whether, how and when you will call sexism out if it happens to you. As Julia shared at the start of this book, if she had her time again she would call out the sexism she faced as a leader earlier. What will be your strategy when it happens to you?

There is no one perfect answer to this question. Much will depend on the moment, your position at the time, and your access to allies and supporters. But war-gaming likely scenarios now, in your own mind or with trusted friends, and working out reactions is smart preparation.

In the lead-up to election campaigns, it is common for political parties to do exercises to test and refine how they will react if something unexpected happens. For example, if a natural disaster strikes, or a period of mourning is called for because a leading national figure dies, or the party leader gets laryngitis right before a major debate, what will the campaign do? Businesses commonly do scenario-planning exercises too. We are advocating you take the same kind of planned, thoughtful and tested approach.

That includes not only working out how you would react if a sexist incident happened, but how you would handle the second-round response. Imagine you call out the sexism and complain about it. What will happen next? We predict that you will come in for a barrage of criticism. This is not some ill-informed guess but is based on looking at the reaction to Julia's misogyny speech in Australia from women and men on the other side of politics and in the news media. She was accused of 'playing the gender card', or starting a gender war, or whining or being self-pitying.

Such negative observations are all too commonly faced by women leaders who raise gender issues. Often woven through them is a dismissive theme that only the pampered and privileged are worried about any of this agenda. It is easy to be guilted into silence by these kinds of criticisms.

However, when we listen to the words of our women leaders, with all their global diversity, there is nothing on which to base the conclusion that sexism is only seen as a burden by advantaged women who have little else to complain about. Even though our leaders come from such different cultures and contexts, the degree of commonality they expressed about the challenges they have faced is striking. Each spoke about judgements based on their appearance and each felt gender-coloured perceptions of them led to self-limiting behaviours. All the mothers spoke of the pressures presented by work and family life, though the sacrifices they needed to make to manage them were very different, with Ellen facing the most difficult of choices.

There were disparate views about being perceived as 'a bit of a bitch' and the degree of support they enjoyed from other women. But the patterns of variation did not follow lines of income, either in the sense of an individual woman's wealth or that of the nation from which she comes.

Of course, culture and context matter, as does intersectionality. Strategies to combat gender and other forms of discrimination will never be the same in every place. But we should not fall for the disempowering rhetoric that somehow it is only women at the top who wonder and worry about sexism and want to see its eradication. Can you think of a time when a white, male political leader was told he should never complain about anything – name-calling by his opponents, inaccurate reporting by the media, lack of assistance from important stakeholders – until the most disadvantaged men on the planet are lifted out of poverty? No, this kind of guilt trip is only laid on women leaders calling out sexism. Let's see it for what it is.

The key lesson here is that, sadly, sexism, shaming and silencing all exist, so plan your reactions to them now.

Lesson Eight – Always remember to role-model the positive. Over time, you will likely move from being someone who looks up to role models, to becoming the woman others watch and strive to learn from. This can be a daunting position to end up in and you may initially find yourself thinking, *What on earth do I have to share that can make a difference to anyone else?* We suspect every woman leader in this book has felt that at moments in her life.

But as you find and develop your voice as a role model, please remember that it is vital to speak positively about being a leader as well as authentically about the challenges. That way you will do the most good for those who are hanging off your words.

On your pathway to power, there are decisions to make about whether and how you will access sponsors and mentors. Our best advice is to start by being very clear about what you want and how much time you have to devote to being in this kind of relationship.

Part of finding clarity is recognising that, in common usage, the word 'mentor' can be rubbery, and the word 'sponsor' is far less known. A mentor can mean a person who listens and empathises, who plays a nurturing and caring role in your life. It can also mean someone who is all business, analytical and dispassionate about how you are performing and what you need to do to succeed. A coach-style mentor can switch between these roles, metaphorically holding your hand in one session and challenging you in the next.

A mentor can be someone who opens doors for you and takes you to events where you can network. A sponsor may also play this role, but moreover they are prepared to use their contacts and own personal brand to endorse you for promotion.

On top of all that, there are so many women-focused courses and conferences that it would literally be possible to go to one every working day of the year. The organisation you work for or community you live in may also have its own women's networks and programs.

What, if any of this, would truly make a difference to you? In making an assessment, be realistic about the time you can devote to being in a mentorship arrangement. For many, such arrangements can go the way of New Year's resolutions. At the start, there is plenty of commitment, energy and enthusiasm. But as the demands of daily life crowd in, what once held so much promise sputters to an ignominious end.

Aim to answer the questions, exactly what do I want from a mentor, and how much time can I commit? Fuelled by that clarity, then seek out the best person. A relationship is unlikely to emerge by simply asking a powerful woman who you meet at an event, for all the reasons we have seen in this book. Getting the right mentor requires the same kind of thoughtfulness and research that goes in to other big life decisions, like where to live, what to study, where to work and so on. There are now many organisations around that help match mentors and mentees. Part of your search should be seeing if one of these bodies is right for you.

What we have discussed so far applies to quite formalised mentoring arrangements. You may prefer to take a more networked approach, organically growing over time a list of political contacts or business associates, acquaintances and friends, who can provide advice and support on an as-needed basis. For some of the busiest and most senior people in your life, this might yield more results than a request for more formalised arrangements. Due to work pressures, many might say no to regular mentoring-style meetings, but people are less likely to decline a request to provide their perspective occasionally.

Set review periods, perhaps annually, where you and your mentor work out whether your relationship has run its course or still works for both of you. To the extent you are taking a more organic approach, do at least an annual stocktake of who is in your network and how best to add to it.

Getting a sponsor is much more likely to happen naturally or as a result of a formal mentoring arrangement deepening than it is to flow from a straight-out request. If you put yourself in the sponsor's shoes, it is easy to see why. Recommending someone for promotion and vouching for them is a risk; why would anyone take that risk for a person they do not really know and are not invested in?

Much can be gained from attending women-focused conferences and events, but there is a trap here and, once again, it is best to be aware. If, time after time, you find yourself at meeting venues and networking occasions with other women while the men who have power are gathering elsewhere, then there will be a limit to what you can accomplish.

In our observation, this is an endemic problem. In political parties, businesses and other organisations, it is assumed that women's equality will be achieved by just facilitating women coming together. There is a need for women to organise together and support each other. However, driving change requires decision-makers to be involved and act. At the moment, those with the power to decide are still disproportionately men. That is why the male political party leader or business chief executive officer or chair of the board needs to be in the room, truly listening to women, responding to women and acting for gender equality. Making this meaningful, not just an exercise in showing up, requires men to think about their role, but women also need to plan how we can best bring men in.

As we collectively work our way through those puzzles, we recommend you think about which of the many potential gender equality and women's events are the best for you.

From our women leaders' stories, it is clear that some women see mentoring, in particular, as more important than others. Our women leaders were not big planners of their mentorship and sponsorship strategies. This is not surprising given the degree of focus on both is much greater now than it was when most of our women leaders started their leadership journeys.

We are urging you to think through your strategy. In doing so, do not restrict yourself to only contemplating powerful women. Look out for positive male role models and sponsors. Some of our leaders were more directly assisted in their careers by stand-out men. Even if your ultimate decision is that you do not want to have a mentor or sponsor, it is better for that to be a deliberate, planned outcome than a default.

Lesson Nine – While working on this book, Julia has thought about what it is she wished she had known when she was starting out in politics. After consideration, she decided it is the power of networking. That might seem like an odd thing to say for someone who now has connections across Australia and around the world.

But when she was first a member of parliament, Julia took the view that you would arrange meetings with people if you had a clear agenda of work to do with them. They were busy, you were busy, and that was most respectful of everyone's time constraints.

It took her a while to realise that many of the up-and-coming male politicians were taking a different approach. Despite being newcomers to parliament, with a bright and breezy confidence they were taking themselves off to meet the chief executive officers and board chairs of Australia's biggest companies, the editors of major newspapers, the owners of television stations and the like. These various meetings had no agenda other than introductions and relationship building. Later in their parliamentary careers, at times of potential promotion or even moments of crisis, these contacts would come in handy.

When she looks back on it now, Julia realises that the main difference in approach boiled down to the men assuming that powerful people in Australia would be interested in what they, as young politicians, had to say. They made a confident assumption about how much space they were able to take up in the world of Australia's powerful elite.

Ngozi has a related message about networking. She is not a career politician like Julia. She did not run for office but was appointed into it. Nevertheless, she found herself in the middle of politics. Because she was so focused on the job, so absorbed by the challenges of reforming the country's financial systems, she devoted very little time to new outreach. Instead, Ngozi relied extensively on the networks she had already built prior to becoming Finance Minister to help her solve problems.

Looking back, she now realises she should have made more effort to broaden her networks and build new coalitions, because these contacts can be critical during challenging times, or avenues of support in times of opportunity.

From both of us, that means our message is twofold. Do not underestimate how valuable getting people to know you is and how much space you should take up. In addition, spend the time needed to network and build coalitions and friendships. It is worth it.

Theresa talked about deliberately setting out to establish a women's network to rival the old boys' club in conservative politics. Another approach is opening up processes so that old boys' clubs are disempowered. In the business world, some use is now made of anonymised processes where the selection group working through job applications cannot see the name, gender, school or university of the person seeking an appointment. That way it is impossible to zero in, deliberately or subconsciously, on those who come from the same social set as the old boys. Politics does not lend itself to this approach, but affirmative-action rules can play a role in disrupting the tendency to tap the male power network and preselect the next man in the queue. A third option is for women to seek to barge their way in to the pre-existing club. By gaining power, women are able to put themselves in a position where they cannot be ignored. We would suggest thinking about deploying each of these approaches. There is merit in all of them.

Lesson Ten – Our final lesson was taught to your authors by the publisher of this book, Meredith. Submitting a manuscript is a bit like handing in an examination paper. You wait for judgement.

When it came, it included the observation that we should write more on sponsorship and mentorship. That many women would want to see that content, and what we had predominantly shared was that neither of us felt we were doing enough. Meredith pointed out we both regularly speak at women's events; we were in the midst of writing a whole book on the subject; Julia is developing a Global Institute for Women's Leadership; Ngozi is sought out regularly for her views on gender equality and development. Yet, even with all of that, Meredith chided us, you are both acting like stereotypical women and highlighting your failures and guilt.

Naturally, in response to her assessment, we edited. But there is something laugh-out-loud ridiculous about two intelligent, dedicated women writing tens of thousands of words about gendered stereotyping and then falling for it in our behaviour.

Earlier in this book, we recommended women leaders regularly access someone with expertise who can periodically give advice on the gendered aspects of how their leadership is being perceived. We did so on the basis that it can be impossible for a woman leader to see this for herself when she is in the middle of it. Now we want to broaden that advice. Meredith has taught us a lesson about how we can all fail to see our gendered behaviours as we pursue our own lives and objectives.

In response, what can we say other than we all need a woman in our lives who periodically says, 'Are you kidding? Listen to yourself!'

Time to man up

Both of your authors have attended international meeting after international meeting at which rooms full of women discuss how best to achieve gender equality. We love feeling the power and passion of those around us. But, as highlighted above, we also know making progress means we have to include men in our discussions.

On that basis, it has been wonderful to see meetings of leaders, like the G20 and the G7, schedule discussions of women's empowerment – to see the most powerful people in the world, overwhelmingly men, showing that gender equality is their business too.

However, as a man you do not need to be the prime minister or president of a wealthy nation to make a difference. From our women leaders, we believe we can glean some lessons for men too. In this section, the lessons are especially for the men who read this book.

First, men can recognise that it is not the sole responsibility of a woman who is subjected to sexist conduct or stereotyping to call it out. In fact, she may often be in the most difficult position to start the discussion. She is the only person who faces being labelled self-interested if she points it out. Perhaps the very conduct or the bias, conscious or unconscious, that needs to be complained about has left her feeling disempowered. She may also have started with less power than others in the room. But even if she is a leader and has more power, she may feel loath to add to gendered perceptions, like 'she's a bit of a bitch', by pulling people up.

That means it is time to man up and take on the job of calling it out. Pointing to sexism does not have to be done in a way that drips with anger and promotes confrontation. It can be as simple as a quiet word with a perpetrator. Or accomplished by saying in a meeting, 'I have been thinking about how important it is to make sure the things we say do not include gender stereotypes', or, 'We all have unconscious biases and we need to talk them through'. If men find the will, then they will find the words, and the more they do it, the easier it will be.

What might start as the thing a man is prepared to do in his own environment ought to become an activity in all environments. Julia has often speculated about what a difference it would have made if, while gendered critiques of her prime ministership were being hurled around, a leading Australian man from outside politics had been prepared to say publicly, 'As Australians we do not do our politics this way. Let's have a political debate that is respectful and free of gender stereotyping.'

Second, think about whose voices are being heard. A study of talking time in groups of five people found that even when three women were in a group, they did not talk for a fair amount of the available time. That only happened when there was a super-majority of four women. In that setting, only 20 per cent of the interruptions made when a woman was speaking were negative, whereas if there was only one woman in the group of five, then 70 per cent of the interruptions she received were negative. If you are worrying about the lone man in the super-majority female groups, there is no need. He held his own. The same research showed that the rules of engagement mattered. If the group of five were told a decision could only be made by consensus, rather than majority rule, then a lone woman talked for nearly her fair share of time.[1] For men, there are two key points to take away from this. Ask yourself as you participate in discussions, am I talking and interrupting more than I should? Are the women not being heard? If the answer to either question is yes, level the playing field. If you are the one who determines how the meeting functions, think about the decision-making model and how you equalise talking time. As a participant in the discussion, make sure you invite women into the conversation.

Third, achieving work and family life policies that are better for balance is not women's work. It too requires shared effort from men and women. Workplaces will change faster if pressure comes from all sources.

There is research to suggest that seeking family-friendly flexibilities can be stigmatised. Some flexible workers may see negative career outcomes such as less access to training opportunities and promotion, with mothers being particularly likely to be affected.[2] But this stigma can be tackled if access to flexible work is expanded so that it is seen as the norm rather than the exception,[3] part of which will mean encouraging more men to work flexibly. We are therefore advocating men be part of the change we all want to see by visibly using the opportunities available under the policies at their workplaces.

A further benefit will be better role-modelling to children that caring for them and doing housework is also a man's job. Ngozi has practical experience to share on this topic. Her husband, despite being a busy physician and surgeon, cooked and cleaned right beside her, and jointly they taught their three sons and one daughter how to cook as soon as they turned twelve years old. The boys learnt that there are very few gender dimensions to having good food and a clean home.

At the time of this book's publication, many millions of families around the world have experienced the twin pressures of working from home and caring for children because of the restrictions introduced to fight the Covid-19 pandemic. Very early data is showing that the division of duties within households during this unusual time has mirrored ongoing gender divisions. For example, in the United Kingdom, mothers spent six hours a day on child care and home-schooling, whereas fathers devoted just over four hours. Curiously, mothers in highly paid jobs that are likely to require intense work bore even more of the load. Women earning over £80,000 a year were engaged for seven hours a day in caring and educating children, while men earning the same amount did less than 4.5 hours.[4] Yet, there is cause for hope. Emerging from this crisis, many businesses will be profoundly rethinking how they approach work and the balance between in-person attendance and virtual and flexible modes. Anecdotally, it seems that the experience of being locked down together at home has provoked much-needed conversations about how best to share domestic work. We urge everyone, and especially men, not to waste the current potential for major and equitable change at home and work.

As we discussed in chapter 4, it is also important that parents encourage girls and boys to think equally about their future potential. Our women leaders have in common that as children they were never told leadership was only for boys. How a girl is nurtured today matters for her vision of herself and her ambitions as an adult.

Fourth, men can and should serve as role models, mentors and sponsors to women at critical times in their career progression and leadership journeys. Be responsive if women seek you out as mentors or sponsors, and take the time to do it well. There is a phenomenon of being 'mentored to death', where women are told to do extra projects, go to evening networking events and participate in women-only company events, all while still being required to do the same amount of labour at work and home.[5] This is a recipe for stress and burnout, not career advancement. Being a mentor or sponsor is a skill that needs to be learned and honed. It is not innate. Seek out training, or study best practice guides. Ultimately, the test you should set for yourself is, did you actually help a woman advance? Supporting even one woman to succeed will change her life and make a difference for the women who follow in her footsteps. It is also likely that the time taken will be rewarded by you gaining deeper insight into how the world looks through women's eyes.

Fifth, every time we highlighted women's lack of access to leadership positions in this book, we could have pointed to the other side of the coin – that men disproportionately hold the power. Men can and should choose to use that influence for change. Gender inequality is embedded in the structures and systems of our societies, as well as in individual attitudes. In order to see real change, we need men to deliberately commit to the reworking necessary to weed out the gender inequality.

Not only do men currently disproportionately hold power, research tells us that they can become disproportionately powerful change agents. Psychological research conducted in 2018 shows that 'men are doubly advantaged in mobilizing followers' to combat gender inequality.[6] What that means is that a male leader articulating an anti-sexism message strikes more of a chord with both men and women. Unfortunately, exactly the same message carried by a female leader is less impactful. This conclusion is in line with earlier research that shows men are advantaged in confronting sexism because they are seen as having greater legitimacy due to the perception they are doing something against their own interests and which might put them at some risk.[7]

Men, if all that does not convince you to get involved, maybe this will: studies have shown that male leaders are more favourably evaluated and encounter positive reactions when drawing attention to gender inequality. So, the truth is you do not need to worry about getting involved. In fact, aside from knowing you are doing the right thing, there is a direct upside!

The media

For journalists in the traditional media, we ask them to be aware of the many issues around women and leadership we have discussed in this book. We offer a few simple suggestions for putting into practice the lessons learnt from our women leaders.

First, after writing a piece on a woman leader, delete her name and instead insert a generic male name. We think this will help highlight any gender bias in the piece. If the leader in question was male, would the article describe what they are wearing? Would it refer to their marital status and number of children? Would it describe them as shrill? Would it use the label unlikeable?

Second, in today's world where journalists also spend time appearing on commentary panel discussions to dissect what is happening in politics, be prepared to be the one who throws out challenges like, 'Is this woman leader really out of touch, or have some sexist stereotypes come in to play in forming our views?', or, 'Do we really need to spend any time discussing clothing choices?'

As individuals on social media we can practise the same discipline. Before tweeting or putting out a post or blog about a woman, quickly insert a man's name. Would you have said the same things?

But once again, there is a structural dynamic here that goes beyond good-willed individual action. Traditional media companies tend still to be male-dominated environments. It is quite rare to see a female editor of a newspaper or a woman as chief executive officer of a television station. There is reason to suspect that the gender bias in what these media outlets produce will never be eradicated until the businesses themselves become more gender balanced.

In addition, while individual journalists being more thoughtful is desirable, ultimately work processes and systems will dictate how much progress is made on getting gender bias out of the media. Media companies do things like analyse their content to determine the legal risk of being sued for defamation. What about bringing the same rigour to spotting and correcting gendered coverage?

None of these things are impossible if media companies invest in the idea and allocate appropriate resources. The foundation stone for change is media companies deciding that the days of splashing photographs and headlines that demean women leaders are over.

Third, for social media companies, there is clearly much work to be done to make the online environment less toxic for women in the public eye, including politics. The anonymity of social media seems to empower a certain type of person to say or express things about women that are clearly unacceptable in civilised society. It would be impossible for an individual to buy space in a newspaper or a commercial spot on television and promulgate a threat to rape or kill a woman leader. Yet anyone can pick up their phone and do precisely that on social media. How can that be fair or right?

No doubt there are technical complexities to getting the misogyny off social media platforms. But there is some progress now being made that only confirms more can and must be done.

For all of us

Many of the actions we have recommended here may feel difficult to translate into the real world. Hopefully the ideas seem meritorious, but implementing them may feel daunting.

For women who are contemplating becoming a leader, the pressures, the exposure and the risk of failure may seem all too much. The thought in your mind might be, *Can't someone else do it?*

For men, including those with the power to make major changes in large organisations, taking action may seem like it will be embarrassing or stressful. The thought in your mind might also be, *Can't someone else do it?*

If too many women and men succumb to this way of thinking then profound change will not come. In moments of doubt, your authors have always found it galvanising to remember and recommit to the purpose that drives them on.

So, in that spirit, let us conclude with a reminder about the vision we are striving to make a reality.

While you are reading this sentence, somewhere in our world, a child will be born. Inhaling a first breath, uttering a first cry, receiving a first cuddle and kiss – this child represents another possibility for all humanity. This child might become a leader who profoundly improves our world.

Should that potential promise be thwarted just because we hold our prejudices too dear or we find the process of letting go too confronting?

The answer each of us gives to that question, in word and deed, defines us and our future.

That is the biggest lesson of all.

Annex

Snapshots of the pathways to power

Jacinda Ardern

1980: Jacinda Ardern born in Hamilton, New Zealand.

2001–2005: Private Secretary to Harry Duynhoven, Associate Minister for Mines & Energy; Executive Assistant to Phil Goff, Minister for Justice; works for Prime Minister Helen Clark.

2006–2008: Works for Prime Ministers Tony Blair and Gordon Brown in the United Kingdom.

2008: First elected as a party list Member of Parliament in New Zealand.

2011: Re-elected to parliament as a party list Member.

2014: Re-elected to parliament as a party list Member.

2017: Re-elected to parliament as the Member for Mount Albert.

2017: Becomes deputy leader of the Labour Party in March, leader in August and prime minister in October.

Michelle Bachelet

1951: Verónica Michelle Bachelet Jeria born in Santiago, Chile.

1973: Military dictator Augusto Pinochet seizes power.

1974: Michelle's father dies after torture in prison.

1975: Imprisoned along with her mother and tortured.

1975: Release and exile to Australia.

1975: Moves to East Germany and recommences medical training.

1979: Returns to Chile.

1983: Graduates from medical school.

1994: Appointed Senior Assistant to the Deputy Health Minister.

1996: Begins studies in military strategy.

1998: Scholarship to study in Washington, DC.

1998: Appointed Senior Assistant to the Defense Minister.

2000: Appointed Minister for Health.

2002: Appointed Minister for National Defense.

2005: Runs as Socialist candidate for president.

2006: Elected for first term as president.

2010: Appointed head of UN Women.

2014: Elected for a second term as president.

2018: Appointed United Nations High Commissioner for Human Rights.

Joyce Banda

1950: Joyce Mtila born in Malemia, Malawi.

1989: Establishes the National Association of Business Women in Malawi.

1999: Enters parliament.

2004: Appointed Cabinet Minister for Women and Children Welfare.

2006: Serves as Foreign Minister.

2009: Takes office as vice-president.

2010: The Democratic Progressive Party (DPP), of which she and the president are members, seeks to fire her.

2012: President Mutharika passes away; Joyce assumes presidency. First and only woman to serve.

2014: Stands again for presidency, not successful.

Hillary Rodham Clinton

1947: Hillary Diane Rodham born in Chicago, Illinois.

1970: Research assistant, Yale Study Center. Awarded a grant to work at Marian Wright Edelman's Washington Research Project.

1971: Legal intern at law firm Treuhaft, Walker and Bernstein.

1973: Staff attorney, Children's Defense Fund.

1974: Staff member supporting the House Committee on the Judiciary during the inquiry into the Watergate scandal.

1975: Becomes a faculty member at University of Arkansas School of Law.

1976: Joins Rose Law Firm.

1977: Co-founds Arkansas Advocates for Children and Families.

1978: Appointed to the board of the Legal Services Corporation.

1979: Becomes First Lady of Arkansas and continues in that position for the twelve years of Bill Clinton's governorship (1979–1981 and 1983–1992).

1979: Becomes the first female full partner of Rose Law Firm.

1983: Becomes chair of the Arkansas Education Standards Committee.

1986: Becomes chair of the Children's Defense Fund.

1987: Becomes the first chair of the American Bar Association's Commission on Women in the Profession.

1993: Serves as First Lady of the United States until 2001.

2001: Serves as United States Senator from New York to 2009.

2008: Runs for presidential nomination for the Democratic Party, defeated by eventual winner Barack Obama.

2009: Serves as the 67th United States Secretary of State until 2013.

2016: Wins the Democratic Party nomination for President.

2016: Defeated by Republican candidate Donald Trump.

Christine Lagarde

1956: Christine Lallouette born in Paris.

1981: Joins law firm Baker & McKenzie.

1987: Becomes a partner at Baker & McKenzie.

1995: Becomes the first female member of the Baker & McKenzie executive committee.

1999: Elected Baker & McKenzie's first female chair.

2005: Appointed France's Minister of Trade.

2007: Briefly serves as Minister for Agriculture & Fisheries.

2007: Becomes first woman to serve as France's Minister of Finance.

2011: Elected managing director and chair of the board of the International Monetary Fund (IMF), the first woman to serve.

2016: Elected for a further five-year term as managing director and chair of the IMF.

2019: Becomes the first woman to be President of the European Central Bank.

Theresa May

1956: Theresa Mary Brasier born in Eastbourne, Sussex.

1977: Commences work at the Bank of England.

1985: Becomes a financial consultant at the Association of Payment Clearing Services.

1986: Serves as local councillor until 1994.

1997: Enters parliament as the Tory representative for seat of Maidenhead.

1999: Serves as Shadow Secretary of State for Education and Employment.

2001: Moves to the Transport shadow portfolio.

2002: Appointed the first ever female chair of the Conservative Party.

2003–2010: Various shadow cabinet positions including Culture, Media and Sport, and Work and Pensions

2005: Founds Women2Win group.

2010: Appointed Home Secretary and Minister for Women and Equality.

2016: Becomes leader of the Conservative Party and Prime Minister of the United Kingdom.

2019: Steps down as prime minister, re-elected as MP.

Ellen Johnson Sirleaf

1938: Ellen Johnson born in Monrovia, Liberia.

1956: Commences paid work, including a secretarial job at the Stanley Engineering Company and assistant to the head accountant at the Elias Brothers' Garage.

1962: Studies at Madison Business College, Wisconsin.

1964: Returns to Liberia.

1969: Speech as a junior official in the Ministry of Finance results in threat of jail.

1969–1971: Earns a Master of Public Administration at the John F. Kennedy School of Government, Harvard University.

1971: Returns to Liberia. President William Tubman of Liberia dies. William R. Tolbert becomes President and his brother, Stephen Tolbert, becomes the Minister for Finance. Ellen is appointed Deputy Minister for Finance.

1973: Commences career at World Bank in Washington, DC.

1975: Accepts invitation from new Finance Minister to return to Liberia and ministry.

1979: Appointed Finance Minister.

1980: Samuel Kanyon Doe executes President Tolbert and seizes control in a military coup. Only four ministers from Tolbert's government spared. Ellen appointed to lead Liberia's central bank.

1980: Returns to Washington, DC and employment in banking.

1985: Selected by her party to be the vice-presidential candidate.

1985: Jailed after giving speech calling President Doe and his team 'idiots'. Still elected senator. Jailed again on false suspicion of being involved in a failed coup attempt.

1986: Freed from prison as a result of national and international campaign pressure, and flees Liberia.

1989: President Charles Taylor overthrows President Doe in the First Liberian Civil War.

1997: Ellen stands against President Taylor and loses. Forced into exile.

1999: Second Liberian Civil War.

2003: Conflict in Liberia brought to an end by the 2003 Accra Peace Agreement.
2006: Becomes president of Liberia – the first woman president elected and the first woman national leader in Africa.
2011: Awarded Nobel Peace Prize.
2011: Re-elected President of Liberia.
2014: Leads her nation through the West African Ebola epidemic.
2016: Elected chair of the Economic Community of West African States, the first woman to hold the position.

Erna Solberg

1961: Erna Solberg born in Bergen, Norway.
1979: Elected to the board of the School Student Union of Norway.
1979: Deputy Member of the Bergen City Council, serving until 1983.
1987: Both Member of the Bergen City Council and deputy member of the executive committee.
1989: Elected to parliament.
2001: Appointed Minister of Local Government and Regional Development.
2002: Appointed deputy leader of the Conservative Party.
2004: Appointed leader of the Conservative Party.
2013: Elected Prime Minister.
2017: Re-elected as Prime Minister.

Notes

Prologue   Why are we writing this book?
1   Julia Gillard, *My Story*, Knopf Australia, North Sydney, 2014, p. 97
2   Ngozi Okonjo-Iweala, *Fighting Corruption Is Dangerous: The story behind the headlines*, MIT Press, Cambridge, Massachusetts, 2018

1   Doing the numbers
1   UN Women, 'Visualizing the data: Women's representation in society', 25 February 2020, unwomen.org/en/digital-library/multimedia/2020/2/infographic-visualizing-the-data-womens-representation
2   Statista, 'Number of countries where the highest position of executive power was held by a woman, in each year from 1960 to 2020', January 2020, statista.com/statistics/1058345/countries-with-women-highest-position-executive-power-since-1960
3   Ibid.
4   Ursula Perano, 'Slow progress for female world leaders', Axios, 10 March 2020
5   UN Women, 'Visualizing the data'
6   World Economic Forum, 'Global Gender Gap Report 2020', report, Geneva, 2019
7   UN Women, 'Visualizing the data'
8   Kalyeena Makortoff, 'Half of new FTSE 100 chiefs must be women to hit gender target', *The Guardian*, 13 November 2019
9   Community Business, 'Women on boards 2020: Q1', 2 January 2020, communitybusiness.org/women-boards-2020-Q1
10   'Global Media Monitoring Project 2015', report, World Association for Christian Communication, November 2015
11   'Improvement toward inclusion in film, but more work to be done', USC Annenberg School for Communication and Journalism, 4 September 2019,

annenberg.usc.edu/news/research-and-impact/improvement-toward-inclusion-film-more-work-be-done

12   Dr Martha M. Lauzen, 'Boxed in 2017–18: Women on screen and behind the scenes in television', Center for the Study of Women in Television & Film, San Diego State University, September 2018

13   World Economic Forum, 'Global Gender Gap Report 2020'

14   Kurt Badenhausen and Forbes Staff, 'The world's highest-paid athletes 2019', *Forbes*, 11 June 2019

15   Alex Marshall and Alexandra Alter, 'Olga Tokarczuk and Peter Handke awarded Nobel Prizes in Literature', *New York Times*, 10 October 2019

16   Caroline Criado-Perez, *Invisible Women: Exposing data bias in a world designed for men*, Chatto & Windus, London, 2019

17   Simon Crompton, 'Should medicine be gendered?', *Science Focus*, 1 May 2019

18   World Economic Forum, 'Global Gender Gap Report 2020'

19   PitchBook and All Raise, 'All in: Women in the VC ecosystem 2019', allraise.org/assets/pitchbook_all_raise_2019_all_in_women_in_the_vc_ecosystem.pdf

20   PitchBook, 'The VC female founders dashboard', updated 6 April 2020, pitchbook.com/news/articles/the-vc-female-founders-dashboard

2   Our framework

1   Stuart J. Ritchie et al., 'Sex differences in the adult human brain: Evidence from 5216 UK Biobank participants', *Cerebral Cortex*, vol. 28, no. 8, August 2018, pp. 2959–75

2   Cordelia Fine, *Delusions of Gender: How our minds, society, and neurosexism create difference*, W. W. Norton & Company, New York, 2010

3   Herminia Ibarra, Robin J. Ely and Deborah M. Kolb, 'Women rising: The unseen barriers', *Harvard Business Review*, September 2013; Alice Eagly and Linda L. Carli, 'Women and the labyrinth of leadership', *Harvard Business Review*, September 2007

4   Elizabeth Judge, 'Women on board: help or hindrance?', *The Times*, 11 November 2003

5   Michelle K. Ryan and S. Alexander Haslam, 'The glass cliff: Exploring the dynamics surrounding the appointment of women to precarious leadership positions', *Academy of Management Review*, vol. 32, no. 2, 2007, pp. 549–72

6   Michelle K. Ryan, S. Alexander Haslam, Mette D. Hersby and Renata Bongiorno, 'Think Crisis–Think Female: The glass cliff and contextual variation in the Think Manager–Think Male stereotype', *Journal of Applied Psychology*, vol. 96, no. 3, 2011, pp. 470–84

7   McKinsey Global Institute, 'The power of parity: How advancing women's equality can add $12 trillion to global growth', report, September 2015; Food and Agriculture Organization of the United Nations, 'The state of food and agriculture 2010–11: Women in agriculture: Closing the gender gap for development', report, Rome, 2011

8   Lori Beaman, Esther Duflo, Rohini Pande and Petia Topalova, 'Female leadership raises aspirations and educational attainment for girls: A policy experiment in India', *Science*, vol. 335, iss. 6068, 3 February 2012, pp. 582–6

9   Jenny M. Hoobler, Courtney R. Masterson, Stella M. Nkomo and Eric J. Michel, 'The business case for women leaders: Meta-analysis, research critique and path forward', *Journal of Management*, vol. 44, no. 6, July 2018, pp. 2473–99

3   Pathways to power: Introducing our women leaders

1   Ellen Johnson Sirleaf, *This Child Will Be Great: Memoir of a remarkable life by Africa's first woman president*, HarperCollins, New York, 2009, chapter 3

2   United States Institute of Peace, 'Truth Commission: Chile 90', 1 May 1990, www.usip.org/publications/1990/05/truth-commission-chile-90

3   World Bank, 'GDP per capita (current US$) – Malawi', data.worldbank.org/indicator/NY.GDP.PCAP.CD?locations=MW. Most recent data 2018

4   Tara Sophia Mohr, 'Why women don't apply for jobs unless they're 100% qualified', *Harvard Business Review*, 25 August 2014

5   Maria Ignatova, 'New report: Women apply to fewer jobs than men, but are more likely to get hired', LinkedIn Talent Blog, 5 March 2019

6   Tomas Chamorro-Premuzic, *Why Do So Many Incompetent Men Become Leaders? (And how to fix it)*, Harvard Business Review Press, Boston, Massachusetts, 2019, chapter 2

4   Hypothesis one: You go girl

1   Carmen Niethammer, 'Finland's new government is young and led by women – here's what the country does to promote diversity', *Forbes*, 12 December 2019

2   'Expanded Norwegian Government headed by four female leaders', Government.no, 22 January 2019, regjeringen.no/en/aktuelt/expanded-norwegian-government-headed-by-four-female-leaders/id2626529

3   Cynthia Hess, Tanima Ahmed and Jeff Hayes, 'Providing unpaid household and care work in the United States: Uncovering inequality', Institute for Women's Policy Research, 20 January 2020

4   Usha Ranji and Alina Salganicoff, 'Data note: Balancing on shaky ground: Women, work and family health', Kaiser Family Foundation, 20 October 2014

5   Alyssa Croft, Toni Schmader, Katharina Block and Andrew Scott Baron, 'The second shift reflected in the second generation: Do parents' gender roles at home predict children's aspirations?', *Psychological Science*, vol. 25, no. 7, July 2014, pp. 1418–28

5   Hypothesis two: It's all about the hair
1   Rachael Combe, 'At the pinnacle of Hillary Clinton's career', *Elle*, 5 April 2012
2   'Justin Trudeau's "Bollywood" wardrobe amuses Indians', BBC News, 22 February 2018
3   Michael Lewis, 'Obama's way', *Vanity Fair*, 11 September 2012
4   'The audacity of taupe: Barack Obama's tan suit creates sartorial stir on social media', ABC News, 29 August 2014
5   Susan Sontag, 'The double standard of aging', *Saturday Review*, 23 September 1972, pp. 29–38
6   Linda Trimble, 'Gender, political leadership and media visibility: *Globe and Mail* coverage of Conservative Party of Canada leadership contests', *Canadian Journal of Political Science*, vol. 40, no. 4, December 2007, pp. 986–9
7   James Devitt, *Framing Gender on the Campaign Trail: Women's executive leadership and the press*, Women's Leadership Fund, New York, 1999
8   Caroline Heldman, Susan J. Carroll and Stephanie Olson, 'Gender differences in print media coverage of presidential candidates: Elizabeth Dole's bid for the Republican nomination', conference paper, American Political Science Association, August 31–3 September 2000
9   Blair E. Williams, 'A tale of two women: A comparative gendered media analysis of UK prime ministers Margaret Thatcher and Theresa May', *Parliamentary Affairs*, published online, 26 April 2020
10   Linda Trimble, 'Gender, political leadership and media visibility'
11   'Sexism cited in reaction to Stronach move', CBC News, 18 May 2005
12   George Jones and Andrew Sparrow, 'A stiletto in the Tories' heart', *Daily Telegraph*, 8 October 2002
13   Melissa Kite, 'Tories fall for Theresa's shoes', *The Times*, 10 October 2002
14   'Theresa's tough look', *Daily Mirror*, 9 October 2002
15   Mathew Norman, Diary, *The Guardian*, 25 March 2003
16   Nigel Cawthorne, *Theresa May: Taking charge*, Sharpe Books, 2018, chapter 4
17   Matthew Norman, Diary, *The Guardian*, 8 April 2003
18   Jill Parkin, 'The great cleavage divide: There's only one real debate at Westminster', *Daily Mail*, 30 November 2007
19   Michelle Duff, *Jacinda Ardern: The story behind an extraordinary leader*, Allen & Unwin, Auckland, 2019, chapter 1

20 Jonathan Milne, 'Nicola Kaye vs Jacinda Ardern', *New Zealand Listener*, 24 September 2011

21 'The audacity of taupe: What did Obama actually say in that tan suit?', SBS News, 30 August 2014

6   Hypothesis three: Shrill or soft — the style conundrum

1   Virginia E. Schein, 'The relationship between sex role stereotypes and requisite management characteristics', *Journal of Applied Psychology*, vol. 57, no. 2, May 1973, pp. 95–100

2   Anne M. Koenig, Alice H. Eagly, Abigail A. Mitchell and Tiina Ristikari, 'Are leader stereotypes masculine? A meta-analysis of three research paradigms', *Psychological Bulletin*, vol. 137, no. 4, July 2011, pp. 616–42

3   Benjamin Schmidt, 'Gender bias exists in professor evaluations', Opinion Pages: Room for Debate, *New York Times*, 16 December 2015

4   Lillian MacNell, Adam Driscoll and Andrea Hunt, 'What's in a name: Exposing gender bias in student ratings of teaching', *Innovative Higher Education*, vol. 40, no. 4, August 2015, pp. 291–303

5   Tomas Chamorro-Premuzic, *Why Do So Many Incompetent Men Become Leaders? (And how to fix it)*, Harvard Business Review Press, Boston, Massachusetts, 2019, chapter 2

6   Laurie A. Rudman and Peter Glick, 'Prescriptive gender stereotypes and backlash toward agentic women', *Journal of Social Issues*, vol. 57, no. 4, Winter 2001, pp. 743–62

7   Herminia Ibarra, Robin J. Ely and Deborah M. Kolb, 'Women rising: The unseen barriers', *Harvard Business Review*, September 2013; Alice Eagly and Linda L. Carli, 'Women and the labyrinth of leadership', *Harvard Business Review*, September 2007

8   Catherine H. Tinsley and Robin J. Ely, 'What most people get wrong about men and women', *Harvard Business Review*, May–June 2018

9   Dina W. Pradel, Hannah Riley Bowles and Kathleen L. McGinn, 'When gender changes the negotiation', Harvard Business School Working Knowledge, 13 February 2006

10 John Crace, *I, Maybot: The rise and fall*, Guardian Books, London, 2017

11 *New Statesman*, cover, 14–20 July 2017

12 Henry Mance, 'Year in a Word: Maybot', *Financial Times*, 18 December 2017

13 Christopher Hope, 'Theresa May suggests that people who mocked her tears during resignation speech are sexist', *The Telegraph*, 11 July 2019

14 Alice H. Eagly, Christa Nater, David I. Miller, Michèle Kaufmann and Sabine Sczesny, 'Gender stereotypes have changed: A cross-temporal meta-analysis of

U.S. public opinion polls from 1946 to 2018, *American Psychologist*, advance online publication, 18 July 2019

15 Alice H. Eagly, Mary C. Johannesen-Schmidt and Marloes L. van Engen, 'Transformational, transactional, and laissez-faire leadership styles: A meta-analysis comparing women and men', *Psychological Bulletin*, vol. 129, no. 4, July 2003, pp. 569–91

7   **Hypothesis four: She's a bit of a bitch**

1   Broken People, 'Original video – Bitchy resting face', YouTube, 22 May 2013, youtu.be/3v98CPXNiSk

2   Caitlin Gibson, 'Scientists have discovered what causes Resting Bitch Face', *Washington Post*, 3 February 2016

3   Melkorka Licea, 'Women are flocking to plastic surgeons to fix "resting bitch face"', *New York Post*, 16 September 2019

4   Tyler G. Okimoto and Victoria L. Brescoll, 'The price of power: Power seeking and backlash against female politicians', *Personality and Social Psychology Bulletin*, vol. 37, no. 7, July 2010, pp. 923–36

5   Ibid., p. 931

6   Michelle Grattan, 'Finessing a flagrant backflip', *The Age*, 26 June 2010

7   Alice H. Eagly, 'When passionate advocates meet research on diversity, does the honest broker stand a chance?', *Journal of Social Issues*, vol. 72, no. 1, March 2016, pp. 199–222

8   Maegan Vazquez, 'How Trump's rhetoric on Kamala Harris has changed and why', CNN, 9 September 2020, https://www.cnn.com/2020/09/09/politics/donald-trump-kamala-harris-rhetoric/index.html

9   Analysis by Chris Cillizza, CNN Editor-at-large, 9 September 2020

10 Joshua Mcdonald, 'Jacinda Ardern's re-election woes', *The Diplomat*, 26 March 2020

11 Joachim Dagenborg, 'Norway's Merkel, Erna Solberg hopes to beat history in re-election bid', *Reuters*, 8 September 2017

8   **Hypothesis five: Who's minding the kids?**

1   Dr Jarrod Gilbert, 'Life, kids and being Jacinda', *New Zealand Herald*, August 2016, republished 19 January 2018

2   Ellen Johnson Sirleaf, *This Child Will Be Great*, HarperCollins, New York, 2009, chapter 20

3   Tony Blair, *A Journey*, Hutchinson, London, 2010, pp. 266–7; Steven Morris, 'Camerons' baby brightens up their summer holiday in Cornwall', *The Guardian*, 25 August 2010

4   Oliver Wright, 'Boris Johnson welcomes son into world – then gets straight back to work', *The Times*, 30 April 2020

5   Rachel Sylvester, 'Being a mother gives me edge on May – Leadsom', *The Times*, 9 July 2016

6   Ibid.

7   Jessica Elgot, 'Andrea Leadsom apologises to Theresa May for motherhood remarks', *The Guardian*, 11 July 2016

8   'Barren Behaviour', *The Australian*, 4 May 2007

9   '29 moments that led to Julia Gillard's downfall', news.com.au, 27 June 2013

9   Hypothesis six: A special place in hell – do women really support women?

1   Madeleine Albright, 'Madeleine Albright: My undiplomatic moment', *New York Times*, 12 February 2016

2   Abby Wambach, Barnard College commencement address, 16 May 2018, barnard.edu/commencement/archives/2018/abby-wambach-remarks

3   Edward H. Chang, Katherine L. Milkman, Dolly Chugh and Modupe Akinola, 'Diversity thresholds: How social norms, visibility, and scrutiny relate to group composition', *Academy of Management Journal*, vol. 62, no. 1, February 2019

4   Stephanie L. Hardacre and Emina Subašić, 'Whose issue is it anyway? The effects of leader gender and equality message framing on men's and women's mobilization toward workplace gender equality', *Frontiers in Psychology*, vol. 9, iss. 2497, 11 December 2018

5   G. Staines, C. Tavris and T. E. Jayaratne, *The Queen Bee Syndrome in the Female Experience*, CRM Books, Del Mar, California, 1973

6   Cristian L. Dezső, David Gaddis Ross and Jose Uribe, 'Is there an implicit quota on women in top management? A large-sample statistical analysis', *Strategic Management Journal*, vol. 37, no. 1, January 2016, pp. 95–115

7   David A. Matsa and Amalia R. Miller, 'Chipping away at the glass ceiling: Gender spillovers in corporate leadership', *American Economic Review*, vol. 101, no. 3, May 2011, pp. 635–9

8   Catherine Reyes-Housholder, 'Presidential gender and women's representation in cabinets: Do female presidents appoint more women than male presidents?', conference paper, American Political Science Association, 29 August 2013

9   Diana Z. O'Brien, Matthew Mendez, Jordan Carr Peterson and Jihyun Shin, 'Letting down the ladder or shutting the door: Female prime ministers, party leaders, and cabinet ministers', *Politics & Gender*, vol. 11, no. 4, December 2015, pp. 689–717

10 Dee Goddard, 'Examining the appointment of women to ministerial positions across Europe: 1970–2015', *Party Politics*, published online, 18 October 2019

11 Herminia Ibarra, Nancy M. Carter and Christine Silva, 'Why men still get more promotions than women', *Harvard Business Review*, September 2010

12 Ibid.

10 **Hypothesis seven: Modern-day Salem**

1 Victoria L. Brescoll, Erica Dawson and Eric Luis Uhlmann, 'Hard won and easily lost: The fragile status of leaders in gender-stereotype-incongruent occupations', *Psychological Science*, vol. 21, no. 11, November 2010, pp. 1640–2

2 John F. Dovido and Samuel L. Gaertner, 'The aversive form of racism' in *Prejudice, Discrimination, and Racism*, Academic Press, Orlando, Florida, 1986, pp. 61–89; Gordon Hodson, John F. Dovido and Samuel L. Gaertner, 'Processes in racial discrimination: Differential weighting of conflicting information', *Personality and Social Psychological Bulletin*, vol. 28, no. 4, April 2002, pp. 460–71

3 'Brazil's Lula: The most popular politician on earth', *Newsweek*, 21 September 2009

4 Brasil de Fato, 'Dilma Rousseff: "Torture is about pain and death. They want you to lose your dignity"', Peoples Dispatch, 18 January 2020

5 Perry Anderson, 'Bolsonaro's Brazil', *London Review of Books*, vol. 41, no. 3, 7 February 2019

6 Ibid.

7 'Brazil leaked tape forces minister Romero Juca out', BBC News, 24 May 2016

8 Dom Phillips, 'Eduardo Cunha, who led impeachment drive against rival in Brazil, gets a 15-year jail term', *New York Times*, 30 March 2017

9 Dom Phillips, 'Brazil's former president Lula walks free from prison after supreme court ruling', *The Guardian*, 9 November 2019

10 Abigail Tracy, 'Republicans' $7 million Benghazi report is another dud', *Vanity Fair*, 28 June 2016

11 Kim Willsher, 'Negligence case against Christine Lagarde is very weak, says prosecutor', *The Guardian*, 16 December 2016

12 Jonathan Watts, 'Dilma Rousseff: Brazilian congress votes to impeach president', *The Guardian*, 18 April 2016

11 **Hypothesis eight: The role-modelling riddle**

1 Lori Beaman, Esther Duflo, Rohini Pande and Petia Topalova, 'Female leadership raises aspirations and educational attainment for girls: A policy experiment in India', *Science*, vol. 335, iss. 6068, 3 February 2012, pp. 582–6

2   Michael X. Delli Carpini, and Scott Keeter, *What Americans Know About Politics and Why it Matters*, Yale University Press, New Haven, 1996; Sidney Verba, Nancy Burns and Kay Lehman Schlozman, 'Knowing and caring about politics: Gender and political engagement', *Journal of Politics*, vol. 59, no. 4, November 1997, pp. 1051–72; Linda L. M. Bennett and Stephen Earl Bennett, 'Enduring gender differences in political interest: The impact of socialization and political dispositions', *American Politics Research*, vol. 17, no. 1, January 1989; R. Robert Huckfeldt and John Sprague, *Citizens, Politics and Social Communication: Information and influence in an election campaign*, Cambridge University Press, Cambridge, 1995; Lonna Rae Atkeson and Ronald B. Rapoport, 'The more things change the more they stay the same: Examining gender differences in political attitude expression, 1952–2000', *Public Opinion Quarterly*, vol. 67, no. 4, Winter 2003, pp. 495–521

3   Christina Wolbrecht and David E. Campbell, 'Leading by example: Female members of parliament as political role models', *American Journal of Political Science*, vol. 51, no. 4, October 2007, pp. 921–39

4   Tiffany D. Barnes, Stephanie M. Burchard, '"Engendering" politics: The impact of descriptive representation on women's political engagement in sub-Saharan Africa', *Comparative Political Studies*, vol. 46, no. 7, July 2013, pp. 767–90

5   Scott Desposato and Barbara Norrander, 'The gender gap in Latin America: Contextual and individual influences on gender and political participation', *British Journal of Political Science*, vol. 39, no. 1, January 2009, pp. 141–62

6   Ed Yong, 'What we learn from 50 years of kids drawing scientists', *The Atlantic*, 20 March 2018

7   Ian McAllister, 'The gender gap in political knowledge revisited: Australia's Julia Gillard as a natural experiment', *European Journal of Politics and Gender*, vol. 2, no. 2, June 2019, pp. 197–220

8   Blair Williams, 'Julia Gillard, the media and young women', research paper, online.fliphtml5.com/vhkx/iebp

9   Shan-Jan Sarah Liu, 'Are female political leaders role models? Lessons from Asia', *Political Research Quarterly*, vol. 71, no. 2, June 2018, pp. 255–69

10 Shaki Asgari, Nilanjana Dasgupta and Jane G. Stout, 'When do counter-stereotypic ingroup members inspire versus deflate? The effect of successful professional women on young women's leadership self-concept', *Personality and Social Psychology Bulletin*, vol. 38, no. 3, March 2012, pp. 370–83; Yael M. Bamberger, 'Encouraging girls into science and technology with feminine role models: Does this work?', *Journal of Science Education and Technology*, vol. 23, no. 4, August 2014, pp. 549–61; Diana E. Betz and Denise Sekaquaptewa, 'My Fair Physicist? Feminine math and science role models demotivate young

girls', *Social Psychological and Personality Science*, vol. 3, no. 6, November 2012, pp. 738–46; Josh Lerner and Ulrike Malmendier, 'With a little help from my (random) friends: Success and failure in post–business school entrepreneurship', *Review of Financial Studies*, vol. 26, no. 10, October 2013, pp. 2411–52; Penelope Lockwood and Ziva Kunda, 'Superstars and me: Predicting the impact of role models on the self', *Journal of Personality and Social Psychology*, vol. 73, no. 1, July 1997, pp. 91–103

11   Florian Foos and Fabrizio Gilardi, 'Does exposure to gender role models increase women's political ambition? A field experiment with politicians', *Journal of Experimental Political Science*, published online, 7 August 2019

12   Frances Perraudin and Simon Murphy, 'Alarm over number of female MPs stepping down after abuse', *The Guardian*, 1 November 2019

13   Beth Rigby, 'Sky Views: The Tories are allowing hatred and misogyny to drive women away', Sky News, 6 November 2019

14   Harriet Brewis, 'Caroline Spelman quits: Tory MP to stand down after "abuse and death threats" which left her "wearing panic button"', *Evening Standard*, 5 September 2019

15   Beth Rigby, 'Sky Views: The Tories are allowing hatred and misogyny to drive women away'

16   Amnesty International UK, 'Black and Asian women MPs abused more online', amnesty.org.uk/online-violence-women-mps

17   Tom Peck, 'Diane Abbott received almost half of all abusive tweets sent to female MPs before election, poll finds', *The Independent*, 5 September 2017

18   Simon Murphy, 'Diane Abbott speaks out on online abuse as female MPs step down', *The Guardian*, 31 October 2019

19   Chimamanda Ngozi Adichie, *Americanah*, Alfred A. Knopf, New York, 2013, p. 359

20   Kelly Dittmar, 'The 2020 primaries are over. Here's what you need to know about the record numbers of women nominees', Centre for American Women and Politics, 18 September 2020, https://cawp.rutgers.edu/election-analysis/post-primary-analysis-women-2020

21   BBC Data Journalism Team, 'Election 2019: Britain's most diverse parliament', BBC News, 17 December 2019

22   Elise Uberoi, 'Ethnic diversity in politics and public life', House of Commons Library, 30 May 2019, commonslibrary.parliament.uk/research-briefings/sn01156

12 The stand-out lessons from eight lives and eight hypotheses

1   Tali Mendelberg, Christopher F. Karpowitz and J. Baxter Oliphant, 'Gender inequality in deliberation: Unpacking the black box of interaction', *Perspectives on Politics*, vol. 12, no. 1, March 2014, pp. 18–44

2   Heejung Chung, 'Gender, Flexibility Stigma and the Perceived Negative Consequences of Flexible Working in the UK', *Social Indicators Research*, published online, 26 November 2018

3   Tanja van der Lippe & Zoltán Lippényi, 'Beyond Formal Access: Organizational Context, Working From Home, and Work–Family Conflict of Men and Women in European Workplaces', *Social Indicators Research*, published online, 5 October 2018

4   Donna Ferguson, '"I feel like a 1950s housewife": How lockdown has exposed the gender divide', *The Observer*, 3 May 2020

5   Herminia Ibarra, Nancy M. Carter and Christine Silva, 'Why men still get more promotions than women', *Harvard Business Review*, September 2010

6   Stephanie L. Hardacre and Emina Subašić, 'Whose issue is it anyway? The effects of leader gender and equality message framing on men's and women's mobilization toward workplace gender equality', *Frontiers in Psychology*, vol. 9, iss. 2497, 11 December 2018

7   Heather M. Rasinski and Alexander M. Czopp, 'The effect of target status on witnesses' reactions to confrontations of bias', *Basic and Applied Social Psychology*, vol. 32, no. 1, February 2010, pp. 8–16

Acknowledgements

It would have been impossible for us to layer book writing on top of our already busy workloads without getting incredible support from others.

Ngozi gratefully acknowledges the contributions of Nicole Mensa and Gloria Kebirungi to the book. Nicole participated in several of the interviews with our women leaders and efficiently transcribed the results. She and Gloria helped with background research, corrections to the manuscript and critiques of the overall concept and approach to the book, bringing fresh perspectives of young women of colour. I would also like to thank my children, Uzodinma Iweala, Okechukwu Iweala, Onyi Iweala and Andrew Spector, and Uchechi Iweala and Chioma Achebe, for their encouragement and enthusiasm.

Julia thanks Roanna McClelland for her help, especially in providing the critique of a younger feminist on our many drafts of this book. Julia would also like to acknowledge her dear friend Josephine Linden. A voracious reader, Josephine provided a fresh pair of eyes when a new perspective was needed most. Thanks also go to Michelle Fitzgerald for her personal support and work to ensure Julia was where she needed to be for the interviews of leaders. Nina Gerace, as always, provided encouragement.

Our combined thanks go to Meredith Curnow and Kathryn Knight, the editorial team from our publisher Penguin Random House Australia. At all times they have shown wisdom and creativity, while providing exactly the right doses of patience and discipline. Karen Reid, also from Penguin Random House, continues to be both great fun and a consummate professional.

Many thanks also go to Rosie Campbell and Laura Jones from the Global Institute for Women's Leadership, who read drafts and provided research tips. If you have been inspired to learn more about women and leadership, please visit GIWL at **www.kcl.ac.uk/giwl**.

About the authors

Julia Gillard was sworn in as the 27th Prime Minister of Australia on 24 June 2010 and served in that office until June 2013. Ms Gillard is the first woman to ever serve as Australia's prime minister or deputy prime minister.

As prime minister and in her previous role as deputy prime minister, Ms Gillard delivered nation-changing policies including reforming Australian education at every level from early childhood to university education, creating an emissions trading scheme to combat climate change, improving health care, commencing the nation's first ever national scheme to care for people with disabilities, addressing the gender pay gap for social and community sector workers, and delivering an apology to all those who had suffered through the practice of forced adoptions.

In October 2012, Ms Gillard received worldwide attention for her speech in parliament on the treatment of women in professional and public life. She currently serves as the inaugural Chair of the Global Institute for Women's Leadership at Kings College in London, which through research, practice and advocacy is addressing women's under-representation in leadership.

Ms Gillard is the Chair of Beyond Blue, one of Australia's leading mental health awareness bodies; is Chair of global funding body for education in developing countries, the Global Partnership for Education; and is Patron of the Campaign for Female Education.

Ms Gillard's memoirs, *My Story* (Penguin Random House), were published in September 2014.

Dr Ngozi Okonjo-Iweala is an economist and international development expert with over thirty years of experience. She is Chair of the Board of Gavi, the Vaccine Alliance and of the African Risk Capacity (ARC). She is co-Chair of the Global Commission on the Economy and Climate and co-Chair of the Board of Lumos, a small-cap renewable energy company. She also sits on the Boards of Standard Chartered PLC and Twitter Inc.

Previously, Dr Okonjo-Iweala was a Senior Advisor at Lazard from September 2015 to October 2019. She served twice as Nigeria's Finance Minister, from 2003 to 2006 and 2011 to 2015, and briefly as Foreign Minister, the first woman to hold both positions. She spent a 25-year career at the World Bank as a development economist, rising to the number two position of Managing Director, overseeing an $81 billion operational portfolio in Africa, South Asia, Europe and Central Asia.

Dr Okonjo-Iweala has been ranked by *Fortune* as one of the 50 Greatest World Leaders in 2015, by *Forbes* as one of the Top 100 Most Powerful Women in the World consecutively for four years, by *Time* as one of the Top 100 Most Influential People in the World in 2014, and by the UK *Guardian* as one of the Top 100 Women in the World in 2011.

Dr Okonjo-Iweala holds a Bachelor's degree in Economics from Harvard University and a PhD in Regional Economics and Development from the Massachusetts Institute of Technology. She is an Angelopoulos Global Public Leader at Harvard University Kennedy School, a Fellow of the American Academy of Arts and Sciences, and has received over fifteen honorary degrees, including from Yale University, the University of Pennsylvania, Brown University, Tel Aviv University and Trinity College, Dublin. She is the author of numerous articles on finance and development, and several books including *Fighting Corruption Is Dangerous: The story behind the headlines* (MIT Press, 2018) and *Reforming the Unreformable: Lessons from Nigeria* (MIT Press, 2012).